PRIVATE NOVELS,
PUBLIC FILMS

Private Novels, Public Films

JUDITH MAYNE

THE UNIVERSITY OF GEORGIA PRESS

ATHENS & LONDON

© 1988 by the University of Georgia Press
Athens, Georgia 30602

All rights reserved

Designed by Richard Hendel

Set in Electra

The paper in this book meets the guidelines for
permanence and durability of the Committee on
Production Guidelines for Book Longevity of the
Council on Library Resources.

Printed in the United States of America

92 91 90 89 88   5 4 3 2 1

Library of Congress Cataloging in Publication Data
Mayne, Judith.
Private novels, public films.
Bibliography: p.
Includes index.
1. Motion-pictures and literature. 2. European
fiction—Social aspects. 3. Motion-pictures—Social
aspects. 4. Motion-pictures—United States—History.
I. Title.
PN1995.3.M37   1988   791.43   87-19239
ISBN 0-8203-1007-7 (alk. paper)

British Library Cataloging in Publication Data available

For my parents

CONTENTS

ACKNOWLEDGMENTS

While working on this book I have received various forms of support. First and foremost, I would like to thank the following friends and colleagues who offered diverse forms of encouragement: Robert Allen, Germaine Brée, Teresa DeLauretis, Anne Friedberg, Mitchell Greenberg, Stephen Heath, Marlene Longenecker, Dana Polan, Eric Rentschler, B. Ruby Rich, Ruth Rosenberg, Ron Rosbottom, Steve Summerhill, Marie-Claire Vallois, and Nat Wing. For support of a more material kind, I would like to thank the National Endowment for the Humanities for a summer fellowship, and the College of Humanities and the Graduate School of the Ohio State University for released time and generous grant support which allowed me to pursue research for this book. Linda Sabo and Jo White typed the manuscript with care and precision. Douglas Armato has been a most encouraging and responsive editor, and Loris Green's contributions as copyeditor have been helpful and perceptive. And finally, special thanks to Terry Moore, with whom I share my enthusiasm for novels, films, and the intricacies of private and public life.

PRIVATE NOVELS,
PUBLIC FILMS

INTRODUCTION

This book examines a familiar topic in film studies—the relationship between film and the novel—from a new perspective. If the most obvious connection between films and novels is cinematic adaptation of novels, the relationship between the two forms has many less obvious, and more complex components. The shared qualities of novels and films occur on many levels, aesthetic as well as social. Both novels and films have a remarkable capacity to incorporate a variety of aesthetic and discursive influences, from the personal diary to the historical chronicle in the case of the novel, from comic strips to melodrama in the case of the cinema. And as narrative forms, novels and films often employ similar devices of narrative and point-of-view. In historical terms, the novel and the cinema—particularly as forms of what is commonly referred to as "classical realism"—have flourished primarily in middle-class societies. As social forms, novels and films have appealed to cross-class audiences, and demonstrate an identification with the values of middle-class culture.

While cinematic adaptations of novels, as well as narrative devices common to the novel and the cinema, are examined in this book, my primary concern is how the social function of cinematic narrative can be illuminated by examining its relation to the Western middle-class novel. The middle-class common denominator will be discussed in terms of the changing relationship between the spheres of private and public life. I argue that as narrative forms, cinema and the novel have responded to the separation between private and public life characteristic of Western industrial societies. The title of this book, *Private Novels, Public Films*, refers, then, to how the Western European novel was shaped by the emergence of private life as a relatively new concept, and to how the cinema, particularly in the United States, was part of the emergence of a new kind of public sphere, one shaped by the institutions of consumerism. Novels and films will thus be compared in terms of their functions as symptoms of fundamental social, economic, and cultural changes. Yet there is much more to the novel-film connection than a common status as symptom. Indeed, the capacity of both novels and films to articulate the contradictions of middle-class society is as central to this study as their re-enactment of social ideals. In the middle-class novel and later the cinema, narrative functions as an encounter with the spheres of private and public life, an encounter which emulates *and* problemizes the division of private and public, as well as the oppositions upon which that division draws—particularly those of gender and of social class.

Throughout the history of motion pictures, writing about the cinema has drawn frequently upon comparisons between film and other forms, other discourses. The scope of the comparison is not limited to the arts, as is amply demonstrated by the importance of psychoanalysis as a frame of reference in contemporary film theory. Sometimes such comparisons are meant to illuminate by showing that film is unique because it is different from other forms; or, conversely, that film is unique because it surpasses the very forms it resembles. The novel and the theatre are the two most common literary reference points in discussions of film, and particularly of the mainstream, fiction film which is the object of this study.[1] While comparison of film and the novel is more characteristic of film criticism in recent decades, comparisons between film and the theatre tended to dominate the earliest writings about the cinema, especially during the period of the silent cinema. Hugo Munsterberg, in *The Film: A Psychological Study*, published in 1916, compares the cinema to the theatre in order to better assess the unique properties of the film medium. The theatre stage thus emerges as a problematic referent for the motion pictures. Munsterberg formulates the problem as follows: "Do the photoplays furnish us only a photographic reproduction of a stage performance; is their aim thus simply to be an inexpensive substitute for the real theatre, and is their esthetic standing accordingly far below that of the true dramatic art, related to it as the photograph of a painting to the original canvas of the master?"[2] Munsterberg concludes that the cinema transcends many of the limitations of the theatre. Thus, while Munsterberg affirms that the unique art of the motion pictures lies in what film can do that the theatre cannot, his study reflects nonetheless a conception of the motion pictures as, first and foremost, a dramatic art.

For many early film theorists, writing about film was a defensive enterprise, so that differentiating film from theatre was above all an effort to define film as a worthwhile form in its own right. Implicit in Munsterberg's account is that the obvious connection of motion pictures to the stage is both appropriate and deceptive, to the extent that film articulates a different *kind* of dramatic aesthetic. Similarly, the comparison of film to other art forms would become a way, not simply of defining what film was not, but of demonstrating the uniqueness of the film medium, precisely because of its connection to other representational forms. Hence Vachel Lindsay's *The Art of the Moving Picture* (1915) reads on one level as a remarkable catalogue of cross-disciplinary possibilities. Lindsay compares different types of films to different art forms, from the Action Film defined as "sculpture-in-motion" to the Intimate Photoplay defined as "painting-in-motion" to Splendor Pictures defined as "architecture-in-motion." Despite his cross-disciplinary enthusiasm, and his insistence that "the photoplay is as far from the stage on the one hand as it is from the novel on the other," Lindsay acknowledges that cinema and the drama "are still roughly classed together by the public. The elect cannot teach the public what the drama is till they show them precisely what the photoplay is and is not."[3]

During the early decades of the cinema, then, the theatrical analogy was firmly established. For later generations of film historians, the relationship between film and the theatre was also central in tracing the early development of motion pictures, both in terms of the emergence of a distinct set of themes and structures associated with moving pictures, and in terms of the creation of a film audience. John Fell has demonstrated how the cinema emerged from a broad tradition of the popular arts in the nineteenth century, including melodrama, comic strips, stereoscopes, and dime novels.[4] According to Nicholas Vardac, the birth of moving pictures was a logical outgrowth of the demand for pictorial realism more and more in evidence in the nineteenth-century theatre. The forms most appropriate to the cinema—melodrama and spectacle—were borrowed from the theatre.[5] And the nineteenth-century stage did more than provide a set of dramatic structures and themes; it also provided a ready-made audience for the motion pictures.[6]

Common wisdom has it that during the first twenty years or so, cinema was perceived as a somewhat sleazy form of entertainment. The view that cinema began as working-class entertainment and gradually appealed to a more diverse, i.e., a more middle-class audience, has been challenged in recent work by film historians.[7] Nonetheless, in the production of motion pictures, novels—that is, the so-called classics of the middle-class tradition, rather than pulp novels—came to represent not only plots and characterizations appropriate for adaptation to the screen, but also sources with the stamp of middle-class respectability. As John Fell has documented so well, film emerged from a broad tradition of popular narrative and dramatic arts in the nineteenth century.[8] Why, then, insist on the particular relevance of the middle-class novel? While the theatrical analogy and the tradition of popular arts explain much about the emergence of the cinema, the evolution of cinema as a narrative form requires a broader frame of reference, one that situates cinema as part of both a popular and a middle-class tradition.

There is, of course, one important nineteenth-century figure in the emergence of motion pictures who was part of the popular and middle-class traditions simultaneously. One of the most famous anecdotes in the history of motion pictures has it that when producers objected that a scene might be incomprehensible to the public, filmmaker D. W. Griffith replied that he did in pictures what Charles Dickens did in words.[9] Sergei Eisenstein's assessment of the importance of Dickens for the cinema remains not only one of the most provocative explorations of cinema's relationship to nineteenth-century predecessors, but also a formulation of the particular importance of the novel in analyzing cinema as a narrative form. Few critics have pursued the strategies of comparison and contrast with as much enthusiasm as Eisenstein, who saw the principles of cinematic form in the works of authors as diverse as Flaubert, Shakespeare, and Pushkin, and who based his observations on examples drawn from the theatre and poetry, as well as the novel.

Yet in Eisenstein's 1944 essay "Dickens, Griffith and the Film Today," the novel emerges with particular force as a model for film narration. Eisenstein suggests that film had a function in Griffith's time comparable to that of the novel in Dickens' era: "What were the novels of Dickens for his contemporaries, for his readers? There is one answer: they bore the same relation to them that the film bears to the same strata in our time. They compelled the reader to live with the same passions."[10] Most significant, perhaps, the comparison between novel and film reveals the centrality of narration, understood in both technical and ideological terms, to the art of the cinema. Commenting on cinema's "ancestral array, going back as far as the Greeks and Shakespeare," Eisenstein stresses the "art of viewing—not only the *eye*, but *viewing*—both meanings being embraced in this term." For Eisenstein, Griffith's use of montage was limited by the director's dualistic vision of the world, whereas Soviet filmmakers would initiate the "esthetic growth from the *cinematographic eye* to the *image of an embodied viewpoint on phenomena*."[11]

Eisenstein's essay is something of a turning point, for it anticipates the replacement of theatre by the novel as the major term of comparison for the cinema, as well as a shift in the very function of comparison, suggesting that the cinema is at the very least equivalent, rather than inferior to, its predecessors. Alexandre Astruc, in his phrase "caméra stylo" (1948), defined the film director as an *auteur* equivalent to a literary author, and George Bluestone, in *Novels into Film* (1957), a study of adaptation, insisted that cinematic adaptations be evaluated, not as mere retellings of novels, but rather as autonomous works and on their own terms. [12]

If cinematic adaptations of traditional novels were designed to bring more respectability to the screen, the coming of sound film would seem to have enlarged the possibilities of filmed novels, and filmed plays too, for that matter. While such films were often disastrous from a cinematic viewpoint, Marie-Claire Ropars has advanced an intriguing argument concerning the strategic function of cinematic adaptation of novels. Initially, the adaptation of novels to the screen may have encouraged little in the way of cinematic experimentation. But according to Ropars, because novels and films share so many affinities as narrative forms, adaptation also led to many encounters that would expand the boundaries of film narrative. [13]

The relationship between film and the theatre has been used to describe both the history and the aesthetics of the cinema. The novel has also served as a paradigm for the historical development of film, a paradigm that is significantly broader than that of the theatre. Susan Sontag, in a 1961 essay, argued that "fifty years of the cinema present us with a scrambled recapitulation of the more than two hundred year history of the novel."[14] Ropars takes that argument considerably further. According to Ropars, analogies and affinities with the theatre (and occasional, limited expeditions into the epic and poetry) were of value primarily in a negative sense, as they demonstrated that cinema was not primarily a dramatic, or a poetic form. Only in confrontation with the novel, Ropars argues, would filmmakers begin to encounter the unique properties of cinematic *écriture*. [15]

Ropars' study was published in 1970, just prior to the development of contemporary film studies. Since the mid-1970s, film study has been characterized by a rigorous theoretical framework and a commitment to the analysis of film as a signifying system. While Ropars' approach to film history is somewhat problematic and mechanistic, *De la littérature au cinéma* occupies a significant shift in writing about cinema and the novel, and suggests how analogies between film and the novel have been defined in contemporary film studies. For Ropars suggests the necessity of evaluating cinematic adaptations, not in terms of their fidelity, or even (as in Bluestone's analysis) in terms of how the cinematic adaptation functions as an autonomous work of art, but rather in terms of how the encounter with a literary source creates a commentary on the narrative process itself. At the same time, central to Ropars' account is the narrative common denominator between film and the novel, an affiliation that surpasses the relationship between a single novel and a single film.

In contemporary film studies, the prominent role accorded the novel in previous decades has been superseded by an emphasis on narration and narrative structure in film. This does not mean that the study of adaptation has disappeared. An alternative approach to adaptation analysis has developed which explores, along the lines suggested by Ropars, how cinematic adaptations function more as commentaries, as readings, as transformations, of literary texts.[16] A parallel area of interest is the influence of the cinema on contemporary literature.[17] The field of narratology—that is, examination of the fundamental properties of narrative across a wide variety of forms—has encouraged comparisons of narrative technique in film and the novel, without the defensive posturing of proving the superiority of one form over the other.[18]

The traditional middle-class novel is influential in another, more pervasive way in contemporary film studies. The notion of classical film narrative, or of the classical realist film text, has evolved from the analogy between film and the novel. The term "classical cinema" is virtually synonymous with the Hollywood cinema, and has come to refer to the period, roughly, between the advent of sound film in the late 1920s and the demise of the studio system in the 1950s. The classical film text refers to recurrent cinematic features, such as structures of crisis and resolution, plots centering on individual characters, and interweaving patterns of binary opposition. While it is by and large agreed that the notion of the classical cinema affirms the affinity between film as narrative form and the middle-class novel, that connection has not been widely explored in contemporary film studies. A major goal of the present book, then, is to explore how an understanding of the classical Hollywood cinema can be expanded by further examining the narrative common denominators between cinema and the traditional middle-class novel.

Much theoretical work on the classical Hollywood cinema has demonstrated that a rigid set of codes governs virtually all commercial, narrative films. Thus, however different such films might be in other ways, they nonetheless conform to a specific and identifiable set of rules. The most thorough examination to date of the classical Hollywood cinema is *The Classical Hollywood Cinema*, by David Bordwell, Janet Staiger, and Kristin Thompson. Through detailed examination of the technological, industrial, and stylistic features of the institution of the Hollywood cinema, the authors emphasize the homogenous nature of the classical tradition. Hence the capacity of cinema to incorporate so many sources and influences has become an ideological force as well as an aesthetic one. Particularly telling in this regard is David Bordwell's discussion of the possibility of a classical Hollywood film which would subvert or violate the norms of the classical Hollywood mode. "In Hollywood cinema," Bordwell writes, "there are no subversive films, only subversive moments. For social and economic reasons, no Hollywood film can provide a distinct and coherent alternative to the classical model. . . . So powerful is the classical paradigm that it regulates what may violate it."[19]

The sheer length of *The Classical Hollywood Cinema* suggests its intended status as a definitive statement. The view of the classical Hollywood cinema as a monolithic institution is persuasive, given the interdependence of art and industry and the totalizing capacities of the cinema as a cultural and ideological form. If the Bordwell-Staiger-Thompson volume seems to rely too exclusively on empirical evidence as the measure of all theoretical claims, other definitions of the classical Hollywood cinema, particularly those that draw upon psychoanalysis, echo the conclusions reached by these authors. Raymond Bellour, for instance, speaks of the affinity between film and the novel in terms of their common oedipal scenarios, where the subject of narration is assumed to be white, male, and heterosexual.[20] Indeed, the very term *novelistic* has been appropriated from Marthe Robert's study of the Western middle-class novel as the enactment of the Freudian family romance.[21] From this perspective, it is the function of cinema to carry on the oedipal tradition of the novel. Colin MacCabe identifies the classic realist text, in the nineteenth-century novel as well as in the cinema, as a set of discursive constraints grounded in the suppression of contradiction.[22] In contemporary film studies, then, the central notion of classical narrative suggests a novel-film connection defined by a monolithic ideology of the male bourgeois subject, incapable of serving any other ends but those prescribed by dominant ideology.

By far the most influential definition of the classical realist text is Roland Barthes's S/Z, an analysis of Balzac's novella, "Sarrasine." Barthes's distinction between two modes of reading, the readerly (*le lisible*) and the writerly (*le scriptible*), has a particularly strong field of application in contemporary film theory. The readerly is a function of the classical text: "The reader is thereby plunged into a kind of idleness—he is intransitive; he is, in short, *serious*: instead of functioning himself, instead of gaining access to the magic of the signifier, to the pleasure of writing, he is left with no more than the poor freedom either to accept or reject the text: reading is nothing more than a *referendum*."[23]

The distinction between the readerly and the writerly is primarily a question of the materiality of language, as well as the difference between a referential and transparent use of language, on the one hand, and an engagement with the complexity and polyvalence of linguistic signs, on the other. The distinction suggests also different ideological uses of language. The readerly is characterized by the unquestioned subservience of literature to a coherent referent, and the writerly, by the opening up of another space which is irreducible to the demands of ideology. In contemporary film theory, classical film narrative and the readerly tend to be interchangeable terms, with the attendant implication that the only cinematic equivalents of the writerly are to be found through films which deconstruct the codes of classical film narrative.

Central to Barthes's analysis is the way in which texts are read. Thus the writerly defines the reader as a producer rather than as a consumer.[24] Barthes's analysis of "Sarrasine" is predicated on its "limited plural," that is, on an ambivalent status which is neither pure "readerly" nor pure "writerly." Barthes's rewriting of "Sarrasine," reading in a "writerly" fashion against the "readerly" grain, raises some perplexing questions about the ambivalent status of classical narrative. Is "Sarrasine" an exceptional, isolated example, or does the "limited plural" inhabit many, perhaps all, realist narratives to one degree or another? Can the "writerly" only exist as a function of a specific kind of textual analysis, or is literature, in its institutional quality, characterized by more complexity than the opposition of readerly and writerly would allow?

In contemporary film theory, the tendency to erect firm and rigid barriers between the readerly and the writerly, between the classical cinema and alternatives to it, reveals a problematic dualism. The way in which the novel is evoked, in discussions of classical film narrative, suggests an institution firmly situated within the camp of Barthes's "readerly." This study aims to rethink the relationship between the classical Hollywood cinema and the middle-class novel, to argue that the structures and functions of narrative that cinema has inherited from the middle-class novel are determined both by the articulation of middle-class ideals and resistance to them. The point is not to rescue classical narrative, but rather to insist that the social framework of narrative is irreducible to convenient clichés about the inevitably passive, transparent and ideologically coherent forms of the novel or the cinema.

Narrative is a process created and shaped by the act of reading, by the interaction between readers, texts, and social reality. Narrative creates imaginary reconciliations between opposing terms. Those reconciliations are not always, however, simple affirmations of dominant ideology. The reconciliations posited in narrative are more appropriately described as fantasies—fantasies in which the terms reconciled are often irreconcilable in everyday experience. Barthes's analysis suggests that classical narrative tends as much towards the writerly as the readerly; the difference is, precisely, a question of reading. Certainly one impulse of classical narrative is the containment of experience within familiar boundaries. At the same time, however, narrative articulates the contradictions of middle-class society.[25]

In order to examine how novels and films share a preoccupation with private and public life, I draw on a number of theoretical and critical frameworks. The separation of private and public life is of particular interest to Marxists and to feminists. My approach to the topic has been particularly influenced by recent feminist scholarship, which has drawn attention to the problematic status of the private and the public as inscribing both the aspirations and the limitations of women's lives in industrial societies.[26] Close readings of individual texts are central to the study, as I attempt to situate those individual narrative structures within broader patterns of cultural meaning. The theoretical project of this book is perhaps best described as an analysis of the mediations of private and public life as they occur in the novel and the cinema. In Marxist criticism, the term "mediation" describes the ways in which socio-economic reality connects both to the realms of the superstructure and to individual experience. Mediation assumes that there is no direct line, no immediate relationship, that connects the economic base with all of the elements of the superstructure—religion, the press, the legal system, education—not to mention the arts.[27]

The model of base and superstructure is not peculiar to Marxist criticism, for a certain kind of feminist perspective is determined by the notion of a patriarchal base upon which a sexist superstructure is erected. The model of base and superstructure relegates literature and cinema to the superstructure along with a host of other objects with which they may have little visible connection. A certain kind of criticism deals only with art perceived as the ubiquitous "reflection" of reality, whether it be the reality of the economic base or of patriarchy. The very notion of mediation has been an alternative to the reduction of artistic and cultural products to mere "reflections." Unlike the term "reflection," the term "mediation" suggests that the path from one social instance to another is full of detours, margins, and complex turns.[28]

The risk in defining mediation as an object of study is in perpetuating the linearity and duality of base and superstructure, cause and effect, whereby narrative becomes a complex reflection rather than a simple one, but a reflection nonetheless.[29] As I have stated, the present study is an attempt to rethink the relationship between film and the novel so as to avoid the simple dualities characteristic of much writing about classical narrative. The term mediation is only useful, I would argue, if it puts into question the simplistic categories of cause and effect. I certainly do not claim, for instance, that the separation of the private and the public somehow "caused" the rise of the middle-class novel and the invention of motion pictures. Because I examine the social functions of readership and spectatorship, the risk of another kind of duality—between the "text" and the "social," as if the two were ever so easily separable—is present as well. I have attempted, rather, to maintain a tension between the different levels which are central to this study. Tension implies dialogue—not hierarchy, and not reflection.

The book follows a chronological pattern, although its historical contours are not meant to be exhaustive—this is neither a history of the private and the public, nor a history of narrative. Rather, it is historical in the sense that the advent of a "new" narrative form, the cinema, can best be assessed by examining how it engages—in both similar and dissimilar ways—with the paradigm of the novel. I argue that the narrative contours of the encounter between the private and the public have taken shape, in analogous ways, at crucial moments of emergence (the eighteenth-century British novel; the early cinema in the United States) and maturation (the nineteenth-century European novel; American cinema of the 1940s).

Chapters 1 and 2 deal with the middle-class novel in relationship to private and public life. In chapter 1, I examine the phenomenon of the rise of the novel in eighteenth-century England and the changing dimensions of private and public life. I suggest that two quintessential creations of the eighteenth century, Clarissa Harlowe and Robinson Crusoe, reveal in both their oppositions and their similarities the itineraries of private and public life. In chapter 2, two nineteenth-century novels are examined in detail. Jane Austen's *Pride and Prejudice* and Honoré de Balzac's *Eugénie Grandet* exemplify two narratives of private and public life: the one a fantasy of reconciliation, whereby an ideal marriage consolidates the potentially conflicting realms of the private and the public; and the other a nightmare of reification, where such consolidation leads only to the destruction of the private sphere. *Pride and Prejudice* and *Eugénie Grandet* are not presented here as necessarily "representative" of virtually every nineteenth-century novel. Not *every* nineteenth-century novel is as centrally concerned with the private and the public as these two are. Rather, these novels are exemplary texts, in that they demonstrate, in bold relief, the narrative ramifications of the private and the public.

In chapter 3, I examine the emerging narrative conventions of the early (pre-1910) American cinema. It has been amply demonstrated that the construction of spectatorship in the early cinema evolved from the popular theatre of the nineteenth century. Nonetheless there are analogies to be made with the emergence of readership in the British novel. While the public sphere of early motion pictures may have been modelled on that of the nineteenth-century popular stage, the narrative dimensions of early spectatorship suggest an equally strong affinity with the components of readership.

In chapter 4, I examine the notion of classical film narrative as a theoretical and critical concept, with particular reference to the influence of literary notions of authorship and readership. Chapter 5 consists of close readings of two films, *Rebecca* and *Mildred Pierce*. These films exemplify the profoundly ambivalent status of classical film narrative in relationship to private and public life. Both films are structured, ostensibly, by a female point of view, one which strains between the functions of reconciliation and reification. Chapter 6, in conclusion, examines briefly the relationship between classical film narrative of the 1940s, and other examples of narrative cinema which depart from the classical Hollywood tradition.

The relationship between narrative and the spheres of private and public life is a particularly appropriate vantage point from which to examine the ways in which novels and films negotiate, in parallel ways, the complex process of both affirming and resisting middle-class ideals. My claim is not that the opposition of private and public is the primary thematic bond between novels and films, but that it encompasses a number of relations crucial to both forms—between men and women, between social classes, between the reader/viewer and the text. The relationship between the private and the public is both a thematic preoccupation and a central factor in the development of readership and spectatorship in the middle-class European novel and the classical Hollywood cinema, respectively. The spheres of private and public life, as both theme and structure within the text, on the one hand, and as major determinations of how the reading of novels and the viewing of films would acquire a social function, on the other, provide a unique vantage point for an examination of the social implications of narrative.

PRIVATE AND
PUBLIC SPHERES

Clarissa and Robinson

In the early eighteenth century and primarily in England, narrative began to assume new dimensions and new functions, shaped by middle-class needs and expectations. This was the time, in the words of Ian Watt's famous study, of the "rise of the novel."[1] Novels occupied a social space, indicated both by their subjects and forms, and by the very function that the reading of novels acquired. More important, novels *created* a social space. It is this capacity of narrative, in the form of the middle-class novel and later the cinema, to respond to the conditions of experience defined by Western capitalist societies which will be explored in this study. Thus I am working from the assumption that the middle-class novel as social form has determined, in a variety of ways, our social and aesthetic expectations of narrative cinema.

In the history of the novel as middle-class art form, there are many individual works that could be cited as exemplary. In eighteenth-century novels like *Pamela, Moll Flanders, Tom Jones, Robinson Crusoe,* and *Clarissa,* key features emerge as emblematic of a middle-class imagination: individual characterization, psychological motivation, attention to the details of everyday life, situations drawn—literally or figuratively—from middle-class experience.[2] From those exemplary works, I begin with two, *Robinson Crusoe* and *Clarissa,* which are of interest to this study for their differences as much as for their similarities. *Robinson Crusoe* and *Clarissa* strikingly illustrate both the common features of early middle-class novels, and the marked differences which separated the journeys of men and women characters. Held up to one another, *Robinson Crusoe* and *Clarissa* are like the negative filmstrip held up to the positive image: they bear the same image, while the one is fundamentally different from the other.

In Daniel Defoe's 1719 novel, Robinson Crusoe leaves England on a series of adventures which eventually lead him to the island where he builds a kingdom, of sorts. His island-kingdom becomes the site for a condensed history of civilization, read and written from a middle-class perspective. Thus, the thread of individual initiative gradually interweaves with those of religious puritanism and white chauvinism, and Robinson becomes a producer rather than a mere survivor. *Robinson Crusoe* has been called the first middle-class novel, but Robinson's world of experience is as much a fantasy of middle-class values as an accurate reflection of them. The fantasy is located in the excessive visibility of principles of production. Whether Robinson is growing corn or writing his journal, building a canoe or instructing Friday, he is constantly and unremittingly a producer. No matter how complex Robinson's activities, they are always identified for the reader as governed by their utility, their productivity. The complexity of experience is distilled and clarified into one fundamental form: that of economy.

Such a narrative process of distillation and clarification entails, of necessity, some absences. Perhaps the most striking absence in *Robinson Crusoe* concerns human relations. In human communication as in the growing of corn and the baking of bread, economy and productivity are the rule. Thus, it is perhaps not too surprising that all Crusoe has to say about his marriage and family is conveyed in one brief paragraph, beginning with a cursory "In the meantime. . . ."

Crusoe's journey takes him away from England, away from "civilized" society; and if his island-kingdom is in some ways a mirror of his homeland, it is in other ways an experiment in the possibilities of obsessive single-mindedness. The single-mindedness takes the form of an expanding set of concentric circles. Crusoe's journey moves constantly outward, not just in the simple geographical terms that take him away from England, but in his own development as a social man, as *Homo Economicus*.[3] The journey of Clarissa Harlowe, in Samuel Richardson's novel of the 1740s, moves inversely, uncovering the complexities of private life, the family, personal relations, love, and marriage. Clarissa's journey moves constantly inward. *Clarissa* is certainly a middle-class novel, although not in the same way *Robinson Crusoe* is. In Richardson's work, the central tensions stem from an aristocratic versus a middle-class view of marriage. Clarissa wants to marry for love; her parents insist that she marry according to their economic designs. Hence the novel describes the tension between the "most important concerns of private life" and socially defined roles and expectations. These tensions occur not only in the conflict between bourgeois and aristocratic views of marriage, but also in the conflicts between economic gain and personal fulfillment, between male aggression and female passivity.[4]

Clarissa searches for an inner life, for a shelter from the social changes threatening to transform drastically every aspect of daily life. Yet for Clarissa, this inner life remains utopian: she is constantly badgered either by the demands of her family, or by the sexual advances of Lovelace. Clarissa's search for personal integrity is especially problematic because it is in direct opposition to the desires of her family. Within the Harlowe family, personal happiness is only possible in direct correlation to the economic and social designs of the male members of the household.

The opposing itineraries of *Robinson Crusoe* and *Clarissa*—the one, a plunge into an economic universe, the other, a retreat from it—can be seen as the narrative equivalents of the concern, in eighteenth-century society, with the differences and the connections between the spheres of private and public life. Private and public: these terms seem, at first glance, like simple synonyms for the individual and the social, or for the "singular" versus the "mass" phenomenon. Surely the narrative concern for the relations between the individual and the social predates middle-class society by quite a few years, as narratives like *The Iliad* and *The Odyssey* make abundantly clear. I use the terms private and public, however, to designate the specific way in which the relationship between the individual and the social is articulated in Western middle-class societies.

"Private" and "public" correspond to "individual" and "social" only in the broadest, and ultimately, most ahistorical sense. In Western middle-class societies, any understanding of the relationship between the individual and society is bound by the separation of the private (the family, friendship, intimate relations) from the public (work, business relations, social institutions).[5]

In his study of the public sphere of Western societies, Richard Sennett notes that the "eighteenth-century usage [of the terms private and public] sets up the modern terms of reference." The first recorded uses of the word "public" in English equate "public" with the "common good of society." Later, "public" came to mean "that which is manifest and open to general observation." "By the end of the seventeenth century," writes Sennett, "the opposition of 'public' and 'private' was shaded more like the way the terms are now used. 'Public' meant open to the scrutiny of anyone, whereas 'private' meant a sheltered region of life defined by one's family and friends. . . ."[6]

The different paths traced in *Robinson Crusoe* and *Clarissa* suggest in specific terms how public space and private space were perceived in eighteenth-century society.[7] In *Robinson Crusoe*, an ideal public sphere is created.[8] The principle of this sphere is economy: anything which does not have an immediate, visible productive function is dismissed in the novel. The primary concern of *Clarissa*, on the other hand, is the family as the major institution of the private sphere. Narrative in *Robinson Crusoe* works to create a sense of the public sphere of capitalist values, whereas in *Clarissa* narrative functions to explore the nature of the private sphere.[9]

If the middle-class novel creates social space, the contours of that space are defined by the spheres of private and public existence. Indeed, few "documents" offer more extensive meditations on the significance of private and public existence than the novel. This is not to suggest that the middle-class novel is a simple mode of expression which reflects, in a one-dimensional and direct way, the social concerns of class society. Narrative is a mode of understanding, a structure within which questions are raised and answers tested, a fiction of possibilities and hypotheses. In narrative, then, the relationship between the two spheres of public and private life is examined, articulated, and thought through. The middle-class novel has a special function in relation to private and public existence, a function defined by the capacity of narrative to create and examine opposing terms and their interrelations.

I have suggested that *Robinson Crusoe* and *Clarissa* occupy different areas of concern: that Defoe's novel articulates a public sphere, Richardson's a private sphere. Yet the space separating private from public spheres is not as great as the differences between these two novels would initially suggest. Clarissa pursues the inviolability of her personal values to the end, but her struggle cannot escape the economic terms against which her personal integrity initially is directed. The novel seems to draw a circle around love, around personal space; yet at the same time documents the impossibility of such inviolability. Clarissa is drawn into a broadening circle where personal and social values are conflated. She preserves her "personal life" by regarding her body as her most prized possession, her virtue as something that cannot be sold, her virginity as something that cannot be given away. Clarissa revolts against the proliferation of economic principles, yet she herself is doomed to accept the terms of commodity exchange.[10] The contradiction underlying Clarissa's predicament is that the inner life can only survive when it is defined within the terms of buying and selling, ownership and free enterprise.[11]

And even though *Robinson Crusoe* may seem to be firmly entrenched within the public sphere, Robinson's life on his island-kingdom is marked by a constant return to his personal origins, to his father. It is, we recall, Crusoe's father who functions, in the early pages of the novel, as the voice of middle-class values. It was he who spoke to Robinson about the "middle-state," describing it as "the best state in the world, the most suited to human happiness."[12] Crusoe's remarkable religious conversion, which occurs during a period of serious illness on the island, is the most striking example in the novel of the constant importance of his father. That conversion is reminiscent of Crusoe's bouts with illness on his first sea voyage, when he also appealed to a father, repenting for having rebelled against him in the first place. The relation of a son to his father thus acquires a symbolic importance for Crusoe, and becomes a principle of survival.

However firmly entrenched *Robinson Crusoe* may seem to be in the public sphere, and *Clarissa* in the private sphere, each novel is characterized by the displacement of one set of concerns onto the other. There is a principle of economy operative in *Clarissa*: instead of being directed toward production, its "normal" field of application, that principle is directed inward, defined in terms of a politics of family life. The refusal of the Harlowe family to disengage familial and business concerns presses Clarissa to defend all the more strongly the sanctity of private life. There is, in both *Robinson Crusoe* and *Clarissa*, a principle of colonization operative; the difference is primarily one of context. Friday becomes (and each utterance of his name reiterates this fact) the property of Robinson. This colonized servant is but one element in the activities of production defining Robinson's existence. Colonization in *Clarissa* has but one object, repeated over and over again: the female body. The terms of desire—sexual on the part of Lovelace, economic on the part of the Harlowes—become more and more difficult to distinguish as Clarissa's body is so obsessively sought after in the novel. As Terry Eagleton puts it, "The 'universal commodity' (Marx), magically unchanging in itself yet source of 'magical' transformations in others, 'pure gold' yet in ceaseless liquidity, Clarissa's body is itself the discourse of the text. It is the signifier which distributes others to their positions of power or desire, fixing them in some fraught relation to her own mysteriously inviolable being."[13]

The economic principle central to *Robinson Crusoe* is thus rendered more diffuse in *Clarissa*, obscured as it is by the nature of sexual desire and familial power. And by the same token, Crusoe's family—in the form of his father—is present throughout *Robinson Crusoe*. If Crusoe becomes a child on the island in relation to the Christian god to whom he prays, then he becomes a father in his turn when he adopts Friday as his servant and surrogate child.[14] The private sphere is not absent from *Robinson Crusoe*; it is merely embedded within the context of production—just as the public sphere is, in *Clarissa*, embedded within the family.

The categories of private and public space are not, then, rigidly separate. But if a comparison of *Robinson Crusoe* and *Clarissa* suggests the interdependence of private and public spheres, there is another separation, linked to private and public space, which resists such fluidity. This is the difference between male and female spheres of activity, a difference most emphatically represented by the relation of each of these characters to language. In both novels, first-person narration dominates: the "I" of Robinson's journal and the personal account that frames it; and the "I" of Clarissa's letters which alternates with the voices of other letter-writers in the novel. Each "I" records a different function of language. Clarissa speaks from within the confines of domestic space, and her letters describe in detail the drama within the Harlowe family and her experiences with Lovelace. For Clarissa, writing functions as personal expression and contact. Letters define the contours of female friendship and of male-female romance. Crusoe's journal, however, serves primarily as a form of record-keeping, a logbook of his productive activities. These two different definitions of writing suggest different modes of identification on the part of the reader. Reading Clarissa's letters suggests an invasion of privacy, a peek into the private concerns hidden from public view, whereas reading Robinson's journal suggests a form of public record from which no private concerns are hidden simply because there are none to hide. Language, in these two novels, has male and female poles of expression.

The difference between male and female occupies more or less the same territory as the separation between private and public spheres: to women belongs the preoccupation with private life, and to men, the shaping of the public sphere. Female and private, male and public: these are, in the history of the middle-class novel, practically synonymous terms. However, if the boundaries between private and public spheres are not always clearly marked and neatly separated, the difference between male and female is affirmed more resolutely. It is significant in this regard that Robinson and Clarissa encounter characters whose sexual identity is ambiguous, like Mrs. Sinclair who assists Lovelace in his plans to rape Clarissa: the woman is described as a monster, as an aberration, as a woman with an overabundance of distinctly male qualities. And surely Friday has what is ultimately an ambiguous sex role in relation to Robinson. Friday is servant, child, worker, slave—not to mention a kind of substitute wife. Yet in the face of sexual ambiguity, Clarissa and Robinson both—as writers and as narrators—keep their sexual identities intact.

Sexual identity on the one hand, class identity on the other: the journeys of Clarissa and Robinson involve, in however different ways, a process of intersection of these two determinations. Put another way, Clarissa and Robinson are figures of the possible relationships between class and sexual identities. Surely one of the most distinctive characteristics of the middle-class novel is, precisely, the attention to the contradictions and consolidations between sexual and class identities. And it is through private and public space that these identities are negotiated: private space, where female and male identities are generated, and where the family is a mirror of sorts of class society; and public space, where female and male identities assume different social forms, and where class identity asserts itself.[15]

Private and Public Spheres

If the relation between private and public spheres is a major preoccupation of the middle-class novel, it is a function of the enormous social changes underlying the emergence of the areas of private and public life as new concerns in the eighteenth century. Three areas thus emerge as central to the social and narrative space of the novel: the economic organization of production, the family, and the definition of male and female roles.

Capitalist development has been marked by an increasingly sharp division of the world into the opposing spheres of work and leisure, the workplace and the home. While it is true that much of the history of capitalist production took place within the family as an economic unit, it is equally true that, as historian Eli Zaretsky writes, "the overall tendency of capitalist development has been to socialize the basic processes of commodity production—to remove labour from the private efforts of individual families or villages and to centralize it in large-scale corporate units. Capitalism is the first society in history to socialize production on a large scale." The mode of capitalist production relies on a separation between the socialized labor of the capitalist enterprise and labor performed within the home. That initial split is tied, as Zaretsky points out, to a second split, "between our 'personal' lives and our place within the social division of labor."[16] "Just as capitalist development gave rise to the idea of the family as a realm separate from the economy, so it created a 'separate' sphere of personal life, seemingly divorced from the mode of production."[17]

As the family began to have a less direct role in production, the very definition of "family" began to change. Philippe Ariès, in his study of the family and childhood, specifies the eighteenth century as the decisive period of change. The family unit gradually reduced to parents and children, and no longer included the extended family, nor servants and laborers. In the process, the former function of the family in public, collective terms gave way to a more isolated, sheltered existence: "In the eighteenth century, the family began to hold society at a distance, to push it back beyond a steadily extending zone of private life."[18] An immediately visible effect of this change was the house. Rooms became specialized, with separate rooms designated for sleeping and eating. This division of the space of the home satisfied, according to Ariès, a "new desire for isolation." It was primarily through the family, in short, that the separation between private and public life was accommodated.

> It is as if the modern family has sought to take the place of the old social relationships (as these gradually defaulted), in order to preserve mankind from an unbearable moral solitude. Starting in the eighteenth century, people began defending themselves against a society whose constant intercourse had hitherto been the source of education, reputation and wealth. Henceforth a fundamental movement would destroy the old connections between masters and servants, great and small, friends or clients. . . . Everywhere it reinforced private life at the expense of neighborly relationships, friendship, traditional contacts. The

history of modern manners can be reduced in part to this long
effort to break away from others, to escape from a society whose
pressure had become unbearable . . . Professional and family
life had stifled that other activity which once invaded the whole
of life: the activity of social relations.[19]

Hence the very design of houses revealed the increasing separation
between the private and the public. If the house reveals what Ariès
calls the "new desire for isolation," it would also reveal, in its internal
divisions, a distinction between rooms essentially open to the public,
like the drawing room, and rooms reserved for the pursuits of private
life, like the bedroom. The activities of reading and letter-writing
would make their own contribution to this separation within domestic
space. We know that libraries were common in middle- and upper-
class homes, and so were closets off the bedroom, where women, in
particular, would read and write letters.[20]

The division of life in industrialized societies into the two worlds of
work and home, of social and personal relations, is one instance of a
fundamental dualism characteristic of western culture. One thinks,
for instance, of another set of terms which formed the center of many
philosophical debates throughout the eighteenth century: the opposition between nature and culture, between, in the terms proposed by
Jean-Jacques Rousseau, the noble savage in vital touch with the
rhythms of the natural world, and the civilized European so corrupted
by socialization as to be out of touch with any sense of a species-
existence. The relation between private and public existence intersects
with this conception of the opposing forces of nature and culture. If
the public sphere is the realm of work and social intercourse, then the
private sphere is perceived as maintaining some measure of contact
with the natural world of emotions, cycles of birth and death, and
affective bonds. Thus, Richard Sennett describes the eighteenth-century view of private and public as follows: "The public was a human
creation; the private was the human condition."[21]

The profound effect of such a division, the precise nature of private
and public spheres, and the relations—real and imaginary—between
them, are better grasped by examining the nature of production as a
determining principle of the public sphere. If such a consideration
seems to lead us away from narrative, it is worth remembering that in
middle-class societies novel-production has always been an industry in
which the boundaries between "production" and "creation" are fluid.

The opening lines of Henry Fielding's *Tom Jones* (1749) are instructive in this regard: "An author ought to consider himself, not as a gentleman who gives a private or eleemosynary treat, but rather as one who keeps a public ordinary, at which all persons are welcome for their money."[22] Fielding is of course describing the new role of the novelist in a society defined by commodity production. No longer simply accountable to a small group of people, the writer produces for a market of readers who are at once "ordinary" and anonymous.

It is a commonplace that the capitalist mode of production is characterized by the distinction between use value and exchange value: use value, the immediate utility of an object (shoes are to be worn, food products to be eaten); exchange value, the worth of one product in relation to others. Unlike pre-capitalist societies, where production was determined exclusively by the use-value of individual objects, capitalist production subjugates use value to exchange value. Products are valued not according to their potential use, but according to how much they are worth in relation to other products. Central to the entire process of exchange is money as the abstract determination of value.

The distinction between use value and exchange value may seem to have only the most remote connection to the spheres of private and public life. But if the public sphere of industrialized societies is founded upon the separation of the workplace and the home, that public sphere is constituted by much more than just the workplace. It is, precisely, exchange value as a *principle* which permeates areas of life outside the immediate area of production, and is instrumental in creating the public sphere of industrialized societies. This process is the basis of narrative development in *Robinson Crusoe*.

In Marxist terms, the process whereby the realm of production connects to the variety of institutions and relations that determine social reality is reification. From this vantage point, the organization of work—a relation of human beings to the objects they produce—determines a two-fold process of reification: relations between human beings take on the appearance of relations between objects, and objects become endowed with human characteristics. Marx wrote in *A Contribution to the Critique of Political Economy*: "A social relation of production appears as something existing apart from individual human beings, and the distinctive relations into which they enter in the course of production in society appear as the specific properties of a thing—it is this perverted appearance, this prosaically real, and by no means imaginary, mystification that is characteristic of all social forms of labour positing exchange-value."[23]

The most famous elaboration of reification is to be found in Georg Lukacs's *History and Class Consciousness.* Lukacs examines the ways in which reification modifies subjective consciousness, and leads human relations to a state of "phantom objectivity," that is, "an autonomy that seems so strictly rational and all-embracing as to conceal every trace of its fundamental nature: the relation between people."[24] As capitalism develops and expands, those features initially a part of commodity production permeate all aspects of society. Hence: "Reification requires that a society should learn to satisfy all its needs in terms of commodity exchange."[25] Capitalist development thus introduces a new form of social relations; Lukacs writes that "for the first time in history—the whole of society is subjected, or tends to be subjected, to a unified economic process, and . . . the fate of every member of society is determined by unified laws."[26] Reification as defined here is a continuous process of penetration: "the structure of reification progressively sinks more deeply, more fatefully and more definitively into the consciousness of man."[27] The distinction that an author like Fielding makes between private and public responsibilities would thus be a symptom of this infiltration of commodity production into all areas of creation.

Lukacs's own work on literary criticism suggests that the middle-class novel has a strategic function in this subjection of society to a "unified economic process." For Lukacs, the very form of the traditional, realist novel, structured by an individual quest, is a search for organic meaning and totality in a world where such values no longer exist: "The novel is the epic of an age in which the extensive totality of life is no longer directly given, in which the immanence of meaning in life has become a problem, yet which still thinks in terms of totality."[28] Thus the novel has a double function, for it reflects the reified values of its own age, and yet preserves links (because of its emergence from the epic) to a utopian past untouched by the forces of capitalist value.

Thus defined, the novel has a utopian burden that borders on idealization and romanticization. The dangers of this particular kind of utopianism are particularly marked in the work of Lucien Goldmann. For Goldmann, reification results from the substitution of exchange value for use value, thus creating, in the "psychic structure" of the individual, "abstract, universal relations between buyers and sellers" in the place of genuine human relations.[29] Like Lukacs, Goldmann perceives a special function of the middle-class novel in reified societies: "The novel form seems to me, in effect, to be *the transposition on the literary plane of everyday life in the individualistic society created by market production.* There is a *rigorous homology* between the literary form of the novel . . . and the everyday relation between man and commodities in general, and by extension between man and other men, in a market society."[30]

The concept of reification requires that the dependence of the public sphere of middle-class societies on commodity production be understood as a complex process. It is essential to recognize, simultaneously, the diversity of the public sphere, and the recurrent features which are particular to capitalist production.[31]

Of the two spheres of private and public existence, the public sphere would appear to be infinitely more diverse than the private sphere. The public sphere comprises not only the city and the factory, but spaces like the marketplace, the store; institutions like commerce and transportation; relations like boss and worker, or buyer and seller. In contrast, the private sphere seems relatively uniform. Even when class differences are taken into account, the private sphere is an easily definable space (the house, the room, the apartment), and an easily definable set of relations, limited primarily to household and family ties.

But if reification is a persistent movement, it can hardly stop suddenly at the threshold of family life. Now one could argue, with Goldmann, that it has been the function of the family to *resist* reification; that the private sphere is in fact the one area of life where use value exists relatively unencumbered by exchange value. "In the private sphere, the sphere of consumption," writes Goldmann, the individual is "alone before the products he consumes; or . . . relations between family members or friends, precisely because they are private, that is, more or less removed from the *immediate* impact of the marketplace, still preserve to a certain extent interpersonal generosity and solidarity." In the private sphere, Goldmann suggests, some measure of contact with natural existence, with human values uncorrupted by capitalist economy, is maintained. Such contact is "the privilege of 'poets, children, and women,' that is, of individuals in the *margins of economic life*."[32]

Goldmann's designation of these "margins of economic life" suggests not only a tendency to romanticize, but also an extremely narrow definition of the economic infrastructure. Indeed, theories of reification run the risk of positing a mechanistic model of production, and of relegating to the category of "symptom" any determination which cannot be defined readily and immediately within the terms of capitalist production. Since the separation of private and public spheres is so closely linked with the separation of male and female realms of activity, a feminist perspective on the relationship between the private and the public is vital. Recent feminist analysis questions the so-called "margins of economic life." In her analysis of Marxist and psychoanalytic responses to the position of women in capitalist societies, for example, Ann Foreman offers a different view than those of Goldmann or Lukacs. Like Goldmann, Foreman stresses the function of the family as receptacle for the values no longer tolerated in a commodity-determined environment: "Although the subjective existence of the individual was destroyed in industry . . . it remained alive in the family relations outside."[33] Foreman's analysis has the advantage of a more complex view of the function of the private sphere; not only the public sphere is directly affected by the changes wrought by capitalist development. The private sphere, when stripped of the functions which in pre-capitalist societies were integrated with production, becomes a site of alienated activity as well:

> As social production became detached from the family, these
> latter relations apparently lost their economic meaning.
> Stripped of this the family became the realm of the personal
> and the sexual, emotions that were considered subjective and
> not susceptible to intellectual analysis. The relations between
> men and women no longer rested, as in pre-capitalist epochs,
> on the industrial roles that each played within society but on
> their own spontaneous and personal feelings of love. But, more-
> over, because the individual's self-confirmation took place
> within the family and not the work situation, it was in these
> terms that individuality became defined. Thus the process of
> alienation and reification which revealed the class dynamic of
> capitalism at the same time plunged individual experience into
> the obscure depths of the emotional and the sexual.[34]

The public sphere of Western industrialized societies is shaped directly and indirectly by the principles of capitalist production. Such a definition of the public sphere evolves from the relations of individuals to the social division of labor. Hence the private sphere could be understood as the area where those needs, denied or deferred in the public sphere, are fulfilled. But concealed within such a definition of private and public space as production-bound is another relationship: that between men and women, between male and female spheres of activity. To identify private and public spheres uniquely in terms of production is to adopt a perspective which in capitalist societies has been primarily that of men.[35] Joan Kelly, summarizing the work of Marxist-Feminist theories of recent years, writes: "Feminist thinkers in the Marxist tradition . . . have shown how the separation of work (production) from leisure (consumption) really exists for men only. As a conception of society, the notion of home as a refuge from the world of work masks a sexual division of labor. It mystifies women's work in the home, obscuring the fact that this domestic labor helps 'reproduce' capitalist and patriarchal society."[36]

We have seen, via Clarissa Harlowe and Robinson Crusoe, how the relation between private and public spheres constructed by each character is bound by the mutually reinforcing identities of class and sex. In considering how the principles of capitalist production create a public sphere, we see again, now in less specifically literary terms, how the relationship between private and public space needs to be evaluated from the perspective of male and female realms of activity. This perspective intersects with a socio-economic view of private and public space, but is not reducible to it. Here, for instance, is how Foreman describes the effect of the split between work and home on male and female identities: "Capitalism split society into two worlds— the world of business, industry and social interchange, and the world of the family. But the two were not symmetrical. Men strove to rule in the first, but failing that were the victors in the second. Women were their foil in both. Family life provided the relief where, after the threats and assaults that social life made on a man's confidence, the woman confirmed his humanity and subjectivity."[37]

The experience of the public sphere is potentially quite different for women than for men. Reification is a useful concept only if it takes into account the different ways in which men and women live the disjuncture between private and public space. If the private sphere functions as a site of a more "natural" human identity, a site of non-alienated activity, then such a function must be *produced*.[38] Historically, it has been the task of women to do so. It is questionable whether the work required to create such a "refuge" can remain impervious to the force of reification.

If the public sphere is the realm determined by production, then the parallel term to describe the private sphere is reproduction, the familial ties of husband and wife, parent and child.[39] But to define the private sphere as limited to the nuclear family has two sets of interrelated consequences, one socio-economic and one sexual. First, we assume that the private sphere is indeed set apart from work relations, and that the family ties are the principal, if not the only means, through which individuals experience personal relationships. And second, we assume that women, whether they work outside the home or not, are defined primarily by their family identity, as wives, daughters, or mothers. Thus men would appear to move freely between the realms of private and public space, whereas women's involvement in the public sphere is bound by the private sphere, the family.

The relation between public and private spheres is an ideological relationship, through which Western middle-class societies are experienced, simultaneously, in the terms of commodity production and the patriarchal family. This is not to say that the split between home and workplace is simply a barrier erected by false consciousness. However, the very nature of that "split" needs to be interrogated.[40] No matter how separate the realms of private and public, they are also profoundly linked. The boundaries between private and public space are not always as clearly marked as the simple distinction between home and workplace would suggest. As we have seen, the apparently opposing worlds of *Robinson Crusoe* and *Clarissa* have more in common than meets the eye, and it is virtually impossible to speak of either novel as structured uniquely by the private or the public sphere.

Recent historical scholarship has shown that the categories of private and public space are not always easily distinguishable, and offers us some illuminating evidence on the specifically *narrative* implications of that overlap between private and public realms. Carroll Smith-Rosenberg has spoken, for instance, of the "female world of love and ritual" which was an essential feature of the lives of many American women in the eighteenth and nineteenth centuries.[41] Within the private sphere of home and female work, women formed extensive networks of communication which were frequently based on the extended family, as well as on friendships formed in neighborhoods and at schools. The very nature of these networks suggests patterns of community which transcend the isolated realms of individual homes, and which challenge the notion of women's dependence on husbands and fathers for any sense of social identity. This "female world of varied and yet highly structured relationships," writes

Smith-Rosenberg, was one in which "men made but a shadowy appearance."[42]

In examining the conditions which allowed these strong patterns of female relationships to occur, Smith-Rosenberg says:

> American society was characterized in large part by rigid gender-role differentiation within the family and within society as a whole, leading to the emotional segregation of women and men. The roles of daughter and mother shaded imperceptibly and ineluctably into each other, while the biological realities of frequent pregnancies, childbirth, nursing, and menopause bound women together in physical and emotional intimacy. It was within just such a social framework, I would argue, that a specifically female world did indeed develop, a world built around a generic and unself-conscious pattern of single-sex or homosocial networks. These supportive networks were institutionalized in social conventions or rituals which accompanied virtually every important event in a woman's life, from birth to death.[43]

One might assume that the "female world of love and ritual" was simply a refuge, like the frequently described function of the private sphere as a refuge from the public sphere. But a refuge from what? From the private sphere itself, as a kind of reflection in miniature of the nuclear family? Smith-Rosenberg notes that through their friendships women formed social networks: "Friends did not form isolated dyads but were normally part of highly integrated networks."[44] These extensive patterns of friendship did not intensify women's isolated position within the private sphere; rather, they removed women from their isolation within individual, nuclear families. Hence Smith-Rosenberg insists that "Women . . . did not form an isolated and oppressed subcategory in male society."[45]

Smith-Rosenberg suggests that the nuclear family is not necessarily the sole, nor even the primary, institution of the private sphere. The separation of male and female realms of activity does not correspond, in simplistic one-to-one fashion, to the separation of public and private spheres. Men had a private sphere, but it did not overlap with that of women. In the letters and diaries studied by Smith-Rosenberg, "men appear as an other or out group, segregated into different schools, supported by their own male network of friends and kin, socialized to different behavior."[46] Thus the "female world of love and ritual" challenges any rigid separation of the private and the public. The friendships examined by Smith-Rosenberg were maintained through letters and recorded in diaries: forms that bridged the potential gaps between private and public. "Women," writes Smith-Rosenberg, "who had little status or power in the larger world of male concerns, possessed status and power in the lives and worlds of other women."[47]

Rigid separation of private and public spheres is challenged from another perspective when we look at the lives of working-class men in London towards the end of the nineteenth century. A particularly direct instance of the reification of everyday life was the concern of the middle class, dating from the eighteenth century, to "police the amusements of the poor,"[48] to provide leisure activities that would insure optimal work performance (i.e., with little alcohol or licentiousness) and would steer workers away from the influence of radical political movements. Attempts to control the leisure of workers became particularly energetic when, in the course of the nineteenth century, working-class life began to take on some of the attributes of middle-class existence. During the first half of the nineteenth century, London workers had extremely long hours and tended to live close to the workplace. Theirs was a work-centered culture, from which women were by and large excluded. In the second half of the century, however, working-class culture began to be oriented more towards family and home. Working hours had been reduced, making more leisure time available. Workers began to live farther and farther away from their places of employment. Increasingly, wives of working-class men did not work outside of the home.[49] Eli Zaretsky has described the nineteenth-century bourgeois ideal of the family as "an enclave protected from industrial society." Increasingly, working class people came to share that ideal: "The proletariat itself came to share the bourgeois ideal of the family as a 'utopian retreat.'"[50]

Yet certain distinct features of working-class existence made a total identification with the bourgeois ideal impossible: "With the shortening of the working week and the separation of living quarters from work place, home and the family occupied a larger place in the working man's life. Yet, despite its growing ideological significance the home remained a crowded and unrelaxing environment."[51] Within this contradictory context, many leisure-time activities were pursued by workers outside the home. Among the leisure institutions were the music hall and the pub.[52] Particularly interesting for our purposes is one leisure institution which was initiated by the middle-class impulse to control working-class recreation. This was the Working Men's Club movement, which was founded in 1862. However much the middle-class reformers attempted, through the clubs, to keep the working class in line, by the 1880s the clubs had become exclusively working-class.[53] The clubs were absolutely closed to women. Peter Bailey describes their function as follows:

> The main function of the clubs was to provide for 'the humbler wants' of its [sic] members, and this they did admirably. They provided a set of permanent premises for recreation to an extent which no other organization or movement could match. Illustrations of club interiors seem cheerless to us, but the rooms were kept clean, well-lit and warm, a far remove from the condition of much working-class housing. They were *genuine recuperative refuges*, free from commercial pressures, ritual drinking, police harassment, district visitors *and the wife and family*. With their lectures, concerts, indoor and outdoor games, excursions and picnics, Christmas clubs, coal clubs and sick clubs, they provided, at modest cost, the facilities of the public library, music hall, pub, playing field, and friendly society combined.[54]

Surely these clubs constituted a private sphere for male workers more than the homes which simply could not provide the same pleasures. Working-class men did not have the same mobility to move freely between private and public spheres as middle-class men of the same period. Hence the time spent at Working Men's Clubs blurs the very distinction between private and public. The clubs began as a form of social control, but soon became a means by which male workers defined themselves as a viable community, and not just as the "other" of bourgeois society. The private sphere which middle-class men might find in their homes simply did not exist in the same way for working-class men; nor, one assumes, for working-class women.

In *Clarissa* and *Robinson Crusoe*, in the lives of American women and of English working-class men, "private" and "public" are at once separate and intertwined entities. If *Clarissa* and *Robinson Crusoe* provide early literary examples of how private and public spheres were a major concern of the middle-class novel, the historical examples I have chosen give us a sense of the social reality of private and public life. But art and social reality are no more easily separable than private and public space, and my historical examples were not chosen innocently in this regard.

Carroll Smith-Rosenberg uses letters and diaries to document the "female world of love and ritual." Clarissa Harlowe was also an avid letter-writer, even if her (fictional) letters functioned to a more precise narrative end.[55] Sylvia Bovenschen has spoken of the writing of letters and diaries as the "pre-aesthetic" realm: a kind of apprenticeship which eventually gave women the possibility of entering into literary production.[56] In the same spirit, I would like to consider the letters and diaries examined by Smith-Rosenberg as part of a "pre-narrative" realm: they are forms of communication which attempted to heal the split between personal and social worlds. I use the term "pre-narrative" because it is, precisely, in the narratives of middle-class novels that such attempts to heal the split between private and public realms are most fully realized. The women's lives studied by Carroll Smith-Rosenberg thus have particular significance in relation to the novel. The leisure activities of working-class men at the end of the nineteenth century are suggestive also, not so much of the novel per se, but of how the social function of cinema would develop, simultaneously, as an extension of the middle-class novel, and as a form of middle-*and* working-class leisure. The points of connection between Clarissa Harlowe and the American women in Smith-Rosenberg's study, between Robinson Crusoe and working-class men in late nineteenth-century London, define the initial trajectory of the present study. While this trajectory is anything but linear, it nonetheless is bound by the emergence and crystallization of middle-class culture from the eighteenth to the late nineteenth centuries as manifested in narrative and the novel form. Each instance of the intersection of the private and the public examined thus far suggests the power of narrative, whether in the specifically literary form of the two novels, or in the narrative patterns of everyday life evidenced in Smith-Rosenberg's, Bailey's, and Stedman-Jones's studies. The novel form has always been regarded as that literary genre most open to the influence of everyday life, and the preoccupation with everyday life is itself tied to the emergence of middle-class culture. The class dimensions of these narratives of private and public life are determined by a middle-class identity defined initially in opposition to aristocratic values, and later, in the course of the nineteenth century, to the emerging industrial working class. The relations of male and female emerge against this background, with gender functioning both as a mirror of class divisions and a powerful system of difference in its own right. The private and the public, then, are key terms for the consideration of a series of oppositions—male and female, fiction and everyday life, aristocracy and middle-class, middle-class and working-class. Narrative is the fundamental process whereby the very foundations of these oppositions are examined, reflected upon, and given imaginative form.

Readership

Beginning in the early eighteenth century, the development of the novel created a new function for narrative, tapping traditional and non-traditional narrative forms and shaping them to the contours of middle-class expectations. Examination of the ways in which novels, and later films, mediate between readers/viewers and their social conditions of existence leads to a consideration of narrative as an *institution*. Here is how Harry Levin, in his study of the realist novel, describes the institutional quality of literature: "Literature has always been an institution. Like other institutions, like the church or the law, it cherishes a unique phase of human experience and controls a special body of precedents and devices; it incorporates a self-perpetuating discipline, while responding to the main currents of each succeeding period; it is continually accessible to all the impulsions of life at large, but it must translate them into its own terms and adapt them to its peculiar forms."[57] This institutional quality of the novel might be described as the *novelistic*. Edward Said writes: "Every novel is at the same time a form of discovery and also a way of accommodating discovery, if not to a social norm, then to a specialized 'novelistic' reading process."[58] The novelistic, then, is ideological form, the articulation of a relationship between human beings and their conditions of existence and experience.

The novelistic in Western culture is shaped by several interrelating spheres of influence. The most fundamental of these is the definition of the novel as emblematic middle-class art form. On the one hand, early novels reflected, in a general way, middle-class aspirations in their themes and plots: the individualism of *Robinson Crusoe*, the puritanism of *Clarissa*, the reconciliation of public image and self-knowledge in *Tom Jones*. On the other hand, the development of the novel was marked by a growing correlation between literary and commodity production. The famous career of Samuel Richardson is exemplary in this respect. A former printer and an avid letter-writer, Richardson was asked by two booksellers to prepare an instruction booklet on letter-writing. Richardson used the sample letters as a format for moral instruction. As literary legend has it, he soon discovered that a story was an appropriate vehicle for moralizing and that the letter format was easily adaptable to this end; *Pamela* was the result. [59] The prototypical status of the novel as, simultaneously, artistic and commodity production, is indicated by the ease with which Richardson moved from technician to creator, and by the itinerary of his literary output from one kind of instruction to another.

The founding social function of the novelistic is thus suggested by the middle-class origins of both the subjects of novels and the conditions of novel-production. Perhaps even more fundamental, however, are the conditions of the reception of the novel, as defined in particular by the eighteenth-century English novel. Novel-reception raises directly the issue of the relations between production and consumption. The public sphere of capitalist society is determined by commodity production, a public sphere which would give novelists newly defined roles as producers of goods to be consumed. The growth of the novel-reading public in the eighteenth century is usually attributed to the simultaneous increase in literacy and in the mass production of novels themselves. Equally important was a more diffuse cultural fact: the phenomenon of leisure time.

Leisure is not simply time spent away from work, but rather the organization of that time according to class-defined and gender-defined expectations. [60] If eighteenth-century Western society was marked by the increasing split between the realms of private and public life, between the world of the home and the world of production, of business and trade, then the development of a novel-reading public is connected to that split. The reading of novels would become a leisure-time activity pursued, primarily, within the home. [61]

Debates about the values and potential moral instruction offered by the novel-form were common in the eighteenth century. The novel was considered by many an inferior art form, both morally and artistically. Underlying these discussions was a profound ambivalence not just about the novel, but about the novel as a symptom of the very function of leisure time. Now within the middle and upper classes leisure meant something quite different if you were a man than if you were a woman. This returns us to the feminist insight, that the separation of life into private and public realms and the attendant implications of the home as a recuperative refuge, exist primarily for men. The issue is then complicated by the fact that middle- and upper-class women were not only separated from the public sphere of business and trade, but were separated as well from labor within the home. To use Thorstein Veblen's phrase, their "conspicuous leisure" was a mark of social status.

There are a number of thorny issues involved in analysis of the audience for the eighteenth-century middle-class novel. It has become somewhat of a commonplace that the primary audience addressed by the novel were women, middle- and upper-class for the most part, but also—the important case upon which Richardson's *Pamela* is constructed—domestic servants. Between the fact that women *read* novels, and the assumption that the genre was *addressed to* them, however, there is a short-circuited argument. There is no denying that female experience, on all levels, became a major preoccupation in the early middle-class novel: women not only read novels, after all, but wrote them and were more frequently than not the central characters. "Female" here may be understood as a sign, of sorts, for the private sphere. Put another way, the significant feature may well be, not so much a sudden accounting for "female experience," but rather the emergence of "female" as a symptom of the profound changes taking place in Western society. For the "female" in the middle-class novel constantly leads us to the private sphere.

And no matter how different the relationship of men and women to leisure, men had leisure time as well. To speak of a female readership is to raise, whether directly or indirectly, the question of male readership. If the female audience was indeed so central, one wonders what novel-reading signified to the many men who also read novels, albeit, perhaps, in the closet.

The central focus of novel-reading had more to do with leisure than with some female-specific genre; or, in other words, it was because of their particular relationship to leisure time that women read novels in the first place. Most often, then, the novel appears to have functioned as a form of escape. In this context, Ian Watt cites Lady Mary Wortley Montagu's remark: "I doubt not that at least the greater part of these are trash, lumber, etc. However, they will serve to pass away the idle time."[62] This seems clear enough. But in Lady Mary's voluminous correspondence, other references to the novel suggest a function more complex and more sophisticated than this somewhat cursory dismissal.

It is, of course, tempting to trivialize the struggle against boredom in which novels were a powerful weapon. In her later years, Lady Mary would write to her daughter that in reading, "I think my time better employed" than an acquaintance who continued to indulge herself in "active scenes." And yet, Lady Mary does seem to hold the pastime in some contempt, when she remarks that "valuable books are almost as rare as valuable men."[63] Lady Mary's choice of words is interesting, for some years before she had offered her daughter the following advice on child-rearing: "If your Daughters are inclin'd to Love reading, do not check their Inclination by hindering them of the diverting part of it. It is as necessary for the Amusement of Women as the Reputation of Men; but teach them not to expect or desire any Applause from it. . . . People that do not read or work for a Livelihood have many hours they know not how to employ, especially Women, who commonly fall into Vapours or something worse."[64] Here again, reading is offered as a way of spending idle hours, but it is also considered an activity analogous to the pursuits of men. The "amusement of women" and the "reputation of men" suggest that reading functions as a buffer of sorts between the increasingly separate realms of male and female activity. There is clearly something more specific to the function of reading than mere escape.

The most obvious way in which novels occupied leisure time was quantitative: novels were lengthy and took quite a while to read. But novels also structured leisure time in a qualitative way. The novel can be seen as a paradigm for the way in which the seemingly open, vast spaces of leisure time would be shaped by submitting experience to the structures of narrative. And, at the same time, the novel would mark the increasing scope of narrative possibilities to include the everyday and the mundane.

If the novel is one form of what might then be called the increasing "narrativization" of experience, then its most obvious counterpart is letter-writing. In several letters to her daughter from Italy in 1748, Lady Mary details the garden of her home-in-exile, from a general overview of the size and capacity of the garden, to a brief history of how it had been used and what changes had been made, to her own position, as writer of the letter and witness to the scene ("I am now writing to you in one of these arbours.").[65] Lady Mary compares English and Italian gardens, and moves on to detail her everyday rituals. In another letter on the same topic, Lady Mary sends a diagram of her garden, an accompanying illustration of sorts. And she describes her attachment to her garden "as a young Author of his first play when it has been well receiv'd by the Town."[66]

Lady Mary has, in a word, narrativized her garden, as she is both narrator and author, "worker" and observer. The garden becomes the site for the intersection of the Italian and the British, of the laws of nature and the rituals of everyday life. The garden is "mapped"—both literally and figuratively—and the geographical metaphor is quite appropriate to describe the work of narrative as that connection of points, a mapping out of possibilities.[67] Perhaps Lady Mary herself sensed a profound connection between the novels she read and the narrative potential, so to speak, of her garden, when she wrote that "Gardening is certainly the next amusement to Reading."[68]

Narrative in the eighteenth century took on certain institutional qualities. Lady Mary's letters provide some interesting examples of how novels might be understood in precisely this sense of a grid through which experiences and impressions are read. If the novel is, vis-à-vis the garden, a paradigm of the narrativization of the everyday, so too do specific novels become in Lady Mary's correspondence reference points and measuring sticks for the world around her. In exile in Italy, for instance, Lady Mary referred to her solitude as "not unlike that of Robinson Crusoe."[69] In another context, the example of Clarissa Harlowe came to mind as a way of describing the inadequacy of her own education: "My own was one of the worst in the World, being exactly the same as Clarissa Harlowe's, her pious Mrs. Norton so perfectly resembling my Governess (who had been Nurse to my Mother) I could almost fancy the Author was acquainted with her."[70] It is interesting to note that, when she wrote about the merits of *Clarissa*, Lady Mary was not particularly impressed. But the institutional quality of the novel has to do with a desire more deep-rooted than simply liking or not liking a specific novel.

Perhaps the most striking instance of this institutional quality of literature occurs when Lady Mary writes to her daughter about a local scandal (in Italy) concerning a beautiful servant and her relations with various employers. Lady Mary introduces the gossip with a reference to *Pamela*:

This Town is at present in a General Stare, . . . and not only this Town but the Capital Bergamo, the whole province, the neighbouring Brescian, and perhaps all the Venetian Dominion, occasion'd by an Adventure exactly ressembling and, I believe, copy'd from Pamela. I know not under what constellation that Foolish stuff was wrote, but it has been translated into more Languages than any modern performance I ever heard of. No proofe of its Influence was ever stronger than this present story, which in Richardson's hands would serve very well to furnish out seven or eight volumes."[71]

One thinks perhaps of the old adage that truth is stranger than fiction. But more remarkable is that the reading of novels should provide such an appropriate vehicle for the reporting of local gossip.

Many of the ways in which Lady Mary refers to novels suggest, quite simply, the powers of realism. In a discussion of Fielding, she slides with ease from the novel (*Joseph Andrews*) to her own household, and in particular, to a servant with the same name as a character in the novel. [72] If indeed Lady Mary responds to the increasing powers of realism, then one might begin to ask the question, again, as to what the fact of being female has to do with it all. In defining the strategic importance of a person or group, in this case women readers, the point is not that their experiences are radically *other* than those of men, but rather that female responses to novels are the extreme instance which allows us to see, in clear and bold relief, the new social function of reading—a function which may well be present, though masked in a variety of ways and by a variety of circumstances, in the responses of male readers. In her letters, Lady Mary mediates between the purely communicative function of letters as personal correspondence, and the function of narrative to create social participation. Of course, men also would have had possibilities of identifying with novels, of using them as grids to read their own experience, of "narrativizing" the events of their own lives. Undoubtedly many men did have responses to novels chiming with those of Lady Mary (one thinks of Denis Diderot's *Eloge à Richardson*, for instance). Yet I doubt if they did to the same degree. The institutional quality of narrative leads us to leisure time, and to the separation of private and public spheres. The role of novels in female leisure was located at the points of tension between private and public space. Reading novels thus provided an activity for women that was otherwise unavailable. The activity was of course available to men; it is just questionable whether it would have spoken to their needs to quite the same degree.

Middle-class narrative emerges from the division in capitalist societies between the home and the workplace, with attendant ramifications in the differences between male and female activity. Its social basis occurs at the intersection between leisure time (itself a product of the private/public split) and the growth of female readership. If women were "marginal" to the official public sphere, then the reading of novels offered a fictional world to be consumed, and an imaginary participation in the public sphere. Readership thus brings private and public space increasingly within reach of each other. A distinct feature of the middle-class novel is the mirroring of readership within novels: Characters like Robinson and Clarissa, and readers like Lady Mary, are similarly engaged in narratives of private and public life.

As exemplary novels, *Robinson Crusoe* and *Clarissa* are suggestive of two fundamental narrative modes of private and public life. The island in *Robinson Crusoe* is a zero degree both of civilization and of narrative. The creation of a public sphere in *Robinson Crusoe* is structured by Robinson's constant return, in one form or another, to his family: he constructs an essentially middle-class existence (prescribed by his father), he prays to a Christian god (who is a symbolic father), and he "adopts" Friday. The narrative evolution of *Robinson Crusoe* is an additive process, for each step further away from England provides the setting for a purer middle-class existence. The absence of any concerns of private life, clearly identifiable as such, is thoroughly compensated by the process which integrates Robinson's struggle for survival with his origins.

The narrative structure of *Clarissa* works in different terms. The bourgeois tragedy of *Clarissa* is that private and public are never truly integrated, except in the heroine's death: throughout the novel we encounter one false connection after another. Mrs. Sinclair's house initially appears like a refuge, but soon is revealed as a space controlled by Lovelace. And if in the Harlowe family private and public spheres are integrated, it is in a terroristic fashion.

In *Robinson Crusoe*, the private and the public are integrated so as to suggest harmonious balance. *Clarissa* traces, in contrast, the impossibility of such integration. Here, the public sphere invades the private sphere. Now balance may well be illusory, and what is reconciliation from one perspective may be something quite different from another. Or the "balance" between private and public spheres may in fact entail the subjugation of one sphere to the other.[73] The two narrative modes are not mutually exclusive, for if Clarissa lives in a world of reified values, a fantasy of reconciliation is still maintained; and if Robinson's world seems to be harmonious, it is because the fragmentation and reification of his existence has been naturalized.

In the nineteenth century, the novel achieved maturity as a middle-class art form. I have chosen two novels which, as early nineteenth-century works, were important in defining the evolution of the novel-form: Jane Austen's *Pride and Prejudice* (1813) and Honoré de Balzac's *Eugénie Grandet* (1833). The two works have been drawn, deliberately, from different cultures, and from authors with different preoccupations. In both novels, the relation between private and public is a central issue. Austen and Balzac are well-known for specific uses of realism: Austen, for her irony; Balzac, for his allegorical use of realistic conventions. My point is not to draw a simple comparison between these two very different authors. Rather, the two novels exemplify the two narrative modes suggested by *Robinson Crusoe* and *Clarissa:* the one, a positive fantasy of reconciliation, and the other, a nightmarish fantasy of reification.

Two

TWO NARRATIVES
OF PRIVATE AND
PUBLIC LIFE

Pride and Prejudice *and Fantasies of Reconciliation*

The famous opening sentence of *Pride and Prejudice* seems firmly to situate the reader in the realm of popular wisdom and received ideas, in the domain of what Roland Barthes calls the cultural code: "It is a truth universally acknowledged, that a single man in possession of a good fortune, must be in want of a wife."[1] But we quickly discover that the popular wisdom evoked here, this "law of society" (in Barthes's words), reflects not so much a universal opinion as the peculiarities of Mrs. Bennet's vision of the world: a world clearly divided between the married and the unmarried, and the marriageable and the unmarriageable. Jane Austen's critics have amply demonstrated how such ironic manipulation of perspective and point-of-view—so succinctly expressed in the opening of *Pride and Prejudice*—is essential to her novels.[2] Equally remarkable in the single, ironic statement which introduces us to *Pride and Prejudice* is the designation of an opposition which will, in the course of the novel, take on a variety of forms. Contained within that sentence is a tension between the "laws of society" and marriages, between social order and individual arrangements, between the private and the public. We soon discover, of course, that Mrs. Bennet has an inadequate understanding of the connections between the two realms. But it is from such inadequacies that the novel develops, until finally we witness, in Elizabeth's marriage to Darcy, a satisfying relationship between the social and the personal.[3]

Mrs. Bennet's perspective is like a wedge driven between truths universally acknowledged, and the desires of single men. In a world whose center is occupied by the Bennet family, the two spheres of universal value and individual desire diverge. It is the function of narrative, in *Pride and Prejudice*, to reconcile these two realms—the "laws of society" and marriage, public and private existence. While we soon discover, in chapter 1, that the only universal truths to be found in the Longbourn neighborhood are those invented by Mrs. Bennet, we are equally quickly made aware that there is at least one thing of universal application, and that is a principle of economy. "This truth is so well fixed in the minds of the surrounding families, that he [i.e., a single man new to the neighborhood] is considered as the rightful *property* of some one or another of their daughters" (p. 1, my emphasis). The laws determining the designs of the families with unmarried daughters may not be quite universal; but this, at least, is sure: economics is the principle by which marriages are created, and universal truths established.

Critics have often pointed out how in Jane Austen's novels, economic livelihood is a constant preoccupation. David Daiches remarks, "how ruthless is the clarity with which Jane Austen observes and records the economic realities," and he even describes Austen as a "Marxist before Marx."[4] Yet in *Pride and Prejudice*, as in all of Austen's novels, one rarely moves beyond the realm of family and personal relationships.[5] *Pride and Prejudice* is concerned with the private sphere, with domestic space. Hence Walter Raleigh could, in speaking of "domestic satire," describe Austen's world as follows: "Man is stripped of the public trappings on which he prides himself, he is bereft of all wider social relations, and appears simply and solely as a member of a family—by that let him stand or fall."[6]

The point, of course, is that the institution of marriage as it exists in *Pride and Prejudice* serves two interests, personal and economic. Frequently the two interests are incompatible; and so marriage often occupies an ambiguous space, in Austen's novels, between private and public concerns. Essential to any understanding of marriage in *Pride and Prejudice*, and of the ambiguity through which it is defined, is the fact that marriage is perceived through the experience of middle-class women. Because there were no male children in the Bennet family, the estate is entailed, and the entail is in this sense symbolic of the economic fate of middle-class women. The Bennet sisters are doomed to lives of penury if they do not marry, and marry well. For the middle-class women of Jane Austen's novels, marriage is as surely a vital source of income as work and investment are to men. Judith Newton describes the significance of the entailed estate from this perspective: "The entail, then, which so obviously benefits Mr. Collins and so obviously restricts the Bennet daughters, is really the epitome of an economic privilege that is granted men in general and of an economic restriction that is imposed on women: for most women, lacking men's access to work and inheritance, economic survival means marriage."[7] If marriage equals livelihood, it is also the only way in which any kind of participation in the public sphere is made available to middle-class women.

The female characters of *Pride and Prejudice* adopt a variety of attitudes towards marriage. For some, marriage is above all an economic arrangement. Indeed, for Mrs. Bennet the arranging of marriages for her daughters is "the business of her life" (p. 3). And for Charlotte Lucas, marriage is as well primarily a business transaction. She describes her marriage to Mr. Collins to her shocked friend Elizabeth: "I am not romantic you know. I never was. I ask only a comfortable home" (p. 95). On the other hand, Lydia Bennet perceives marriage in uniquely personal terms, as the institutionalized form of romantic courtship. That such a view is incompatible with the more practical concerns evidenced in Charlotte's attitude, is indicated by the fact that Lydia's marriage to Wickham eventually leads to financial hardship. The firm conviction that marriage is both a socio-economic arrangement and a source of personal happiness distinguishes Elizabeth Bennet from all of the characters in the novel. Her sister Jane has similar ideals, although they are not as actively pursued. Thus the search for a "marriage of true affection" (p. 74) that rests on firm economic ground is left to Elizabeth.

Marriage also functions, in *Pride and Prejudice*, as a form of social regeneration. Austen's novels are almost all concerned with the conflicts and potential resolutions between aristocratic and middle-class views of the world. Mark Schorer accurately describes the social setting of *Pride and Prejudice* as "one in which a feudalistic order that does not know that it is dying and a bourgeois or mercantile order that is not yet confident that it is quite alive, meet and conflict and sometimes merge."[8] The marriage of Elizabeth and Darcy is, in class terms, a "kind of symbol of economic merging, of one class rising and another sinking."[9] As it is drawn in *Pride and Prejudice*, then, marriage serves two primary functions. First, it defines the identities of women's lives in an economic sense (Charlotte), in a personal sense (Lydia), and sometimes both; and second, marriage is a class alliance through which the best of middle-class and aristocratic experience are joined.[10]

Narration in *Pride and Prejudice* occupies a hypothetical space between private and public existence. The narrative unfolds at all levels as a search for an integration between private and public existence, and as an attempt to define the very nature of private and public life. While it is true that *Pride and Prejudice* is concerned with the representation of private space, of the domestic sphere, there is nonetheless a curious quality to that sphere: throughout most of the novel, it is barely represented at all.[11] We do not have much of a sense of the Bennet house, except that Mr. Bennet spends a great deal of time in his library. Mrs. Bennet frequently speaks of family dinners, but never do we witness a meal amongst the Bennet family.[12] Private space is present as a structure, but it is nonetheless an absent space. The development of the novel corresponds to a process of anticipation: we, like the characters of the novel, wait for the representation of a private sphere in which a sense of personal fulfillment is created. Such fulfillment comes, finally, at Pemberley, where rooms exist in great detail and where a meal is finally served. An authentic private sphere is created and represented.

The attempt to create an authentic private sphere is accompanied by an attempt to define the proper terms of the public sphere. The lives of the characters in *Pride and Prejudice* are so thoroughly determined by economic considerations, that the boundaries separating private and public space are confused. Social institutions are only significant in terms of their marriage potential. There are two such institutions in *Pride and Prejudice*, the church and the military. There is a direct line from each of these to Mrs. Bennet: the military regiment is initially stationed at Meryton, her home town; and Lady Catherine de Bourgh, the powerful matriarchal figure of the church, is an aristocratic version of Mrs. Bennet. The reflection of Mrs. Bennet within each of these institutions suggests that the boundaries between social law and individual desire are just as confused in public institutions as they are within the Bennet family. Indeed, the social institutions of the church and the military only come to life in direct proportion to their marriage potential. The military functions primarily as a source of possible husbands for Kitty and Lydia, and the only soldier who is individualized, Wickham, is of primary interest as rival to Darcy. Similarly, characters representing the church—Lady Catherine and Mr.

Collins—exist first as potential vehicles to a suitable marriage for Elizabeth (with Collins), and then as obstacles to her marriage to Darcy. The function of Pemberley as a *social* institution regulates the distorted influence exercised by the military and the church. For Pemberley is an estate, a social center, as well as a home, and once Elizabeth and Darcy are established there, a certain order is reaffirmed: Wickham will never be received at Pemberley, and Lady Catherine is but an occasional visitor. Once Pemberley is regenerated, a social hierarchy is re-established.

The marriage of Elizabeth and Darcy allows the integration of ideals and a restoration of order. Throughout *Pride and Prejudice*, we see a series of static oppositions of male versus female, class versus class. Through marriage, such oppositions are reconciled. In other words, marriage is the major means by which differences are managed. That the inhabitants of *Pride and Prejudice* are divided along class lines is evident from the outset. Aristocrats and bourgeois have different standards, different forms of behavior, different ideals. This much is a given in the social universe of *Pride and Prejudice*. Much more vital, in the class divisions and their reconciliations, than the opposition aristocrat/middle class, is the division that exists within the middle class itself. Of all of the middle-class characters in *Pride and Prejudice*, there is one couple singled out as relatively free of the negative features characterizing the behavior of many members of the Bennet family. These are the Gardiners, who are instrumental in the Elizabeth-Darcy affair: Elizabeth accompanies them on the holiday which first brings her to Pemberley. Mr. Gardiner is the brother of Mrs. Bennet, "greatly superior to his sister as well by nature as by education" (p. 106). Mr. Gardiner lives "by trade and within view of his own warehouses" (p. 106). The Gardiners are as middle-class as the Bennets, but there is nonetheless a difference in their values. Mr. Bennet is a member of the gentry, and his income derives from his estate and from an inheritance on his wife's side. Mr. Gardiner, in contrast, has a more active relationship to work. The Gardiners are, in other words, "new" middle-class as opposed to the traditional middle-class identity of the Bennets. That the Gardiners are so closely identified with Elizabeth and Darcy's marriage suggests that Elizabeth herself is more closely allied with this middle-class identity than with that of her own immediate family.

Hence the class alliance of Darcy and Elizabeth's marriage is more than the simple reconciliation of class differences. The influence of the Gardiners is to accentuate that which is most positive in a middle-class identity. In addition, the Gardiners are partially responsible for changes in Darcy's aristocratic snobbery. Through them, he learns the significance of the differences between middle-class identities. When Elizabeth first visits Pemberley with her aunt and uncle, she experiences a pang of regret for having refused Darcy's offer of marriage. "With these rooms I might now have been familiarly acquainted! Instead of viewing them as a stranger, I might have rejoiced in them as my own, and welcomed to them as visitors my uncle and aunt" (p. 182). However, Elizabeth's thoughts are quickly interrupted by the memory of Darcy's class identity: " 'But no'—recollecting herself— 'that could never be: my uncle and aunt would have been lost to me: I should not have been allowed to invite them' " (p. 182). This first visit to Pemberley is marked by the unexpected appearance of Darcy himself. When Elizabeth introduces him to the Gardiners, she correctly anticipates his surprise that "she had some relations for whom there was no need to blush" (p. 189). While Darcy had already decided to ignore class differences in proposing to Elizabeth, his encounter with the Gardiners makes it clear that middle-class identity is not to be simply ignored in toto, but rather to be reckoned with according to the same discrimination that allowed Darcy to single out Elizabeth in the first place.

Perhaps even more rigidly separated than class from class, are women and men. Critics have remarked that *Pride and Prejudice* describes a world in which women wait, while men enter and leave.[13] Put another way, women are on display, while men observe. This difference is strikingly in evidence at the balls, which are rituals of men watching and women being watched. Within the Bennet house there is a separation between male and female realms as well. Sketchily described as the house is, there are at least two distinctly separate rooms at Longbourn: the library and the breakfast room. Mr. Bennet's library is first mentioned when Mr. Bingley comes to call. Bingley "had entertained hopes of being admitted to the sight of the young ladies . . . but he saw only the father" (p. 6). The library is a male space, literally out of sight of the Bennet women. Later in the novel, when Mr. Bennet has made clear that he is no more favorable to a marriage between Elizabeth and Collins than is Elizabeth herself, he requests "two small favours" of his wife: "First, that you will allow me the free use of my understanding on the present occasion, and secondly, of my room. I shall be glad to have the library to myself as soon as may be" (p. 85). While Mr. Bennet retreats into the library, the women of the house gather in the only comparable "female" space, the breakfast room. Similar to this "sexual architecture" of the Bennet household are the arrangements that Charlotte has made at Hunsford as Mr. Collins's wife. In order to accommodate herself to her marriage while retaining distance from her husband, Charlotte has adopted a strategy not unlike Mr. Bennet's appropriation of the library. During her visit to Hunsford, Elizabeth notes the arrangement: "The room in which the ladies sat was backwards. Elizabeth had at first wondered that Charlotte should not prefer the dining parlour for common use; it was a better sized room, and had a pleasanter aspect; but she soon saw that her friend had an excellent reason for what she did, for Mr. Collins would undoubtedly have been much less in his own apartment, had they sat in one equally lively; and she gave Charlotte credit for the arrangement" (p. 127).

However separate the realms of male and female activity, Elizabeth maintains a certain mobility between female and male space. In particular, within the Bennet home, she is the only family member who freely enters her father's library. Elizabeth's mobility has another, more literal implication as well, for Elizabeth travels extensively in *Pride and Prejudice*. Of her travels, Joseph M. Duffy says that "the larger external movement of travel in the novel coincides with the great theme of exploration of the new region of love."[14] The journey is, in short, a process invested with many layers of meaning, and the activity of travel functions as a metaphor for narrative itself. When the Gardiners propose a trip to the Lakes with Elizabeth—a trip which will later be shortened due to Mr. Gardiner's business concerns, and will therefore take Elizabeth to Pemberley—Elizabeth comments on the proposed journey: "Oh! what hours of transport we shall spend! And when we *do* return, it shall not be like other travellers, without being able to give one accurate idea of any thing. We *will* know where we have gone—we *will* recollect what we have seen" (p. 117). Elizabeth already anticipates the return home, a return which will be full of distinct memories. Indeed, more than she herself is aware, the results of Elizabeth's travels will be like a process of memory expanded: not only will present and past be linked, but the journey will allow the reconciliation of a whole series of oppositions—male versus female, class versus class.

The Longbourn house serves as a point of departure for two different journeys. The first takes Elizabeth to Netherfield in order to be with Jane, who has fallen ill. Between Longbourn and Netherfield lies Meryton, frequently visited by Lydia and Kitty. From the Bennet home to Meryton, it is an easy walk of one mile. The young ladies, we are told, go there three or four times a week (p. 20). The distance to Netherfield is longer; this is a distance that spans class distinctions. Hence, when Elizabeth walks to Netherfield, she arrives "with weary ancles, dirty stockings, and a face glowing with the warmth of exercise." (p. 24). The shocked reactions of the Bingley sisters emphasize the enormous symbolic distance from Longbourn to Netherfield.

Hence if the narrative of *Pride and Prejudice* might be read somewhat like a map, then the geography of the novel is class-bound: to the male/female architecture of an individual house corresponds, on a larger scale, the class divisions of towns and neighborhoods. This "class geography" takes on another form as well, which is the opposition between city and town. The Bingleys leave Netherfield abruptly to return to London. It is an upper-class privilege to have access to the city, but more important, to have the mobility to move freely from city to town. The Gardiners live in London as well, but Gracechurch Street is far from the Bingleys' area of the city. In a country village, in other words, the distance between houses is walkable; in the city, such distances are comparatively greater.

The most important trip that Elizabeth makes leads her first to Hunsford to visit Charlotte, and then to Pemberley. When Elizabeth arrives at Pemberley with the Gardiners, they approach the house through an enormous wooded area. Elizabeth "had never seen a place for which nature had done more, or where natural beauty had been so little counteracted by an awkward taste" (p. 181). Nature and taste: Elizabeth's first impressions of Pemberley concern the balance, the harmony of the estate, the reconciliation of a potential opposition between nature and culture.[15] The juxtaposition of house and garden is strategic. When Elizabeth was visiting at Hunsford, it was necessary to go through a park in order to get to Lady Catherine's house. The mention of the park is but a brief interlude; but it is essential that Elizabeth's access to the house representing a different class be facilitated. The park separating Hunsford and Rosings is a far cry from the dusty road and fields dividing Longbourn house and Netherfield; and it is a park that serves as prelude to the woods that mark Elizabeth's introduction to Pemberley.

Elizabeth's entry into Pemberley involves a series of stages: the initial view of the woods, the discussion with the housekeeper in which

Darcy and Wickham are both revealed to be other than they initially appeared, and the introdution to Darcy's sister Georgiana. Pemberley becomes, simultaneously, the site for reversal of what has preceded in the novel, reconciliation of what has been at odds, and fulfillment of what has been denied.[16] Put another way, at Pemberley all of the elements of the novel are put into perspective. Elizabeth sees Darcy and Wickham in a different light; the Bingley sisters are finally revealed, unequivocally, as fools. What more appropriate place for such readjustments to take place, than the mansion from whose windows a view of nature never afforded in any of the other houses in *Pride and Prejudice* is perceived: "Its windows opening to the ground, admitted a most refreshing view of the high woody hills behind the house, and of the beautiful oaks and Spanish chestnuts which were scattered over the intermediate lawn" (p. 198). The impressions of Pemberley which are recorded for us are those of Elizabeth, and the integrated splendors of Pemberley match her own development of perspective. As Alistair Duckworth writes, "Elizabeth's journey through the park . . . is a spatial recapitulation of her association with Darcy from her first prejudiced impressions of his external appearance, through a recognition of other (and seemingly contradictory) views, to a final arrival at the central core of his character."[17] And what better celebration of this resolution than a meal: that family ritual so talked about in *Pride and Prejudice* but never witnessed until Elizabeth's arrival at Pemberley. "The next variation which their visit afforded was produced by the entrance of servants with cold meat, cake, and a variety of all the finest fruits in season. . . . There was now employment for the whole party; for though they could not all talk, they could all eat; and the beautiful pyramids of grapes, nectarines, and peaches, soon collected them round the table" (p. 199).

In order for the marriage of Elizabeth and Darcy to function as a balancing force between aristocracy and middle class, between male and female realms of activity, Elizabeth has to undertake the journey which leads finally to Pemberley. Travel, with its spatial and geographical implications, is a metaphoric activity in *Pride and Prejudice*; as is another "itinerary" of sorts, and that is reading. Alistair Duckworth notes that the "library motif" in *Pride and Prejudice* is a means by which differences in character are underscored.[18] An early discussion between Darcy and Bingley about books shows Darcy's superior character by virtue of his insistence on the importance of a good library. For Mr. Bennet, the library is above all a retreat. Lending libraries give Kitty and Lydia the opportunity to meet officers; and Mary and Mr. Collins share a pedantic stuffy attitude towards books.

More central than the reading of books is the reading of letters. Through letters, plot information is supplied (Lydia's departure with Wickham) and character deficiencies are revealed (Miss Bingley's snobbery and Lydia's fickleness). Of all of the letters written and sent in *Pride and Prejudice*, the most important is, of course, the letter which Darcy sends to Elizabeth after she has refused his proposal of marriage. In it, Darcy describes the objections he has towards her family, and he explains his views on the two events which had set Elizabeth against him: Bingley's involvement with Jane, and the Wickham affair. That Darcy's views cannot be simply dismissed is due not only to the absolute correctness of his perspective, but also to his ability to express those views in writing. Thus Darcy's insistence that his is a "faithful narrative of every event in which we have been concerned together" (p. 152) applies not only to the truth of the events told, but to the truth of their telling. Darcy's letter cannot be read in the same way as other letters: Elizabeth reads and re-reads the letter, "soon knowing [it] by heart," examining every sentence (p. 159). Between Elizabeth and Darcy, reading and re-reading are more than the communication of information; they are forms of understanding. Hence Elizabeth's comment on the letter: "Till this moment, I never knew myself" (p. 156).

By reading Darcy's letter and in her subsequent changes in perspective, Elizabeth performs an apprenticeship that will allow her, at Pemberley, to see the very possibilities of reconciliation. Readership, as defined through Elizabeth, is an itinerary of self-encounter and ultimately, of self-discovery. In reading Darcy's letter, Elizabeth juxtaposes past events and her present interpretation of them, her family as seen by her and as seen by others. She engages in an examination of contradictions. The result of this process of readership recalls the language Elizabeth used to describe travel: "And when we *do* return, it shall not be like other travellers, without being able to give one accurate idea of any thing" (p. 117). Elizabeth returns, and unlike other readers, she is full of accurate ideas. She does know where she has gone, and recollects what she has seen.

Reading and travel: these are the narrative processes through which we arrive at the reconciliation of class and sex differences. In order for the reconciliation to occur, both Darcy and Elizabeth must go through a process of separation. Elizabeth, prompted by Darcy's letter, finally disentangles her own affection for her family from the way in which they appear, objectively, to others. And Darcy adopts a similar attitude towards Wickham: despite his personal hatred for the man, he recognizes the humiliation that will be suffered by the Bennet family if a marriage without a suitable financial settlement occurs. In other words, both Darcy and Elizabeth separate public image from private feeling. Only once such a separation is made can a genuine resolution take place.

Pride and Prejudice offers the fantasy of an ideal relation between private and public spheres: through marriage, separate spheres are joined together and held in harmonious balance. The union of Darcy and Elizabeth seems to mediate the terms which, in the lives of other characters in the novel, are separate: male and female, aristocracy and middle class, private and public space. In the marriage between Elizabeth and Darcy, neither passion nor cold logic, personal desire nor public image, are allowed to dominate exclusively. Narration in Austen's novel articulates a desire for an integrated existence, in which personal and social life are as neatly juxtaposed as the Pemberley mansion and its surrounding park.

Eugénie Grandet *and Nightmares of Reification*

Balzac's novel of 1833 might also be seen as a fantasy, but *Eugénie Grandet* traces a nightmarish fantasy of reification: if private and public space are reconciled, it is a reconciliation of defeat, of subjugation of the private to the public sphere. Central to *Eugénie Grandet* is a process by which all realms of personal life are invaded and overwhelmed by the forces of capitalist value.

The social worlds represented in *Pride and Prejudice* and *Eugénie Grandet* seem, at first glance, radically different. To be middle-class in *Pride and Prejudice* means perhaps inferior connections, but it also means the kind of industriousness and good breeding exemplified by the Gardiners. Balzac's creation of a middle-class identity has little to do with breeding or work; to be bourgeois means to invest, to profiteer, to have a keen sense of greed and cunning. Hence in Balzac's world, middle-class values can lead only to the destruction of the human psyche, to the reduction of all human relations to objectified entities. This process of reification is centered, in *Eugénie Grandet*, on the daughter of a greedy capitalist. In the Grandet household, gold is a literal object of worship, and it eventually becomes the common denominator for all relations. Eugénie wants to marry her cousin Charles for love, but her father forbids it. Eugénie withers away, consuming memories of the past, accumulating more and more gold, and living a life isolated from any human contact. Critics have often pointed out that in Balzac's novels, the power of capitalism is measured by its ability to destroy the connections between human beings and the cycles of nature. Hence Linda Rudich speaks of the "danger of non-reproduction" in *Eugénie Grandet*: "Grandet's 'religion' is powerful enough to kill the natural principle of reproduction, both Eugénie's maternity and family continuity, because money as capital has the unnatural property of self-reproduction."[19]

The differences between the middle-class worlds of *Pride and Prejudice* and *Eugénie Grandet* can, of course, be attributed to a number of factors: the historical and cultural differences between the French and the English middle classes, the different historical moments in which these novels were written, and the different perspectives of a middle-class woman, on the one hand, and a man sympathetic to the old order washed away by capitalism, on the other. Yet in spite of all these differences, *Pride and Prejudice* and *Eugénie Grandet* contain strikingly similar narrative elements. That both novels are concerned with family life, and with the intersections of class and sex within the family is not particularly striking, since these are features common to the eighteenth- and nineteenth-century novel in general. More specifically, similar motifs appear in both novels, like the journey (Elizabeth travels in *Pride and Prejudice*; in *Eugénie Grandet*, Charles makes a decisive journey), and a house split along male and female lines.

There is a decisive moment in *Eugénie Grandet* which is similar to Darcy's arrangement of Wickham's marriage to Lydia in *Pride and Prejudice*. Eugénie Grandet also makes financial arrangements which allow a marriage to take place. Charles is Eugénie's cousin, the son of Grandet's brother. He comes to visit from Paris after his father has killed himself due to bankruptcy. During this visit, Eugénie falls in love with her cousin. Grandet arranges for Charles to travel to the West Indies in order to make his fortune. Discovering her cousin's penury, Eugénie gives him the collection of rare gold coins that her father has given her, and in exchange Charles gives her a gold box and portraits of his parents for safe-keeping. Eugénie maintains her devotion to Charles even though she does not hear from him for many years. The letter she finally receives announces her cousin's marriage to someone else. However, the debts incurred by Charles's father were never paid: Grandet, dead by the time of Charles's return, had only pretended to pay them off. Charles's marriage cannot take place unless the enormous sum is paid. Eugénie makes the necessary arrangements, and the wedding goes ahead as planned. Whereas Darcy's arrangements allowed the reconciliation of love and money, Eugénie's arrangements for her cousin are the final mark of the very impossibility of any such reconciliation. And so Eugénie resigns herself to a marriage of convenience, insists on remaining a virgin, while the "pale cold glitter of gold" takes the place of "all warmth and colour in her innocent and blameless life" ("L'argent devait communiquer ses teintes froides à cette vie céleste, et donner de la défiance pour les sentiments à une femme qui était tout sentiment").[20]

Examination of *Pride and Prejudice* and *Eugénie Grandet* reveals different narrative arrangements of similar novelistic material, and in this sense the two novels are exemplary. Examined in relation to one another, *Pride and Prejudice* and *Eugénie Grandet* demonstrate a strikingly symmetrical narrative reversal. For while *Pride and Prejudice* articulates a vision of order, based on the reconciliation of private and public spheres, *Eugénie Grandet* puts forth a vision of disorder, a vision of a private sphere of family life and personal relations completely invaded by the public sphere.

That the public sphere of Balzac's novels is manifestly that of capitalist value is well-known. One thinks of Engels' evaluation of what he called Balzac's "complete history of French society," from which: "I have learned more than from all the professed historians, economists, and statisticians of the period together."[21] It is also well-known that Marx greatly admired Balzac's work, and that admiration has become somewhat of an emblem of how Balzac's novels bear witness to the extent to which human behavior has been brutally modified by capitalist development.

If the phenomenon of reification is central in the development of the public sphere of capitalist societies, throughout Balzac's novels, reification functions as a narrative principle. Indeed, the very development of *Eugénie Grandet* is the progressive reification of human relations: the more money one has, the less one has any intimate contact with human beings. Thus there is one founding principle of the public sphere of Balzac's novelistic world, and that is money. As one critic puts it, money replaces blood, in Balzac's work, as the "vital fluid of the social metabolism."[22]

The opening paragraphs of *Eugénie Grandet*, in which the streets and houses of the provincial village of Saumur are described, introduce us to a realm of disorder, where human beings seem to have adopted the gloomy façades of the houses they inhabit:

> Life makes so little stir in them [these houses] that a stranger believes them to be uninhabited until he suddenly meets the cold listless gaze of some motionless human being, whose face, austere as a monk's, peers from above the window-sill at the sound of a stranger's footfall. (p. 33)

> La vie et le mouvement y sont si tranquilles qu'un étranger les croirait inhabitées, s'il ne rencontrait tout à coup le regard pâle et froid d'une personne immobile dont la figure à demi monastique dépasse l'appui de la croisée, au bruit d'un pas inconnu. (p. 27)

The beginning of the novel recalls Eric Auerbach's comments on Balzac: "Every milieu becomes a moral and physical atmosphere which impregnates the landscape, the dwelling, furniture, implements, clothing, physique, character, surroundings, ideas, activities, and fates of men."[23] This confusion between human beings and objects is not unlike what the narrator calls a "perpetual duel . . . between celestial forces and terrestrial interests" (p. 35; "un duel constant entre le ciel et les intérêts terrestres," p. 29), between nature and business.[24] Weather conditions are described in terms of their economic functions, thus: "It's raining gold louis" (p. 36; "Il pleut des louis," p. 29). Between nature and economy, between human beings and houses, the boundaries have become unclear. And so it is, as well, with the distinction between private and public life:

> Everything—expenses, purchases, and sales, to the very profit each will make, is known in advance, and so these people find themselves free for ten hours out of twelve to pass the time in happy diversion, in observation of their neighbors, comment on their affairs, and constant spying on their comings and goings. . . . Consciences are clear there, or at least open for inspection, and the apparently impenetrable, dark, and silent houses are completely lacking in secrecy. (p. 36)

> Là, tout étant prévu, l'achat, la vente, le profit, les commerçants se trouvent avoir dix heures sur douze à employer en

joyeuses parties, en observations, commentaires, espionnages
continuels. . . . Là donc les consciences sont à jour, de même
que ces maisons impénétrables, noires et silencieuses n'ont
point de mystères. (p. 29)

The life of an individual family has no independent existence: "Life is
lived almost entirely in the open air" (p. 36; "La vie est presque tou-
jours en plein air," p. 29). The opening lines of *Pride and Prejudice*
also introduce a potential confusion between universal truths and individual arrangements. However, that confusion stems from the par-
ticularities of Mrs. Bennet's view of the world. In the provincial village
of Saumur, the confusion of realms is an objective feature of the lives
that are lived there.

But the Grandet family does not "live its life in the open air," for
Grandet has two sacred possessions to protect: his gold and his daughter. The Grandet household may be a space relatively separate from
the village, but Grandet's simultaneous "ownership" of his daughter
and of his gold stems from a confusion between the human and the
non-human. Hence the public sphere of the town is reflected in the
Grandet home:

> In this face were written a dangerous craftiness, a calculated
> rectitude, the selfishness of a man who, day by day, concen-
> trated all his emotions on saving money, and on the only being
> in the world who meant anything to him, his daughter and sole
> heiress, Eugénie. (p. 44)

> Cette figure annonçait une finesse dangereuse, une probité
> sans chaleur, l'égoïsme d'un homme habitué à concentrer ses
> sentiments dans la jouissance de l'avarice et sur le seul être qui
> lui fût réellement de quelque chose, sa fille Eugénie, sa seule
> héritière. (p. 35)

Visits to the Grandet house are frequent, but limited to the Des
Grassins and the Cruchot families, who alone are permitted to enter
the house. Through these visits, some sense of the connection between the Grandet household and the village as a whole is created.
Indeed, that connection is purely economic, for the families who visit
the Grandets are interested only in arranging what would be an advan-
tageous marriage with Eugénie. With these visits, one is reminded,
somewhat, of the function of the ball in *Pride and Prejudice*; but

whereas matrimonial possibilities are handled rather ineffectually by Mrs. Bennet, there is no question, when visitors come to the Grandet house, but that Monsieur Grandet is in total and absolute control. "Old Grandet towered above the other actors in this drama, exploiting the false affection of the two families and drawing enormous profits from their pretense of friendship. He made its meaning clear" (p. 66; "La figure de Grandet exploitant le faux attachement des deux familles, en tirant d'énormes profits, dominait ce drame et l'éclairait," p. 51). Visits from the Cruchots and the Des Grassins, then, might be seen as a bridge between the home and the neighborhood, the personal and the social. But the desires of these families, with marriage on their minds, are but pale reflections of Grandet's own desires to invest and make a profit.

These regular visitors to the Grandet home are made in the image of Monsieur Grandet. The arrival of Charles from Paris, however, suggests the intrusion of a different kind of public sphere. For Charles is distinctly Parisian, a man of fashion, immediately identified as "other" in this room of provincials. He has a different relationship to wealth than does Grandet, for Charles's wealth (soon revealed to be illusory) is measured in terms of what can be seen, in terms of appearances.[25] Thus Charles stands in marked contrast to the bare, sparsely furnished Grandet home. Eugénie responds to Charles as if she were experiencing the unknown for the first time: "It seemed to Eugénie, who had never in her life seen such a paragon of beauty, so wonderfully dressed, that her cousin was a seraph come from heaven" (p. 73; "Eugénie, à qui le type d'une perfection semblable, soit dans la mise, soit dans la personne, était entièrement inconnu, crut voir en son cousin une créature descendue de quelque région séraphique," p. 57). The worlds of community and home are so conflated in Saumur, and Grandet so controls the environment in which Eugénie lives, that Charles functions as an "other" she has never encountered, as a representative of another public sphere she has never experienced.

The introduction of Charles as "other" simultaneously introduces the possibility of an alternative to the world in which Grandet is the unquestioned center. We soon discover that Grandet controls the economic future of Charles. The appearance of Charles in Saumur, and Eugénie's subsequent attraction to him, open up the essential question posed in *Eugénie Grandet*: Can Eugénie ever achieve a genuine separation from her father? Put another way, the question is two-fold: Can an authentic private sphere, free of economic consideration, exist; and is there, in the world of capitalist values, any public sphere except that represented and controlled by Grandet?

Grandet the capitalist is indistinguishable from Grandet the patriarch, and the lines drawn between male and female are synonymous with those that separate the capitalist from his subjects. *Eugénie Grandet* is unlike *Pride and Prejudice* in this respect, for in Austen's novel, the separation of male and female realms, exemplified by the Bennet house and by the ball, is co-existent with, but not reducible to, the sense of "class geography" that pervades the novel. In *Eugénie Grandet*, there is a single reference point for sex and class, and that is the Grandet house. Sex and class divisions occupy the same space.

The central room in the Grandet house is the parlor:

> Few people know how important a part this room plays in the life of the small towns in Anjou, Touraine, and Berri. The parlour is hall, drawing-room, study, boudoir, and dining-room, all in one; it is the theatre of family life, the centre of the home. (p. 49)

> Peu de personnes connaissent l'importance d'une salle dans les petites villes de l'Anjou, de la Touraine et du Berry. La salle est à la fois l'antichambre, le salon, le cabinet, le boudoir, la salle à manger, elle est le théâtre de la vie domestique, le foyer commun. (p. 39)

The Grandet parlor is sparsely furnished, and the only luxurious items in it are those that "had been included in the bargain when the house was bought" (p. 51; "Cette luxueuse décoration . . . avait été comprise dans l'achat de la maison," p. 40). If the parlor is the center of the home, it is a center which is defined primarily in economic terms. As it is first presented to the reader, the parlor has two functions. It is where visitors are received, and where the Grandet women perform their needlework. The position of the Grandet women in the parlor defines their position in relation to the world. They are passive onlookers:

> In the window nearest to the door stood a straw-bottomed chair, raised on blocks of wood so that Madame Grandet as she sat could look out at passers-by in the street. A worktable of

bleached cherry wood filled the other window recess, and Eugénie Grandet's little armchair was set close by. (p. 51)

Dans la croisée la plus rapprochée de la porte, se trouvait une chaise de paille dont les pieds étaient montés sur des patins, afin d'élever madame Grandet à une hauteur qui lui permit de voir les passants. Une travailleuse en bois de merisier déteint remplissait l'embrasure, et le petit fauteuil d'Eugénie Grandet était placé tout auprès. (p. 40)

The parlor might be described as the "female space" of the Grandet house. To be sure, Grandet rules the parlor as he rules the rest of the house. Eugénie and her mother share a private space of subjugation and oppression, a private life bound by the sparsely furnished parlor and given rhythms by the domestic labor they perform.

Even though the entire Grandet house could be defined as "male space," given the tyranny of the patriarch-capitalist, there is one room which functions as Grandet's private space, of sorts. This is Grandet's secret workroom, separated from the rest of the house, which no one is allowed to enter. Here work and pleasure are combined for Grandet, as he counts and contemplates his treasure of gold:

The old cooper would come to commune with his gold, to caress and worship, fondle and gloat over his gold. The walls were thick, the shutters close. He alone had the key of this laboratory where, as it was said, he pored over plans on which every fruit tree he possessed was plotted, and calculated his yield to the last shoot in his vineyards, to the last faggot of his timber. (p. 88)

Là . . . venait le vieux tonnelier choyer, caresser, couver, cuver, cercler son or. Les murs étaient épais, les contrevents discrets. Lui seul avait la clef de ce laboratoire, où, dit-on, il consultait des plans sur lesquels ses arbres à fruits étaient désignés et où il chiffrait ses produits à un provin, à une bourrée près. (p. 68)

The spatial dimensions of the Grandet house are marked by these two extremes, the parlor and the workroom, and in between them lie two other rooms of importance, Eugénie's bedroom, and the room where Charles sleeps. If any sense of female space within the Grandet house is limited by the absolute control of the father, Charles's arrival marks the beginning of a resistance to Grandet's tyranny. Eugénie decorates Charles's room with as many objects as she can find, attempting to create a sense of female space within the house. Eugénie even directly confronts her father. One morning at breakfast Grandet puts the sugar away, and when Charles looks round for more, Eugénie "replaced it on the table, looking her father calmly in the face as she did so" (p. 113; "reprit la soucoupe au sucre que Grandet avait déjà serrée, et la mit sur la table en contemplant son père d'un air calme," p. 87).

If Eugénie resists the power of her father in these small domestic ways, the relationship between the women in the Grandet house appears differently once Charles arrives. Charles spends time with the women in the parlor, and their labor is shown through a different perspective:

> Charles stayed in the parlour with the mother and daughter, and experienced a pleasure he had never known before in holding skeins of thread for them to wind, in watching them sew and listening to their talk. He found something that appealed to him strongly in the simplicity of the almost cloistral life they led, in which he had discovered the beauty of the nature of these two women who had never known the world. (p. 170)

> Charles demeurait entre la mère et la fille, éprouvant des délices inconnues à leur prêter les mains pour dévider du fil, à les voir travaillant, à les entendre jaser. La simplicité de cette vie presque monastique, qui lui révéla les beautés de ces âmes auxquelles le monde était inconnu, le toucha vivement. (p. 130)

This may be a romanticized view of the women's lives. Nonetheless, Charles's presence creates the possibility of a female space that Grandet does not absolutely control (the scene occurs while Grandet is in his fields). When Charles leaves for the West Indies, he becomes the center of a kind of fantasy life shared by the three women—mother, daughter, and servant Nanon—of the Grandet home:

> The absorbing interest of their secret bound the three women together in a closer intimacy, and infused new life into their dull domestic existence, which had been so monotonous before

Charles' coming. For them Charles still dwelt under the dis-colored grey rafters of the parlour and came and went as before. (p. 184)

Cette vie domestique, jadis si monotone, s'était animée par l'immense intérêt du secret qui liait plus intimement ces trois femmes. Pour elles, sous les planchers grisâtres de cette salle, Charles vivait, allait, venait encore. (p. 141)

When Charles reciprocates Eugénie's love, their relationship suggests, on two levels, the promise of an integrated existence. Eugénie's love for Charles gives her a sense of connection, of relationship to the world around her: "she herself was one with her surroundings" (p. 93; "les harmonies de son coeur firent alliance avec les harmonies de la nature" p. 72). Simultaneously, love promises a mediation between social and natural existence. Prior to Charles's arrival, Eugénie had "passed her life by that window . . . looking in the silent street outside to see scarcely one passer-by in an hour" (p. 73; "[sa] vie s'était écoulée sous ces crasseux lambris sans voir dans cette rue silencieuse plus d'un passant par heure," p. 57). Eugénie's discovery of love leads her to a different vantage point, emblematic of the promises contained within her relationship to Charles. Eugénie still looks through a window, but now it is the window in her room—a space more removed from the watchful eye of Grandet—through which the garden is visible. This is hardly the large woods that surrounds Pemberley, but there is a similarity between Elizabeth's and Eugénie's experience of the house and the garden. The garden holds many memories for Eugénie, and the sight of it provides the focus for Eugénie's fantasies of an integrated existence.

The Grandet house is thus divided along two axes. From within, one axis separates the secret workroom from the parlor. In between those rooms are two other rooms, belonging to Eugénie and Charles, where a certain transgression of Grandet's power occurs, for each is a focus of female activity hidden from Grandet. Another axis separates interior and exterior space, the house and the garden. The garden, with all of its mythical associations, is a hypothetical space outside of business transactions. The garden functions primarily as the site of Eugénie and Charles's romance. But it is also in the garden that Grandet announces to Charles that his father committed suicide. The scene inspires the following reflection on the part of Grandet:

'You have lost your father!' It was nothing to tell him that.
Fathers usually die before their children. But: 'You have no
money at all!' All the woes in the world were summed up in
those words. (p. 115)

'Vous avez perdu votre père!' ce n'était rien à dire. Les pères
meurent avant les enfants. Mais: 'Vous êtes sans aucune espèce
de fortune!' tous les malheurs de la terre étaient réunis dans ces
paroles. (p. 89)

For both Eugénie and Charles, the garden becomes a special image
marked by its associations with separation, for each of them, from
her/his father. The memory of the garden is imprinted on Charles's
consciousness in connection with his father's death:

In the crises of life, when we are overwhelmed by joy or sorrow,
we see our surroundings with sharpened senses, and they remain for ever afterwards indelibly part of our experience.
Charles scrutinized with strained intentness the box borders of
the little garden, the faded autumn leaves floating to the
ground, the crumbling walls, the grotesquely twisted branches
of the apple trees, picturesque details which were to remain in
his memory for ever. (p. 115)

Dans les grandes circonstances de la vie, notre âme s'attache
fortement aux lieux où les plaisirs et les chagrins fondent sur
nous. Aussi Charles examinait-il avec une attention particulière
les buis de ce petit jardin, les feuilles pâles qui tombaient, les
dégradations des murs, les bizarreries des arbres fruitiers, détails
pittoresques qui devaient rester gravés dans son souvenir. (p. 89)

This is a condensation of the process which, for Eugénie, will be
stretched out over years. Her past is condensed within the space of the
garden. Seated on the garden bench, "her solitary, lonely, true, endur-
ing love entered into every thought, and became the very substance,
or as our forefathers would have said, the 'stuff' of her life" (p. 184; "ce
fut l'amour solitaire, l'amour vrai qui persiste, qui se glisse dans toutes
les pensées, et devient la substance, ou, comme eussent dit nos péres,
l'étoffe de la vie," p. 141). Gradually the garden, as a site of memory,
becomes self-sufficient, as if Eugénie's dreams and fantasies have no

more direct connection to a real past or a real future. For example, Eugénie is seated on the garden bench when she receives the long-awaited letter from Charles: "It was a bright fresh morning, and the poor girl was pleasantly engaged in passing in review her memories of the great and small events of her love-affair and the catastrophes that had followed" (p. 231; "La pauvre fille se complaisait en ce moment, par la plus fraîche, la plus joyeuse matinée, à repasser dans sa mémoire les grands, les petits événements de son amour, et les catastrophes dont il avait été suivi," p. 176). Reading the letter from Charles, she comes to a passage where he speaks of his memory of the little wooden bench. This is how she responds: "Eugénie jumped up, as if she had sat down on blazing coals, and went to find a seat on one of the courtyard steps" (p. 233; "Eugénie se leva comme si elle eût été sur des charbons ardents, et alla s'asseoir sur une des marches de la cour," p. 177). Eugénie's life has become characterized, in other words, by a total split between self and other, between memory and reality. The fantasies which are lived in the space of the garden reinforce the split between private and public space, and the promise of connection disintegrates.

The two metaphoric itineraries of travel and reading that appear in *Pride and Prejudice* are present in *Eugénie Grandet* as well, tracing a process whereby individuals resign themselves to lives as simple agents of capitalist value. Charles's voyage to the West Indies could be called a voyage of self-discovery, but the self discovered is concerned only with economic gain. Charles becomes a slave trader: "He perceived that the best way to make money in the tropics, as in Europe, was to buy and sell men" (p. 226; "il s'aperçut que le meilleur moyen d'arriver à la fortune était, dans les régions intertropicales, aussi bien qu'en Europe, d'acheter et de vendre des hommes," p. 172). While it hardly makes sense to decide who, in the novel, is more thoroughly capitalist, Charles or Grandet, Charles does have a more *direct* relation to capitalist exploitation than his uncle. Linda Rudich describes Charles as a "new capitalist," whose "brutality and cynicism on an imperial scale make old father Grandet's avarice a monstrous comedy compared to what will come."[26] The difference between the two identities is reminiscent of the two different middle-class identities found in *Pride and Prejudice*. By the same token, the image of Eugénie becomes, for Charles, but a distant memory, until finally, "she had a place on his ledger as a creditor for 6,000 francs" (p. 227; "elle occupait une place dans ses affaires comme créancière d'une somme de six mille francs," p. 173). In short, Charles's journey affirms the all-encompassing nature of capitalist value.

More significant than the voyage per se is the way in which Eugénie follows her cousin's travels:

> Eugénie bought a map of the world in the town's only book-shop. This she pinned beside her mirror, so that she could follow on it the course of her cousin's voyage to the Indies, so that night and morning she might go in her imagination aboard that distant vessel, and see her cousin, and ask him all the innumerable questions she longed to ask. (p. 183)

> Elle prit, chez le libraire de la ville, une mappemonde qu'elle cloua près de son miroir, afin de suivre son cousin dans sa route vers les Indes, afin de pouvoir se mettre un peu, soir et matin, dans le vaisseau qui l'y transportait, de le voir, de lui adresser mille questions. (p. 140)

The map and the garden signify the impossible connection between the personal sphere of love and the public sphere of money-bound relations. And like the garden, the map eventually is cut off from any vital connection with the past or the future. Between her map and the garden, Eugénie does have a personal life of sorts, but it too is ultimately defined in a reified way, with objects replacing human beings rather than connecting to them:

> Her isolation, her father's displeasure, were trifles easily borne, for had she not her map of the world? From her window could she not still see the little bench, the garden, the angle of the old wall? Did not her lips remember the sweetness of love's kisses? (p. 200)

> Sa réclusion, la disgrâce de son père, n'étaient rien pour elle. Ne voyait-elle pas la mappemonde, le petit banc, le jardin, le pan de mur, et ne reprenait-elle pas sur ses lèvres le miel qu'y avaient laissé les baisers de l'amour? (p. 153)

The sending and the receiving of letters also functions as a process through which the private sphere collapses to become a simple reflection of the public sphere. By and large, the letters written and read in *Eugénie Grandet* are deceptive, revealing an aspect of a character that has been concealed. The person revealed in a letter is different from the person known: hence, reading is yet another process of the reified imagination, whereby image and object are separated. Eugénie discovers a letter from Charles to his lover Annette in which he writes, coldly and methodically, of a marriage to Eugénie as a good financial arrangement. When Eugénie finally receives the long-awaited letter from Charles, it is a masterpiece of deception. Charles has already made arrangements to marry, but nonetheless tells Eugénie that a marriage between them is still a possibility. This decisive letter is somewhat like Charles's earlier letter to Annette, but there is no longer another side to him that comes to life in the garden. Eugénie, however, has finally learned how to "read," and she understands that Charles no longer reciprocates her love. And so Eugénie herself finally writes a letter (arranging the payments of her cousin's debts), which, along with her own marriage, marks her resignation to a world of duplicitous arrangements and financial greed.

By far the most essential narrative gesture in *Eugénie Grandet*, however, more central than travel or reading, is the exchange of gifts. Here as with all other strands in the novel, Grandet stands at the center of all exchange. But if business transactions pervade the world of *Eugénie Grandet*, the exchange of gifts has a special function. There are two terms here: exchange, implying money and business, the exchange value for which gold is the universal symbol; and gifts, implying personal expression, things given freely, without the hope of investment, interest, or profit. For Grandet, of course, nothing is given freely. Just as surely as Grandet possesses both gold and his daughter, every gift offered by the old man is an investment disguised, an addition to his own supply of gold. Grandet always gives Eugénie a rare gold coin for her birthday (ironically, to add to her dowry), and enjoys watching her accumulate money.

For Grandet, gold exists to be contemplated, not to be exchanged for something else of use. Put another way, the use value of gold *is* its exchange value. In marked contrast to the gifts offered by Grandet to his daughter are those he offers to his servant Nanon. She is the recipient of "gifts" that have no other distinction than the fact that they have already been used, and will continue to be put to use by her. Grandet gives Nanon his old shoes; and most notably, he gives her his old gold watch as a present for twenty years of service. In her turn, Nanon gives things that will be of genuine use, and the gesture of giving on her part is devoid of any overtones of investment or profit.

Nanon is the representative of the old feudal order, bound (in Balzac's view) by devotion rather than by money. Hence it is Nanon who, when Eugénie is being punished with a bread-and-water diet by her father for having given her gold to Charles, saves her own money and makes a pâté for Eugénie to supplement her diet.

Eugénie's greatest transgression against her father is the gift that she makes of her gold to Charles. In exchange—and this is, properly speaking, the only genuinely symmetrical exchange of gifts in the novel—he gives her a gold chest and two portraits of his parents for safe-keeping. Eugénie gives Charles the means to leave France and make his fortune; Charles gives Eugénie an object to be invested with memories. Each object is a link to the family: the gold is from Grandet, the chest from Charles's mother. Thus the exchange functions as a kind of vow of separation from the family. But whereas Charles is, indeed, "safekeeping" the memory of his mother with Eugénie, Eugénie in her turn is violating the law of her father.

Ultimately, it is the itinerary of the gold box which is more important and decisive than the itineraries of any of the characters of *Eugénie Grandet*. The shape of the characters' lives is determined by the destiny of that gift. However resolutely Eugénie protects her treasure from her father, threatening to kill herself with the same dagger that he wants to use to cut open the box, she cannot escape the inevitable degradation implicit in *any* exchange of money. Eugénie spends many hours alone in her room, contemplating the box, studying the portraits, remembering and fantasizing. In this respect she begins to resemble her father, locked in his secret room, contemplating his own treasures. True, gold is its own value from Grandet's perspective; but as we have seen, Eugénie moves more and more towards a similarly fragmented view of objects. When Grandet discovers the gold box, he says to Eugénie: "Charles gave you this in exchange for your beautiful coins, eh? But why didn't you tell me? That was a good stroke of business, little girl. You're your father's daughter, so I see" (p. 209; "Charles t'a donné cela contre tes belles pièces. Hein! pourquoi ne me l'avoir pas dit? C'est une bonne affaire, fifille! Tu es ma fille, je te reconnais," p. 160). And so Charles might as well be Grandet's son, for when he finally writes to Eugénie, he treats the exchange as a simple business transaction, exactly in the terms set out by Grandet.

Hence all human relations, all forms of exchange, are ultimately reducible to an economic common denominator. Gold is worshipped and fetishized in the Grandet household. However much Eugénie resists that worship, her resistance is futile and doomed to failure. Her personal life becomes little more than the financial arrangements she makes so that the man she loves can marry well.

My readings of *Pride and Prejudice* and *Eugénie Grandet* are ideological in the sense that the novel form, in both cases, is assumed to respond to a culture divided into private and public realms. Yet *Pride and Prejudice* and *Eugénie Grandet* are very different novels in terms of their ideological positions. In *Pride and Prejudice* middle-class values and aspirations are celebrated, while in *Eugénie Grandet* they are criticized. Both novels define middle-class values as the power to integrate and connect the realms of private and public life. In one instance the narrative thus engendered has a regenerative aim, whereas in the other its scope is tyrannical. Yet however different their ideological positions, the two novels share another kind of ideological vision, shaped by similar patterns of crisis and resolution, structured by the posing and reposing of binary oppositions. Elizabeth Bennet and Eugénie Grandet may embody radically different visions of female identity, and their narrative journeys may lead them in opposing directions. Yet they embody nonetheless a similar conception of character as the focal point of the reader's identification and the narrator's point-of-view.

Both *Pride and Prejudice* and *Eugénie Grandet* are examples of that ubiquitous entity, the "classical realist text" or "classical narrative." The very word "classical" suggests the institutional quality of literature, the familiarity of easily recognizable structures and conventions. *Pride and Prejudice* and *Eugénie Grandet* are a part of the realist tradition of the nineteenth-century European novel. The visions of the two novels may differ concerning the desirability of middle-class values, but they share fundamental assumptions about language, narrative, and the social universe.

What we call realistic in the novel is a complex system of illusion and identification. Illusion, because the novel more than any other literary form is based upon the assumption that language reproduces the world and is at the service of a coherently defined universe. Identification, because our comprehension as readers is shaped by a perspective functioning at once as a social and as an individual voice. There has been much attention in recent years to the ideological foundations of realism, that is, to realism as a narrative form that presents a socially determined view of the world as unquestionable and universal. A central notion in these discussions is intertextuality, the mechanism by which the authority of a particular text is measured by its relations with other texts. Underlying the notion of intertextuality is the assumption that textuality informs our perception of the world. Hence Lady Mary might be described in terms of an "intertextual imagination," of sorts, when she immediately recognizes Pamela and Clarissa in her own backyard. Realism, then, is a relation between various texts, from social code to literature per se, rather than a relationship between the text and a world yet uncaptured by representation. Through intertextuality, the ideological dimensions of realism can be understood as textual strategies whose purpose is the containment of experience within intelligible boundaries, boundaries defined by the dualistic structures of language and culture. Realism is not a stripping away of textual density to allow a transparent illumination of the "real world," but rather an intertwining of the authorities of various texts. These work together on multiple levels to produce the "realistic effect."

Just as the novelistic "real" is determined by the interplay of different texts, so the novel creates a perception of the world, understood as a text to be deciphered and interpreted. Realism is certain practice of reading, enveloping both an attitude toward the text and toward the world. The realist text is an accumulation of discursive registers; and the novel-form taps a variety of sources, a variety of discourses, from individual psychology to social gesture, from the historical chronicle to the personal diary. These registers are accumulated in a distinct and yet unobtrusive way. They are culture disguised as nature, the already-written presented and understood through the practice of reading as experience being written.

The means of description used in the realist text are, for Roland Barthes, devices of visualization and framing: "Every literary description is a view. To describe is thus to place the empty frame which the realistic author always carries with him (more important than his easel) before a collection or continuum of objects which cannot be put into words without this obsessive operation."[27] Realistic description is a highly selective, often rigidifying process. As the comparison with framing implies, the reader is given a specific place, an assigned vantage point as a spectator within the text. Similar operations assign the reader a compendium of roles: she/he listens, tastes, smells, is roused to anger or sympathy. In short, the reader is guided from one kind of observation to another in such a way that the boundaries between observation and participation seem to disintegrate.

While the nineteenth century tends to be referred to as the age of the realist novel, neither the realist novel nor the nineteenth century is a static homogeneous entity. The narratives of private and public life in *Pride and Prejudice* and *Eugénie Grandet* are mature visions, culminations of a preoccupation evidenced throughout the early middle-class novel. At the same time, these narratives are moments of transition to other narrative visions of private and public life which characterized the nineteenth-century novel. If the development of industrialization changed dramatically the relationship between private and public life, then the evolution of the novel in the nineteenth century is marked by reflections upon the nature of those changes. The narratives of private and public life exemplified in *Pride and Prejudice* and *Eugénie Grandet* explore the ramifications of what were relatively new features of life in Western societies, and particularly in the village and provincial communities where these novels take place. *Pride and Prejudice* and *Eugénie Grandet* are shaped by the division between the aristocracy and the emerging middle class. In the course of the nineteenth century, the social dimensions of the novel are shaped increasingly by the division between middle class and working class, with attendant implications for narratives of private and public life. The separation of private and public life had far-reaching effects on European society in the nineteenth century, but the separation of the two spheres would become, if not a fact of life, then at the very least part of the fabric of everyday existence.

With the advent of motion pictures, the complex oppositions that are the very substance of nineteenth-century narrative found a particularly responsive form. In the next chapter I turn to a consideration of how, during the first fifteen years of motion pictures, the composition of film audiences and the emerging conventions of "primitive" films established a social function for the cinema analogous to that of the nineteenth-century novel. In order to suggest, in a preliminary way, the visual contours of narrative central to the cinema, the example of photography is relevant. When held at a specific angle, the silvered surface of a daguerrotype reveals a crisply defined portrait of nineteenth-century life. When shifted slightly, however, the image fades to a negative blur, mirroring the viewer captured in the act of seeing. The connection between the novel and the cinema is located at once in the gesture that adjusts the picture, in the clear realistic image, and in its reflection of the viewer.

THE TWO SPHERES
OF EARLY CINEMA

Immigrants and Spectators

We have seen how the middle-class novel responded to the changing dimensions of existence in a society increasingly split into the worlds of home and workplace, private and public spheres. The novel developed when such separations were relatively new features of life in European society. By the 1890s, when motion pictures were first exhibited, the separation of private and public existence was by and large a fact of life. But the cinema did respond to a new phase in the relationship of private and public spheres. Home and workplace had become separate entities as accommodations to the development of industrial production. But in the late nineteenth century and especially at the beginning of the twentieth century, that emphasis on production shifted to an emphasis on the search for new markets, and therefore to an emphasis on consumption. Increasingly, modern capitalist development has been oriented towards not just the production of goods, but towards the stimulation of goods-production by the creation of needs, which can then only be satisfied by capitalist products.

The result has been a fundamental change in the relationship between the public sphere of work and the private sphere of the home. For the home has become less of a "haven" and more of a site of consumption. To be sure, throughout the nineteenth century the home was also the place where the products of capitalist society were consumed. But the family still maintained many of its productive functions, and to a large extent remained self-sufficient for food and clothing. And it was not really until very late in the nineteenth century that capitalist production had much direct impact on the home via labor-saving devices and technology. With the development of a consumption-oriented society, the family became much more dependent on the sphere of production. Eli Zaretsky writes that "as capitalism developed the productive functions performed by the family were gradually socialized."[1] This socialization included the growth of public institutions, like schools and hospitals, that assumed functions previously centered within the family.

The most obvious symptom of this change in socio-economic organization was the growth of advertising. In their study of monopoly capitalism, Paul Baran and Paul Sweezy write that a century ago, "before the wave of concentration and trustification which ushered in the monopolistic phase of capitalism, advertising played very little part in the process of distribution of products and the influencing of consumer attitudes and habits."[2] By the 1890s, however, advertising had become more common, and it became more and more influential with every successive decade of the twentieth century.[3] Advertising and its systematic use of images and texts are the emblems, in the twentieth century, of a consumerist culture.[4]

Images and texts are also the basic elements of cinema, and given the chronological parallel between the emergence of cinema and the emergence of modern advertising, it is tempting to consider the cinema as a product of the new consumerist culture.[5] Such a definition of cinema is particularly appropriate when we consider the success of cinema in appealing to a working-class audience. Even when working-class people adopted bourgeois ideals of the family, the real conditions of working-class life made the gap between the ideal and the real apparent. Consumerism and its primary agent, advertising, proved more successful in creating the illusion that certain ideals were shared equally by middle-class and working-class people. Zaretsky writes that the "emphasis on consumption was an important means through which the newly proletarianized, and still resisting, industrial working class was reconciled to the rise of corporate capitalism."[6] Hence consumerism offered the image of a homogeneous population pursuing the same goals—"living well" and accumulating goods. The movie theatre seemed to offer an ideal space for the exhibition of this image, for workers and middle-class people alike needed only to pay a small admission price in order to share equally in the spectacle offered on the screen.

The cinema responds to that cultural development through which the private sphere becomes increasingly and progressively reified. Essential to cinema's role within this development of consumerist culture has been its function as a form of cross-class leisure. Hence, through the cinema, narrative possibilities were made available to a wider population. This is not to say that the novel remained, throughout its nineteenth-century development, an exclusively middle-class art form. There were in fact a sizeable number of working-class readers in the nineteenth century. However, class distinctions were a feature of novel readership, if for no other reason than the primarily "private" conditions of reading. The cinema changed all that, eventually creating a cinematic equivalent of the classical text characterized by an appeal to a diverse class audience.

The development of consumerist culture makes it increasingly difficult to separate the realms of the private and the public, the realms of personal relations and production. We know that the separation of private and public spheres has always been ideological. With the "female world of love and ritual," as well as in the Working Men's Clubs, distinctions between the two realms are not so easily made. But whereas those nineteenth-century phenomena offer examples of resistance to an artificial separation of the personal and the social, the development of the ideology of consumerism makes reification the value to be celebrated. I will argue, however, that while cinema quickly became an agent of the new culture of consumerism, it also kept alive fantasies of resistance to that culture.

The conditions of "spectatorship" in the cinema are formed by a peculiar and persistent fusion of the narrative visions represented by *Pride and Prejudice* and *Eugénie Grandet*. While it took many years for cinematic forms and structures to emerge that can be considered in any way "equivalent" or "parallel" to the novel, spectatorship developed from the beginning on the model which, two centuries before, defined readership in the early middle-class novel. In this chapter I will examine how, in the early years of moving pictures, a form of spectatorship emerged which would eventually allow the cinema to acquire the social functions which, in the eighteenth and nineteenth centuries, were characteristic of the middle-class novel. By the "early years" of moving pictures, I mean the first fifteen years of development, from the first exhibition of moving pictures in Paris and New York in 1895 and 1896, through to the early films of D. W. Griffith (1908–1910) in which the contours of a "novelistic" cinema are clearly defined. I will focus on the development of cinema in the United States. While French cinema was much more influential and important in these early years (the French film industry dominated the world film-market up until World War I, and many—if not most—of the films seen in the United States were French), the combination of a developing consumerist culture and the particular composition of early film audiences in the United States created a unique context for this new narrative form.

If women are, in the eighteenth century, the most important examples of how novel-reading fit into a growing middle-class culture, a similarly strategic vantage point on the growth of cinema as a cross-class cultural phenomenon is offered through the immigrant workers and families who went to the early moving pictures. In considering the development of an audience for moving pictures, we encounter some of the same thorny issues as with the early audience for the middle-class novel. Urban immigrants, particularly Jews and Italians, have been mythologized (somewhat problematically, as we shall see) as the key audience for early films. Often the fact that immigrants went to the moving pictures has become the basis of a short-circuited argument whereby it is assumed that the movies were specifically made for a working-class audience. Recent historical scholarship has suggested that however important the immigrant audience, the middle class was never far away, and that in any case exhibitors were always keen to attract the middle-class clientele.[7] Now if I consider the immigrant audience strategically important, it is not because immigrants represent the "other," but rather—as in the case of women readers in the eighteenth century—because their responses to the motion pictures allow us to see, in sharp and clear terms, how the cinema would acquire a new social function, in cross-class terms, at the same time that it perpetuated an established function of narrative in relation to private and public existence. For immigrants were perhaps the only Americans for whom the separation of private and public existence had not yet become a fact of life: uprooted from societies where the separation between home and industry had barely occurred, if at all, they experienced the split between private and public existence as a new and unfamiliar feature of everyday life.

In speaking of this immigrant audience, yet another problem arises. Film historians who speak of the immigrant audience often seem to assume that it was predominantly male. This may be due to the unfortunate assumption that if the sex is unspecified, then it must be male. That early equivalents of stag films drew all-male audiences seems certain, but these were but one instance in a diverse range of films. If immigrant workers were drawn to the moving pictures primarily because of the pressures of long workdays at exhausting work, then it is well to remember that immigrant women (the daughters of immigrant families in particular) had their share of jobs outside the home. And if immigrants were drawn to the moving pictures as families, then it would seem that the "immigrant" in "immigrant audience" is divided rather equally between men and women. Recent historical scholarship has indeed suggested that during the nickelodeon era, moving-picture theatres tended to be located in immigrant neighborhoods populated by *families* rather than single workers; and that for immigrant women, the motion pictures were a popular form of entertainment approved of by their families.[8]

Unlike other institutions of working-class leisure like the Working Men's Clubs and the music halls, which were exclusively working-class and more often than not exclusively male, the cinema appealed to a heterogeneous audience. An important predecessor of cinema in this respect was American vaudeville. Vaudeville houses were one of the most important exhibition outlets for the motion pictures, and by the 1890s American vaudeville had already created a unique cross-class, male and female audience.[9] Particular to the cinema as collective spectacle was a special kind of transaction between viewer and screen. Examination of that transaction, particularly in terms of immigrant viewers, indicates the special function of cinema in relation to the spheres of private and public life.

It has become a widely accepted fact of film history that immigrants comprised the most important audience for this new form of entertainment. William Everson reflects the opinion of many when he writes that "it is a matter of record that key audiences for the new movies were the vast number of immigrants who had come to America."[10] This is not to say that immigrants were the only audience for moving pictures. One possible reason that the immigrants who went to motion pictures were so often commented upon is that they had never really, in the minds of showmen and entrepreneurs, been perceived as an audience. Here is how Russel Nye describes this "new audience": "Five, ten, and fifteen cent prices brought theatrical entertainment to audiences that neither vaudeville nor the popular stage had ever touched. Nickelodeons and cheap movie houses, located in the city's poorest and most congested districts, supplied exactly what the urban masses wanted."[11] The immigrant is often mythologized in accounts of early movie history. Lewis Jacobs says: "The movies gave the newcomers, particularly, a respect for American law and order, an understanding of civic organization, pride in citizenship and in the American commonwealth. . . . More vividly than any other single agency [the movies] revealed the social topography of America to the immigrant, to the poor, and to the country folk."[12] Garth Jowett echoes Jacobs's assessment: "Especially for the immigrant worker, the movies provided more than just an idle way of filling in time, but also acted as a guide to the newcomer on the manners and customs of his new environment."[13]

Hence by most accounts the moving pictures provided immigrants with a form of acculturation into American life. Surely the most practical aspect of this "socializing machine" was its ability to aid in the learning of English. Russel Nye says that "subtitles, of course, taught thousands of immigrants to speak English,"[14] and Billy Bitzer, who eventually became D. W. Griffith's cameraman, told of visiting nickelodeons on the Lower East Side, where "we noticed that immigrants learned English by reading the titles aloud."[15]

And then there is perhaps the most obvious function of moving pictures in the lives of immigrants—"escape." Garth Jowett describes the "extra relief" that movies provided in "a dreary, work-laden life."[16] Russell Merritt offers a more realistically straightforward account: "Amidst the famous horrors of overcrowded tenement barracks, sweatshop work that paid coolie wages, and continuing typhoid epidemics, movies were treated as a simple refuge—a variant of the race track, the lottery, the fortune teller's, or the saloon. Movies offered the worker a chance to come in from the cold and sit in the dark."[17]

Judging from the accounts of film historians, then, films seemed to play three major roles in the lives of immigrants: they were a form of socialization and apprenticeship into American life; they were makeshift "schools" for the learning of English; and they were an escape from the realities of work and tenement life. The mythologized view of these functions suggests that movie houses and nickelodeons were the back rooms of the Statue of Liberty. It is as if moving pictures had a well-defined role within the melting-pot of American society, and as if immigrants went to the moving pictures as passive subjects eager to be integrated into the mainstream of American life.

Simplistic notions of "socialization" and "escape," particularly when they are used to describe the immigrant experience as passive victimization, are in and of themselves as inadequate to analyze spectatorship in the cinema as they are to describe readership in the eighteenth century. Russell Merritt offers a de-mythologized perspective on the immigrant audience which suggests in more specific terms the importance of movie-going in immigrant lives:

> The films were offered as spectacles that induced the onlooker to marvel at the unnatural, whether in the form of a slapstick chase, a comic dream, a wondrous adventure, or an historic disaster. Those who saw them did not learn much; it was rather the act of going to the movies that mattered most. By perceiving what was general in their own situation, immigrants could identify with others who shared that situation. Like the societies, the schools, and the press, the nickelodeon was a means through which the immigrants came to know each other.[18]

The strategic role of the immigrant as spectator, on the one hand, and the function of moving pictures as collective spectacle, on the other, are two sides of a relationship that can be best understood within the changing spheres of private and public life. The immigrants who went to the early moving pictures experienced the changes taking place in American culture in particularly striking and particularly painful ways. The juncture, let us say, of immigrants and motion pictures represents the drastic effects of the culture of consumerism on the relationship between private and public spheres.

The immigrant population which went to the moving pictures was urban, and for the most part these spectators were "new immigrants"—that is, part of the largely Jewish and Italian immigration that peaked at the turn of the century. The immigrant laborers often had longer working hours and less pay, poorer working conditions and more difficulties (because of linguistic and cultural barriers) adapting to the workplace, than other Americans who also worked in factories and whose lives were also transformed by the increasing rationalization of labor. These "new immigrants" had, for the most part, left societies where industrialization had made but a limited appearance, and where family and community ties were strong: "The bonds of family and traditional community, bonds—despite their contradictions—born of a sensuous proximity to nature, became jeopardized in a world whose self-proclaimed destiny was the transcendence of nature itself."[19] Immigrants entered a culture that was not only industrialized, but in which industrialization was permeating all areas of everyday experience. For some citizens, this industrialization represented emancipation. But the experience of immigrants illustrates the painful process in such transitions. The nature of this process cannot be understood solely in terms of what happened to immigrants at the workplace. For the totality of their lives, in terms of the home and the workplace, family and community, was transformed—just as the development of a consumerist culture was the permeation of industrialization into all realms of experience. Elizabeth Ewen has described the transformations that occurred in the homes of immigrant families, where women in particular attempted to preserve some of the family traditions, even though the conditions of tenement life made such preservation difficult.[20] Hence Ewen describes the home as a struggle between "custom and progress, barbarism and civilization."[21]

To assume that immigrants went to the moving pictures, in part, to *escape* the realities of tenement life is to ignore the ways in which family life was, for immigrants, a resistance to the forces of industrialization. Often such resistance was the province of immigrant women, mothers who performed domestic labor while their husbands and children worked in factories: "In a strange country, immigrant women created a world within their own community. Barred from access to the larger culture by reason of language, class, custom and gender barriers, immigrant women on the Lower East Side depended on each other. This created a web of personal, social and familial relationships that mediated the world of culture left behind and the alien culture they had stepped into."[22]

But not all immigrant men who worked in factories came to the United States with their families. There is a difference in this respect between Jewish and Italian immigration, for amongst Jews the proportion of men and women immigrants was about the same, and entire families tended to emigrate; whereas amongst Italians, about 80% of the immigrants around the turn of the century were men, many of whom repatriated after several years.[23] But even when immigrants did not live with their immediate families, family-like arrangements were the rule. This was evident not just in extended families, but in the lives of single men and women workers who boarded with other families. Of single Italian women workers, Louise Odencrantz wrote: "Even when they live nominally as boarders with distant relatives or friends, they often regard themselves as part of the household, sharing alike in its prosperity and adversity. . . . there was often a tie of relationship with the family with whom they lived."[24] Such participation in family life was true of male boarders as well: "The male boarder occupied a unique position. . . . Once he moved in he quickly became a familiar. He even had the authority to spank misbehaving children. Wherever the family went, the boarder went, too. He could often step between a quarelling husband and wife. Families with a marriageable daughter picked a boarder with the ideal of marrying her off."[25]

This is not to say that immigrant homes were idealized refuges, but rather that the home had a complex status, and was not simply one more place to get away from (as is sometimes implied in discussions of the "escape" value of movies for immigrants). Elizabeth Ewen writes: "the home was not a 'haven' from the outside world; instead it showed the imprint of the economic universe that structured its reality."[26] The lives of immigrants at the turn of the century were characterized by the extreme effects of exploitation and alienation, whether at the factory or at home. Moving pictures provided a "release" from these pressures, but more important, gave leisure, simultaneously, a quality of community and individual fantasy. Moving pictures provided a space where families could share in a sense of community; and where, at the same time, they were exposed to the "private sphere" of an increasingly consumerist culture.[27]

The response of immigrants to the moving pictures reflects the particular strains between family and community, home and workplace, that characterized the immigrant experience. But the immigrant experience is not the exception; rather, it is the extreme instance that shows most clearly the nature of the changes that were taking place on all levels in American society. As Stuart and Elizabeth Ewen have argued: "It is no accident that what we understand to be *mass culture*; a social landscape marked by consumer industries, consciousness industries, and mass media, develops at this nodal point where a formerly rural, or otherwise nonindustrial people were being transformed into a permanent, mass industrial population."[28]

The "public space" of the early moving pictures was shaped by a variety of influences. Vaudeville performances consisted of relatively self-contained scenes, ranging from jugglers to dancers, comics to mimes, and shaped the public sphere of motion pictures in two ways. By 1890, vaudeville was definitely a form of entertainment which crossed class lines. Cinema adopted and developed further this exhibition model. Second, increasing standardization characterized the nineteenth-century development of vaudeville. As Robert Allen writes, "performers were considered components in a system, whose value was determined by the efficacy with which they fulfilled their purpose on the bill."[29] Such standardization was due in part, of course, to the increasingly monopolistic control of the vaudeville industry. Along with such standardization came an increasingly passive, uniform relationship between spectator and stage.

Cinema appears a likely successor to vaudeville from the viewpoint of standardization. As Allen writes, the vaudeville performer "was hired to perform a specialized task with machine-like regularity, three or more times each day for six days each week for as many weeks as there were theatres in the circuit. That he would to some degree be replaced by a machine is not, therefore, surprising."[30] And what Peter Bailey says of the London music-hall could just as easily be said of American vaudeville: "Leisure was now less to be explained than exploited, and the eventual success of the reformed music hall in turning its customers into disciplined consumers adumbrated a new formula for capitalist growth that was to make the mass leisure industries of the present century more formidable agents of social control than anything experienced in Victorian society. . . . In this sense, the contest for the hearts, minds and pockets of the new leisure class had only just begun."[31]

Thus vaudeville provided a context for the public space of the movie theatre as both cross-class entertainment and as standardized performance. Another important predecessor to the moving pictures is the kinetoscope, which indicates some of the particular implications of this public space in which images are flashed on a screen. The kinetoscope was a peepshow where one person at a time looked into a machine in which short moving pictures unrolled, and was thus built on the essential principle of motion pictures, but without the screen. The transition of the moving image, from a compartment designed for individual contemplation (the "film" began with the insertion of a coin), to a large screen seen by an entire audience, is a key moment in the development of "mass audience" and "mass culture." The kinetoscope is based on a simple principle of voyeurism: one person peers at an image. Kinetoscopes were set up in a variety of contexts, including not just parlors specifically designed for the purpose, but also department stores, saloons, drugstores, and hotels.[32] Within the institutions of consumerism, an entertainment machine was in operation, satisfying one pair of eyes at a time. The first moving pictures were shown by and large in makeshift contexts: backrooms and converted storefronts. However makeshift, the first movie "theatres" were a public institution in their own right: the relation of a pair of eyes to the image was, quite literally, brought out into public view. Image-consumption became a public institution. The contemplation of images that had been, with the kinetoscope, purely individual, became collectivized spectacle. Benjamin Hampton says that peep show customers were suspicious of the novelty of motion pictures on a screen, in part because they "dubiously regarded pitch-dark rooms where pickpockets could go through you easy as an eel through water."[33] Suspicions of pitch-dark rooms and pickpockets aptly summarize the new conditions represented by the advent of the movie theatre. While you are watching the screen, someone else may be watching you. There are, in the same space, *other spectators* who are only dimly perceivable in that "pitch-dark." In short, movies are projected in a public space requiring a certain anonymity if they are to be watched comfortably. Yet it is the very nature of the spectacle that it be *collectively* experienced.

It is essential, I think, to account for the immigrant response to the moving pictures as twofold: on the one hand, moving pictures provided an indoctrination into the ideals of consumerist culture; and on the other, the transaction between viewer and screen made film viewing a fantasy responsive to the immigrant experience. Elizabeth Ewen has aptly summarized the nature of immigrant response to the moving pictures: "Moving pictures were the most universal form of cheap and satisfying entertainment in urban immigrant communities. As escape, education or pleasure, they constituted a major source of ideas; they presented a beguiling view of American dress, manners, and sexual freedom. And they pointed to a mode of existence predicated on a commitment to individual survival in a consuming world."[34]

Moving pictures idealized the increasing reification of the private sphere. Other benefits of the consumer society may have been unavailable to immigrants, but the movies offered, at least, a spectacle to be consumed. The very experience of going to the moving pictures made a connection between private and public spheres. This is not to say that such connections were elsewhere unavailable, but rather that the fantasy component of the movies gave a unique imaginary shape to private and public space. Since the mythologies of early cinema tend to portray the immigrant-spectator as little more than a passive consumer of the moving-picture show, the roles of "fantasy" and "imagination" in the film-going experience are open to misunderstanding. Fantasy may imply "escape," but it is also a potential form of resistance, an imaginary refusal of real conditions of existence. Consider, for example, the "daydream" that garment-industry worker Adriana Valenti described: "I'd make up stories in my mind while I'm working. I'd say, 'What kind of a person's going to wear this dress. Is she in good health, is she a good person? Where is she going to go? . . . because on each ticket you put your name or number so you know who made it. Like you're creating something and someone is going to enjoy it. And then I'd think—what kind of a person? Is she going to be careful? Is she going to keep it well? It's not mine. I only made it and got paid for it."[35] Of this daydream, Elizabeth Ewen says: "In her daydream Adriana Valenti was able to establish a more direct relationship between the creator/producer and the consumer/enjoyer than was possible in reality. Her reverie pierced the exploitative nature of the work to grasp the real meaning of work as creation and of consumption as pleasure."[36] So, too, did the moving pictures produce such fantasies of a "direct relationship between producer and consumer"—fantasies in which the daydreamer looks at the screen as the product of her/his imagination, a screen on which the products of consumer society are visible in either everyday or magical contexts. The imagination that links viewer and screen is shaped by the capacity to make connections between realms of experience which are otherwise fragmented.

In the early conditions of spectatorship, then, the itinerary from private to public space which characterized the early conditions of readership is reversed. This reversal, as well as the transitions from kinetoscope to motion picture house, and from vaudeville stage to screen, are key moments in the development of cinema as a narrative form. Yet the evolution of narrative cinema has also been, on another level, continuous with the novelistic tradition. The development of more sophisticated "story films" in early motion pictures occurred only when film exhibitors recruited a more middle-class clientele. Even when films seemed to be primarily working-class entertainment, exhibitors were eager to attract a middle-class audience in order to gain respectability, and therefore larger audiences, for the film medium. Russell Merritt has shown how central the conscious recruitment of women viewers was to the creation of a middle-class audience. In order to attract the "affluent family trade," appeal was made to the "New American Woman and her children": "If few professional men would as yet, by 1908, consider taking their families to the nickelodeon, the woman on a shopping break, or children out from school, provided the ideal life line to the affluent bourgeoisie. . . . In a trade hungry for respectability, the middle-class woman was respectability incarnate."[37]

The phenomenon recalls the strategic importance of women readers, for different reasons, in the eighteenth century. And as women viewers began to be more numerous, film producers looked to the literary classics—including authors like Zola, Hugo, Tolstoy—for film sources, in an effort to create an art form that was more legitimate—that is, more appealing to the middle-class.[38]

If the novel filled the gaps of the leisure time of women, the cinema responded to another kind of leisure time. The earliest U.S. film viewers—urban, proletarian, immigrant—never before had been referred to as an "audience." The cinema became, precisely, a means of giving shape to their limited leisure time. That I could suggest even the most remote connection between those women isolated from the means of production who took to reading novels with unlimited leisure time, and the early audiences who went to the movies with limited leisure time because of demeaning and exploitative jobs and oppressive living conditions, might seem scandalous. But however great the distance between eighteenth-century women and turn-of-the-century immigrants in the American city, some fundamental similarities define the early conditions of readership and spectatorship.

Both novel and film have given the illusion of social participation to groups relegated, for one reason or another, to the margins of meaningful activity. Each group occupies a particularly delicate position in the split between private and public life. For women in industrialized society, the public sphere exists primarily as a magnification of the personal; and for those immigrants who came to watch the movies at the turn of the century, any definition of "personal life" was complicated by long working hours, poor living conditions in crowded tenements, and the shock of being severed from one culture and suddenly dropped into another. But seated in the movie theatre, the immigrant is offered one kind of private space: screen images to be consumed, fantasies that allow for intense personal identification.

In their early definitions as social forms, the novel and cinema accentuated different moments of a narrative itinerary. The novel gave women readers the illusion of social participation, while the cinema gave immigrants a sense of the fulfillment of personal fantasies. The private conditions of reading seem to merge with the social world of the novel; while the public conditions of film-viewing are balanced by individualized fantasy and contemplation. If readership offers participation from the vantage point of the private sphere, spectatorship is, in its early definition, a reversal of that process, offering an imaginary private sphere from the vantage point of public space. Spectatorship and readership alike are accommodations to the changing relationship between private and public life.

Viewer and Screen

Cinema acquired a function vis-à-vis the spheres of private and public existence through the social institution of film viewing long before private and public life affected the content and structure of the films themselves. The issue of when, how, and why the cinema became a *narrative* form has been controversial. While historians have argued about which film is the first "narrative film," to so label films (like Porter's frequently-cited *The Great Train Robbery* [1903] or *Life of an American Fireman* [1903]) obscures rather than clarifies the development of narrative cinema, particularly as an institution. The key moments in the development of narrative film are elements of a constellation, and not parts of a linear chain. The transition from the individualized peep-show of the kinetoscope to the collective spectacle of the moving pictures; the appeal of motion pictures to an immigrant audience; the creation, through vaudeville exhibition, of a cross-class audience; the conscious recruitment of a larger middle-class audience through women: all of these moments are crucial to the development of film narrative.

The evolution of film as a narrative form is marked by the increasing preoccupation, in films made between 1902 and 1906 (that decisive period when the "story film" became well-established) with elements which would eventually become the essential components of the systems of film narrative.[39] Noël Burch has defined the status of certain early films: "In many ways and on many levels these [pre-1906] films seem to be acting out, at the level of narrative, of gesture, at the iconographic, scenographic levels, the symbolism of those fundamental strategies which were to develop over the next quarter of a century (ca. 1907 to ca. 1932) and which came to constitute what is still (abusively) called The Language of Cinema (I prefer to call it the Institutional Mode of Representation)." Burch describes, in this context, the significance of the many "voyeur" films of the period. In some films a maid or bathing attendant would look through a keyhole:

"We are already dealing with a step towards the system of découpage which was indeed ultimately to make of the spectator an invisible, ubiquitous voyeur, roaming 'at will' through the film's imaginary space-time in accordance with what was, from the very first, the logic of his/her desire." Another kind of voyeur film showed a man, hidden behind curtains or a screen, spying on a woman undressing. Here, "the frequent presence of a voyeur on the screen constituted a veritable inscription in the film of a predominantly male audience's relationship to the stripping woman, and it is in this sense that the film acts out a structure of desire which will ultimately come to be 'hidden' (repressed?) in the 'language' of the close-up, the lascivious pan, etc."[40]

Hence many early films contained figures of the conditions of film viewing and film representation. Thus the films articulate what would later become, with the development of the codes of narrative cinema, embedded within narrative. I am struck by another, related, set of figures present in early films. Often the relatively simple narrative structures of the films rely on an opposition between two kinds of space, overlapping with what Burch calls the "acting out . . . of those fundamental strategies which were to develop over the next quarter of a century." At the same time that early films acted out the future of cinematic form, an infrastructure emerged marking the connections with a narrative past. And it is through these figures evoking a narrative past that the relation of private and public space becomes a structuring principle of early film narrative.

Consider, for instance, *The Story the Biograph Told* (1904). There are five symmetrically organized shots in this brief comedy. At the Biograph film office, a man delivers a camera and shows an office boy how to operate it. Another man enters the office with his secretary, who sits on his lap. As they begin to embrace, the boy—unnoticed by them—films the scene. There is a phone call from the man's wife (super-imposed on the image, and very difficult to "read") (shot one). At a movie theatre, the man from the office enters a box with his wife. On the screen, visible to our eyes, the film begins (shot two). The movie screen then appears isolated from the rest of the theatre, and we see the film that was taken by the boy in the office: a reverse angle, at closer range, of the man and his secretary.[41] We return to the previous view of the screen and the movie theatre seen in shot two, and now the wife begins to beat her husband over the head (shot four). Finally, we return to the Biograph office, where we see the man and his secretary. The wife enters the office with a male secretary, and forces the guilty (female) secretary to leave (shot five).

The film is perfectly symmetrical: two shots of the office, two shots of the movie theatre, and at the center of the film, another film. Within the office—a public sphere—a man and a woman kiss and hug: they create, let us say, a somewhat artificial "private space." And within another public space, the movie theatre (the two public spaces linked by virtue of the Biograph common denominator), the consequences of that "private space" emerge through a private sphere particular to the cinema.

Spatial tension is generated, then, around the poles of private and public space. Cinema is the culprit, so to speak, the agent through which a secret act is brought to public knowledge. Another kind of spatial tension concerns the representation of the secret affair between boss and secretary. First we see the scene frontally, with the surroundings of the office and the boy with his camera clearly visible. Then we see the scene from a reverse angle, from the perspective of the boy and the camera. It is as if the witnessing of such a "private sphere" requires the spectator to have a fluidity of vision, the capacity to assume one angle of vision and then another. The articulation of space, particularly in terms of alternation, and the implicit assumption of a point-of-view for the spectator are key features in the evolution of cinema as a narrative form.

In *The Story the Biograph Told*, narrative unfolds from the juxtaposition of two spheres, the office and the movie theatre; the coexistence, within each of these, of public and private space; and finally, two views of the private sphere: the one, still immersed in surroundings identifiable as public space, within which the camera and its "director" are visible; and the other, a vision of private space unencumbered, as it were, by such details. These "two spaces" appear in other films of the period, and this articulation of two spheres reveals the common ground between the cinema and the narrative space of the middle-class novel.

In *Uncle Josh at the Moving Picture Show* (1902), both spheres are located within the movie theatre. There is the screen, on the one hand, and there is the box from which Josh watches, on the other. Between these two spaces several transactions occur, with the stage lying between the box and the screen functioning as an intermediary area. Uncle Josh watches three films. The first is of a woman dancer (*Parisian Dancer*). Josh stretches to see where the image is coming from, and then becomes engrossed in the spectacle and jumps on stage to dance along with the image. The second film is *The Black Diamond Express*, one of those famous films from the early cinema which shows a train rushing forward, frightening the audience, as it frightens Uncle Josh. Josh now retreats from the stage as the train appears to rush towards him, and he cowers in his box. Finally, Josh becomes so excited and angered by the third film on the program (*The Country Couple*) that he tears down the screen. In this film, a couple hugs and kisses. Perhaps the man, in Josh's view, takes unfair advantage of the woman; or perhaps—more likely—Josh is merely excited at the scene of seduction. But here he "transgresses," let us say, the space of the stage. He is no longer an innocent participant. Nor does he run away in fear. He attacks the screen and fights with the rear-projectionist located behind the screen. But that "transgression" in fact identifies how the two spaces are linked. Cinema provides the sense of transgression of the boundaries between the public space of the movie theatre and the glimpses of private life offered on the screen.

Grandpa's Reading Glass (1902) brings the two spaces into the home. A simple alternating structure informs the film. A family is seen in the parlor, and images are intercut of what is seen, and therefore enlarged, with the help of Grandpa's reading glass gleefully applied by the children to a variety of objects. Hence we see, "enlarged," a page from a book—the initial object of the reading glass—and then a series of close-ups: a girl with a kitten, a human eye, a baby. Each object is isolated (with a mask) from the space of the parlor, creating within the film almost a kind of guessing-game as to which object in the room will be isolated next. This is hardly the containment of private space within the public sphere of a movie theatre that we see in *Uncle Josh at the Moving Picture Show* and *The Story the Biograph Told*. The private sphere is a room in a familiar domestic scene, but it is also a process by which particular objects within the room are isolated. In other words, a *cinematic* private sphere is created, connecting a familiar scene with a unique way of perceiving it. In this connection between the whole and its parts, a scene is presented in its entirety and then dissected through the playful eye of children with a reading glass. The structure resembles the reverse angle in *The Story the Biograph Told*, where we first have an overall view of the romance between boss and secretary and then an isolated view, more privileged in its perspective. In *Grandpa's Reading Glass*, the dual perspective is brought into the home, into the private sphere itself.

A *Search for the Evidence* (1903) offers one of the most interesting representations of narrative space to be found in the early cinema. A man and a woman, whom we assume to be a wife and a man of the law (a detective, perhaps), walk down a hotel corridor and peek through the keyholes of one room after another. Here as in the other films two spaces are juxtaposed. The difference in this film is that we see the man and the woman looking and then, through a keyhole mask, we see what they see. The space of the corridor from which they look is neither public nor private; it is adjacent to private space. The scenes glimpsed by these observers are little tableaux of private life. A man walks a baby while his wife sleeps; an old man, apparently drunk, hangs from a chandelier. A doctor attends to a bedridden sick woman as a nurse looks on. Three men play cards, and a waiter enters the room (the first penetration, as it were, from the corridor into the private sphere). A woman is seated in front of a bureau, and looks at herself in the mirror. The scenes of private life precede the climax of the film, the discovery of the "evidence": a man and a woman who are having an affair, the man being the husband of the woman doing the search. When seen as the preludes, as it were, to the "evidence," the scenes leading up to the climax form a curious little patchwork. For in all of these scenes, something is missing. That something is not quite "romance," but nonetheless a sense of male-female intrigue and desire. In the scenes that lead up to the "evidence," there is an alternation operative, between scenes where women are present (but always asleep, sick, or alone) and scenes where private space is male-defined (the old man, the three men playing cards). In short, there is an absence in these scenes of heterosexual private life, so that the final scene provides not only the "evidence" sought by the man and woman in the hall, but also a more diffuse resolution of male and female. The final private space of the film marks the end of the search conducted by the man and the woman. It also is an articulation of male-female desire as a more general principle of narrative resolution.

There is, of course, another male-female couple in the film, united by their search rather than by sexual desire. The woman does most of the looking, but once she sees the evidence, the man takes her place at the keyhole and peers at the same scene. Hence a symmetry is created: a man and a woman are looked at, and a man and a woman look. Surely a case could be made for the strategic importance of the *male* look, the look that authorizes the penetration of the space of the room. More important, the "male look" is inscribed within the public sphere, for it is likely that the man is a representative of the law.

And finally, the penetration of the room allows—as in *The Story the Biograph Told*—a different view of private space. We are no longer bound by the keyhole mask, but are given a full lateral view of the room as the man and woman enter. This is unlike the reverse angle of *The Story the Biograph Told*, in that the different angle in A *Search for the Evidence* allows the "lookers," the "voyeurs," to be integrated into the space of the room. They disrupt the private sphere, to be sure, but they also become the object of our look.

The space of the hallway in A *Search for the Evidence* is the site of voyeurism, defined first as the look of jealousy (hence a function of the personal) and then validated by the public sphere of the law. Hence, within the hallway, the differing looks of men and women are defined within the spheres of the public and private, respectively. On the other side of the hallway, there is tension between different kinds of private space: on the one hand, a series of fragments in which male and female are separate; and on the other—the payoff, in a sense—the space of male-female desire. The difference between the final scene glimpsed through the keyhole and the scenes preceding it, is determined simultaneously by the looks of the two people in the hallway, and by the look of the spectator in the movie audience. In other words, the "real" spectator in A *Search for the Evidence* is both inside and outside the film. The space of the movie theatre is identified as public space, for we assume the position of the man and the woman in the hall as they penetrate the private space of the room. Yet the separation of private and public spheres *within* the film dissolves as the entire filmic space becomes a private sphere to be looked at and consumed within the public space of the movie theatre.

In *The Skyscrapers of New York* (1906) and *The Tunnel Workers* (1906), there is another related representation of the two spheres. *The Skyscrapers of New York* begins with a series of newsreel-like images of buildings under construction, where workers occasionally wave at the camera. These are images of the city, of work, of the public sphere. And then, quite abruptly (at least to the eyes of a modern viewer) a fiction begins which, even though extrapolated from the images of labor and the city, is quite clearly separate from them in tone and presentation. The fiction tells the story of "Dago Pete" who "starts a fight and is discharged," and who then "robs the contractor to get even." The film concludes with a fist-fight, ostensibly on top of the tall buildings under construction, and the last-minute rescue of the contractor. Hence the fiction of the film is integrated with the documentary-like images with which the film begins. Two spaces are juxtaposed in this film, one of which at least is a clearly defined public sphere. I am not suggesting that the fiction of the film must therefore be seen as the counterpart, private space. Rather, the very impulse to create another space, within and departing from the public sphere of labor, buildings, and the city, indicates the narrative imagination of the early cinema.

In *The Tunnel Workers*, however, the relationship between documentary images and fiction does coincide with the relationship of public and private spheres. The film opens with a family scene to introduce the fiction of the film. A man, wife, and child are shown in their house. When the man leaves for work, another man peeks through the window and talks to the woman and child. The jealous husband witnesses the scene. The fiction seems to be momentarily suspended in mid-air when a lengthy series of documentary-like images of tunnel workers appears on the screen. One would almost assume this to be a newsreel, especially with titles like "the greatest superstructural feat." Real workers file past the camera on their way to work, and file past again when their work-day ends. They look at the camera with the self-conscious amusement of non-actors being filmed. And then, just as suddenly as "Dago Pete is discharged" in *The Skyscrapers of New York*, we return to the fiction that began the film, now occurring in a stage-set tunnel. The two rivals are tunnel workers. A fight breaks out between them; but suddenly there is an explosion and they are both trapped in the tunnel. At the conclusion of the film, one man is recuperating in bed and the other comes to visit him. They shake hands, reconciled despite the woman who came between them.

In both of these films, documentary and fiction footage are baldly juxtaposed, creating a relationship between two spheres in which the ragged edges are left intact. Private and public spheres form an infrastructure for the two kinds of images presented in these films. *The Tunnel Workers* and *The Skyscrapers of New York* show us the differences between two spheres—differences which would become less overtly accentuated in the evolution of film narrative. The fascination with the very nature of the transaction between viewer and screen that we see in *The Story the Biograph Told, Uncle Josh at the Moving Picture Show,* and *A Search for the Evidence,* would, similarly, become naturalized, and its implications embedded within film narrative.

These early films suggest, in skeletal form, the evolution of cinematic narratives of public and private life. Over and over again, figures of vision emerge as primitive forms of mediation between the public and the private: the stage in *Uncle Josh at the Moving Picture Show,* the "lens" in *Grandpa's Reading Glass,* the keyhole in *A Search for the Evidence,* the camera and the film screen in *The Story the Biograph Told.* Thus the transaction between viewer and screen is simultaneously a connection between private and public spheres, a threshold space. I am reminded, in this context, of how, in *Pride and Prejudice* and *Eugénie Grandet,* activities like reading and letter-writing embed the early conditions of readership within the novel.

Narrative resolution in these films is sketchily but nonetheless clearly represented in terms of male-female desire. *Uncle Josh at the Moving Picture Show* only becomes a film *about* the transaction between viewer and screen when he sees a male-female couple in a film, and in *A Search for the Evidence* the room is not penetrated until the male-female couple has been found. Even the ragged edges between fiction and documentary images in *Tunnel Workers* are rendered less visible by the romantic intrigue, its crisis (the tunnel explosion), and resolution (the reconciliation of the two rivals). The formula of male-female desire coincides with the relationship of private and public space, on the one hand, and of viewer and screen, on the other.

It is virtually impossible to consider the evolution of film narrative without evaluating the contribution of D. W. Griffith. That Griffith was the most important single figure in the development of early cinema has become practically a truism in film history, and to consider Griffith's films in terms of the increasing narrativization of cinema is hardly a unique approach. It is well-known that if there is any one figure most responsible for a "syntax" of film narrative—from the use of close-ups to alternating montage, from the production of serious dramatic films to the increasing thematic complexities of film narrative—it is Griffith. [42]

An archetypal plot structure is repeated obsessively in Griffith's early films. An outsider threatens the life of a woman or child (almost always identified within the family as wife or daughter or son) until order is restored (usually with police assistance) with a man (father, husband, or lover) restored to his position of propriety, and the intruder punished. This is, of course, standard melodramatic fare, and can hardly be considered a Griffith invention. But what is unique about Griffith's use of melodramatic formula is the way it is tapped to create a sense of cinematic/narrative space, building on the example of earlier films as well as on the heritage of the middle-class novel. *Where Breakers Roar* (1908), for example, begins with two events: first, a group of young men and women (in couples) go to the beach for a picnic; second, a madman escapes from the insane asylum and attacks a man on the road. As the film develops, so does the encounter between the madman and the group of young men and women on the beach. One particularly amorous couple is singled out for our attention, and they are teased by their companions. The singling out of this particular couple coincides with the knowledge that the madman is getting closer and closer to the beach. He arrives at the beach, chases after the couples, and gets into a boat with the young woman. A rescue occurs at the last minute, and the young man and woman are happily reunited.

Where Breakers Roar is different from films like *The Story the Biograph Told* and *A Search for the Evidence*, but there are also two spheres in Griffith's film: one identified with the madman, and the other with the couple. Incorporated into the two spheres is a transaction between, if not a viewer and a screen, then a looker and an object of the look. In earlier films, the representation of private and public spheres is contained within the relation between spectator and spectacle. Such implications are more deeply embedded within the two spheres of *Where Breakers Roar*. The man who intrudes upon the security of the couple is an "other," a marginal figure. Our position as viewers in relation to the couple is based on both identification with the threat posed by the madman, and identification with the madman as the figure whose journey brings us closer, as it were, to the couple. He penetrates literally the sphere that we penetrate symbolically; and our identification with him is masked by his thorough "otherness." Thus Griffith's madman is an Uncle Josh in disguise.

The viewer is situated, simultaneously, within a couple's private space—as a result, sensitive to the threat of the madman—and within the public sphere of the madman—that is, within the space of an outsider who is looking in, who is spying on a private sphere. The psychological and ideological center of these two spheres is the family. The formula of *Where Breakers Roar* is typical in this respect: the threat is aimed towards a woman or child, and the restoration of order is always the re-establishment of the male in his rightful place as father, lover, husband.

But the logic of familial/patriarchal discourse is not always presented so transparently as in *Where Breakers Roar*. In *Faithful* (1910), a well-to-do young man named Adonese is on his way to visit his sweetheart, when the car he is driving accidentally runs into a simpleminded man named Faithful. Adonese gives the man a coin and buys him a new suit to make amends. But Faithful won't leave Adonese alone, and shows up virtually everywhere that Adonese goes. "I can't be happy without you," Faithful says. Most irritating is Faithful's intrusion on Adonese's romance. Indeed, it appears as though Adonese will never again be alone with his lover, and she begins to be thoroughly fed up with Faithful's constant presence. But at the conclusion of the film there is a sudden reversal. A fire breaks out in the woman's house, and because of Faithful's persistent devotion he is quick to arrive on the scene to save her life. When Adonese arrives he hugs Faithful, grateful at last for his excessive attentions. Faithful is thus no longer a threat to the couple, but is rather their protector and ally.

Faithful is "other" in the sense that we perceive him as a disrupter of the private sphere. Yet like the madman and like Uncle Josh, Faithful is also a figure of the transaction between viewer and screen, through which a private sphere is penetrated. That Faithful does not constitute a real threat makes this film a comedy rather than a drama. But Faithful's "otherness" is more than his simplemindedness. He is "other" because of his identification with Adonese, and the attendant implications of gay sexuality. When Faithful saves the woman at the end of the film, we are offered proof of his own heterosexual manhood, however latent. This "spectator within the film" has been integrated *into* the realm of the family (or the family-to-be). Hence this conclusion through integration is an alternative to the banishment and punishment of the intruder in *Where Breakers Roar*.

If the system of looks developed in Griffith's films is profoundly patriarchal, then we would expect the outsider, in order to represent a "real" threat, to be male. In *An Awful Moment* (1908), however, the intruder is a woman. The film opens with a courtroom scene in which a judge finds a woman guilty of a crime. She goes to the judge's house and breaks in through a window. She drugs the judge's wife and sets up a rigged gun so that when the bedroom door is opened, the gun will go off and kill the wife. The scheme is discovered in the nick of time and the wife is saved. At the end of the film, the family is happily reunited while the guilty woman is taken away by police. The woman intruder in this film is clearly ethnic, and probably a gypsy; the home that she invades is white, wealthy, and proper. Hence the relation between the two spheres has specific class contours. That a woman should represent a threat to the family is possible only when her "otherness" is doubly marked, through class and ethnic differences.

In Griffith's films the two spheres retain an imprint of the relation between viewer and screen from earlier films, as if the development of cinematic narrative incorporates a memory of its past. If the relation between viewer and screen is embedded within evolving narrative structures, there is another process whereby the object of fascination shifts away from the "screen" (in earlier films) and onto specific objects invested with narrative density. Hence a single object becomes a fetish, a focus for the condensation of levels of meaning. The process is particularly well-illustrated by the period film *Golden Louis* (1909). Based on the "Little Match Girl," the film shows a little girl who is sent by her mother out into snowy streets to beg. The little girl falls asleep in the snow. A wealthy man takes pity on her, and we see a close-up of his hand as he extends a gold coin to her. The use of a close-up here is of course fundamental, for it isolates and fetishizes the gold coin. Another man passes by the little girl, and we see another close-up of the gold coin, now in her shoe. After some hesitation, the man takes the coin. He goes to a gambling casino where he wins a great deal of money. In the meantime, the little girl wakes up and staggers on her way. The man soon goes in search of her, but when he finds the girl she is dead. He throws his winnings away and clings to the child's dead body, as passers-by scramble for the money.

The coin is the focus of spatial oppositions in the film. The child and the coin represent two different sets of values: the child will either survive or not survive, whereas the coin will either reproduce or not reproduce (through the man's gambling). The gold coin is an object which simultaneously detracts attention from the little girl and displaces possession of her. The man steals the coin and wins money, but fails to possess the girl's body (or rather, can only possess her when she is dead—transformed into an inanimate object like the coin). In this film, the two realms—a public sphere defined by money, a private sphere of human interaction—remain distinctly separate. The isolation of the single object becomes a sign of that separation, and the golden coin is "narrativized" to become a point of condensation for all other oppositions of the story—class, sexual, parental.

Another aspect of this narrative function of objects occurs in *His Trust* (1909) and the 1910 sequel, *His Faithful Trust*. Subtitled "Faithful old Negro servant," the films take place in the South during the Civil War. A Confederate soldier leaves his wife and child to go to war, and he entrusts them to the care of his black servant. Shortly after the news that the man has been killed in action, Union soldiers plunder the house and set fire to it. George, the "faithful servant," goes into the burning house to rescue the child, and then he returns to save the father's sword which had been returned home along with the news of his death. George takes the mother and child to his humble slave cabin, and sleeps outside. In the sequel to the film ("four years later") the mother dies, but George remains faithful to his "trust." He provides for the child, pretending that the money is from her own estate. When the child grows up, she wants to go away to school, and George again provides the money. But he cannot afford the price for too long, and almost steals money from an "English cousin" who comes to visit. Luckily, the "English cousin" falls in love with the daughter and they marry. The film concludes with a visit to George and a handshake from the lawyer. He leaves, and George sits alone in the cabin holding the soldier's sword.

This two-part film reverses somewhat the Griffith formula of family discourse. For George is the figure who, were he not a worthy stand-in for the absent father, would have been the threat against the sanctity of the family. He becomes, instead, the family's protector until a suitable marriage is arranged for the daughter—until, that is, the "real" family, the white upper-class family, is reconstituted.

The central narrative object in this film is the father's sword. At the beginning of the film, when the soldier leaves, and later, when we see him in battle, the sword is but one element in a larger context. But after the father's death, the sword becomes symbolic of the "trust" of the black servant. When the sword is returned to the wife, she has it placed in a position of honor above the fireplace; and when Union soldiers burn the house, George first rescues the child, then the sword. George offers his home to the wife and child, and the sword is hung in his cabin, marking their possession of the slave cabin, and serving as a continuing reminder of the duties entrusted to George. And finally,

George is left with only the sword, after the marriage of the daughter and a handshake from the lawyer.

The sword is the center of a sub-text within the film. Within the general outlines of the story, the sword follows its own itinerary, one which is intertwined with other narrative elements and yet autonomous at the same time. There are no close-ups to isolate the sword, as there were of the gold coin in *Golden Louis*, as if the function performed by the close-up in that earlier film is now being performed by narrative structure itself.

The function of the sword as narrative object has other dimensions as well. Griffith has told a particularly racist story of his childhood from which at least part of the inspiration for *His Trust* and *His Faithful Trust* seems to have been drawn. One of the former slaves who remained on the Griffith family plantation had seen the close-cropped hair of northern men, and proceeded to give a similar haircut to Griffith's brother. Griffith writes that his father pretended to be outraged, put on his Confederate uniform complete with sword, and had the former slave summoned. "Then," says Griffith, "drawing the sword, he went through the technical cuts and thrusts and slashes, threatening the darkey all the time with being cut up into mincemeat. The old Uncle was scared pale, and I took it seriously myself until a wink and a smile from father enlightened me." Griffith sums up the experience in an interesting way: "So that sword remains the first memory I have of existence."[43] Griffith's memory of his father's sword mediates between subjectivity and objectivity, between inner and outer selves. The appearance of the sword as a central part of the film suggests the complex narrative structures that are at work, tying childhood and adulthood, past and present, public and private selves. Griffith's childhood memory in relation to the text mirrors the relation between viewer and film. Obviously this does not mean that Griffith's viewers had similar scenarios of father, sword, and slave in mind. However, the very fact that a childhood memory should be a structuring principle of narrative suggests the increasing capacity of cinema to function in ways similar to the novel, within a different set of "reading" conditions.

The sword links the past of the war to the present destiny of a single family. The sword also gives concrete shape to the position of George as both provider for the family and marginal to it: the daughter gets married, and George gets the sword. The sword functions as a sign of

George's relation to and yet separation from both the family and the public sphere of history. And the sword is, as well, an object for our own identification with the screen. The sword represents the transaction between viewer and screen, and could thus be seen as an updated version of Grandpa's reading glass, that is, both an object embedded within narrative and a condensed figure for several levels of narrative meaning.

There is an initial opposition established in the film between "inside" and "outside," between the domestic interior where the soldier says goodbye to his wife and child and entrusts them to George's care, and the space outside the home, a public sphere where Confederate soldiers march past on their way to war. This is a direct representation of private and public life, unchanneled through the relationship of viewer to screen that we see in earlier films. The transaction between viewer and screen that functions as a configuration of private and public space in earlier films has not disappeared, however, but has become integrated into this narrative opposition of private and public space. For George is, in the early scenes of the film, the viewer, the spectator within the film, who has an ambiguous relation both to the home he is chosen to protect (even though the fact that he is black constantly marks him as other), and to the war being fought by white men. Private and public spheres are separate, but given an imaginary cohesion through the sword, for it is only as retainer of the sword that George has access to history.

The conclusion to Griffith's film—former slave George and a Confederate sword—is also an appropriate conclusion to the early history of spectatorship. Within his own private sphere, George lives an imaginary relation to the private and public spheres of white folks. That this is a film replete with conservative and racist ideology is beyond question. Contained within that ideology are the signs of where cinema has come from. George is marginal in some of the same ways as the early immigrant audiences. But now, that marginal figure has become an object of contemplation contained within the film itself.

Four

READERS, SPECTATORS, AND CLASSICAL FILM NARRATIVE

Classical Film Narrative

As a film *auteur*, a director whose mythical persona evokes that of the novelist in the nineteenth century, D. W. Griffith is suggestive of how the evolution of film narrative was influenced by the nineteenth-century novel. In Griffith's films, narrative acquires an increasingly institutional quality, and thus with Griffith we can begin to speak of the classical cinema. The concept of classical narrative, or the classic realist text, which is so central to Barthes's S/Z and to contemporary literary criticism, has found a particularly responsive reception among contemporary theorists of the cinema. Indeed, according to some accounts, narrative cinema functions as a normative classic realist text— that is, as more "classical" than most nineteenth-century novels ever were. Raymond Bellour, for instance, sums up what has become common wisdom in contemporary film theory, when he says that "the American cinema, like the 19th-century novel, very clearly sets into play an art of narrative founded on representation, conflict, enigma, hermeneutics, suspense, all the things that Barthes defined so well in S/Z." As narrative forms, then, cinema and the novel are structured in similar ways. But Bellour adds a qualification which is characteristic of how the notion of "classical narrative cinema" presumes a much more unified and simplistic model than in the nineteenth-century novel. Bellour describes novels as "more diversified, more different from each other than the films. The American cinema is a machine of great homogeneity, due to its mode of production which is both me-chanical and industrial."[1]

While the concept of a classical text suggests a certain attitude to-wards reading (or viewing), and a continuum of response, the term "classical narrative cinema" has, in contemporary film theory, come to refer to American cinema of the period, roughly, from the early 1930s to the end of the 1950s. While no one would argue that the classical narrative cinema has somehow disappeared or vanished, the term is used infrequently in discussions of contemporary cinema, even though the understanding seems to be that as a narrative model, at least, the classical cinema is still very much with us. Two moments are generally considered key in the definition of the classical cinema, mo-ments marked by the intersection of the "mechanical and the indus-trial" to which Bellour refers. First, the domination by the United States of the worldwide film industry was firmly established after World War I; and second, the advent of sound cinema, in the late 1920s, encouraged more and more adaptations of literary works, and seemed to establish firmly cinema's reputation as the most realistic of art forms. Hence the development of the classical cinema appears not only to strengthen the bonds between film and the middle-class novel, but to magnify the basic characteristics of classical discourse. For if the cinema, like the middle-class novel, is founded upon the mediation between art and industry, the cinema makes the novel pale as a com-modity form. Technical innovation, especially in the American cin-ema and especially after World War I, has been so dependent on the profit principle that the cinema at times seems to resemble a vulgar Marxist fantasy. And the continued development of cinema coincided with the increasingly monopolistic nature of the American film enter-prise. As realistic arts, film and the novel have much in common. But in the cinema, realism is often considered not a function, but an in-herent quality. It is often assumed, in other words, that cinema is by nature realistic, and that film images are simply chunks of the world cut out and transposed to the screen.

The very notion of a "classical cinema" suggests that film has devel-oped a variety of narrative devices that evolve from the principles of realism. Thus film has acquired a status similar to that of the novel by virtue of its own emergence as a realistic narrative form. The middle-class novel shaped the early conditions of spectatorship in the Ameri-can cinema. The notion of the "classical cinema" implies a consolida-tion of narrative techniques, creating a peculiarly cinematic form of realism. The development of synchronized sound may represent a privileged moment in the development of cinematic realism; but the classical cinema is no more reducible to a set of techniques than is the novel. Rather, cinematic realism is best described as an intertextual system, a complex working of illusion and identification. Literary realism involves a certain practice of reading, and cinematic realism in its turn is a way of seeing that incorporates an attitude towards both the text and the world. Central to any definition of cinematic realism is an evaluation of just what that process of "seeing" entails in an aesthetic and an ideological sense. And the novel provides an important frame of reference for such a definition: aesthetic in the sense that so many of the techniques of cinematic realism are analogous to the forms of narration in the traditional novel; and ideological in the sense that cinematic realism, like its novelistic counterpart, functions as an imaginary participation in a world beyond the limits of the screen.

In this context, screen and page, images and words, are corollary rather than comparable elements. It has been sufficiently illustrated that there is no language of images that corresponds to verbal language, hence no minimal unity of cinematic signification that can be isolated.[2] However, in a less direct but nonetheless significant way, film utilizes a *logic* of images, which evolves from a similarity between the status of images and the status of language in the traditional novel.

I would argue, however, that the classical cinema does not simplify narrative to the extent suggested by Bellour. A fitting anecdote here is the famous response of novelist Maxim Gorky to the first program of Lumière films shown in Paris in 1896: "Last night, I visited the kingdom of shadows."[3] In Dana Polan's words: "The kingdom of shadows is an apt description of two sides of the cinematic experience." Polan writes: "Gorki captures something of the contradictory quality of cinema. On the one hand, a film, when projected, is physically nothing more than lights flickering on a screen—shadows, mere ephemera. And yet, those shadows, that mechanical act of projection, become caught up in another projection—the mental projection of audiences who gift this insubstantial material with a life and psychical force, and turn the emptiness of shadows into the fullness of a kingdom."[4]

As a "kingdom of shadows," film is a narrative art of ambivalence. In contemporary film theory the contradictory nature of film narrative has had less to do with classical narrative, and more to do with the desire, described by Roland Barthes, for an intersection between Marx and Freud: "How can the two great *epistemes* of modernity, namely the materialist and the Freudian dialectics, be made to intersect, to unite in the production of a new human relation?"[5] In contemporary film theory, the intersection of Marxism and psychoanalysis has been directed towards examination of the very phenomenon of the cinema itself. A function of projection and a screen surface, the cinema evokes the metaphors of the screen and the camera obscura in Marx and Freud. Hence the cinema consolidates ideological and unconscious form. As Stephen Heath writes, cinema "brings historical materialism and psychoanalysis together in such a way that the consideration of film and ideology begins from and constantly returns us to their conjuncture."[6]

A key term in this endeavor to understand how the cinema "brings historical materialism and psychoanalysis together" has been "apparatus"— "In the first moments of the history of cinema," Stephen Heath writes, "it is the technology which provides the immediate interest: what is promoted and sold is the experience of the machine, the apparatus."[7] Hence questions of the ambivalent quality of film, of film as the contradictory phenomenon suggested by Gorki's phrase "kingdom of the shadows," have tended to focus on the apparatus. Historically, then, it was "no accident" that cinema and psychoanalysis emerged simultaneously. The evolution of cinema as a nineteenth- and twentieth-century form has found in contemporary film theory its most persuasive analogy with psychoanalysis. This is not to say that questions of narrative (or of historical materialism, for that matter) have been marginalized, but rather they have been identified as functions of the cinematic apparatus. Put another way, the nineteenth-century discourse central to contemporary investigations into film narrative has been psychoanalysis, and if the middle-class novel has a role to play in these discussions, it is primarily as a background, as a nineteenth-century symptom for which psychoanalysis also functions as a kind of master narrative.

Christian Metz's *The Imaginary Signifier* has been the most influential articulation of the relationship between cinema and psychoanalysis. Central to his discussion of the cinematic apparatus is the nature of cinema as an institution: "The cinematic institution is not just the cinematic industry . . . , it is also the mental machinery— another industry—which spectators 'accustomed to the cinema' have internalized historically and which has adapted them to the consumption of films."[8] Throughout Metz's essays, the nineteenth-century novel is referred to as one of the components which film spectators have "internalized historically." "Since its birth at the end of the nineteenth century the cinema has, as it were, been snapped up by the Western, Aristotelian tradition of the fictional and representational arts, of *diegesis* and *mimesis*, for which its spectators were prepared—prepared in spirit, but also instinctually—by their experience of the novel, of theatre, of figurative painting, and which was thus the most profitable tradition for the cinema industry."[9] The power of cinema as defined here is not so much its continuation of a tradition defined specifically by the novel, but rather its incorporation of a wide range of discourses.

Yet at the same time the middle-class novel seems to identify, for Metz, more precisely than other forms (and the theatre in particular), the social conditions of spectatorship. Metz writes, for instance, that "the classical film has taken, relay fashion, the historical place of the grand-epoch, nineteenth-century novel (itself descended from the ancient epic): it fills the same social function, a function which the twentieth-century novel, less and less diegetic and representational, tends partly to abandon." Or: "those attending a cinematic projection do not, as in the theatre, constitute a true 'audience,' a temporary collectivity: they are an accumulation of individuals who, despite appearances, more closely resemble the fragmented group of readers of a novel."[10] The novel thus seems crucial in defining the reception of the cinema, the conditions of reception of the cinematic institution. Yet in Metz's account (as in Bellour's) the novel is invoked as a relatively homogenous entity.

Discussion of the cinematic apparatus in contemporary film theory has focused on the problem of the subject, that is, on how spectators are addressed by the cinema, and how subject position is inscribed in film in a variety of ways. Central to this discussion has been Emile Benveniste's distinction between *histoire* and *discours*, story and discourse—corresponding roughly to the distinction between narrative as a series of events that occur, and narrative as a mode of narration or enunciation.[11] A novel may be evaluated both in terms of the actual series of events that it recounts, and in the stance adopted by the narrator(s) or the narrating intelligence. Film narrative, however, seems to be characterized by the absence of any distinct mode of narration; or rather, as Metz puts it, cinema is characterized by a "fundamental disavowal" of its status as discourse: "This fundamental disavowal is what has guided the whole of classical cinema into the paths of 'story,' relentlessly erasing its discursive basis, and making it (at best) a beautiful closed object which must remain unaware of the pleasure it gives us."[12]

From the vantage points of both authorship and readership, the middle-class novel has been the basis for some of the most persuasive myths central to the classical cinema. It has been stated over and over again, in condemnations of the cinema as an inferior art form, that if the cinema is heir to the novel it is a bastard child. But if the classical cinema descends from the middle-class novel, then such kinship—like all relations—must be produced. Throughout film history, there are striking examples of films which act out the complex heritage of the middle-class novel in instructive ways. But if any period of American cinema can be singled out for its appropriation of the middle-class novel, it is the 1940s. A variety of forces—sociological, aesthetic, historical—intersected in the 1940s to create, simultaneously, a continuation and a redefinition of the narrative tradition. In American cinema of the 1940s, the middle-class novel became the basis for cinematic narratives of ambivalence.

Authorship

Discussions of the classical narrative cinema assume some kind of relationship between film and the novel on the basis of an ideological and narrative common denominator. In contemporary film theory, this relationship has been more of a general observation about the cinema; discussions of individual films tend more to focus on the question of adaptation. While adaptation analysis has been much maligned (often for good reason), there persists a gap in contemporary film theory between an understanding of classical film narrative as an institution, and the specific ways in which individual films and/or novels fit into that institution.

The tradition of adaptation-study has been one of the major critical ways in which the middle-class novel has maintained a mythical presence in the classical narrative cinema. We know that a great percentage of American films have been adapted from novels, and that the adaptation of traditional novels was an important marketing strategy to recruit middle-class audiences to the movies. The large body of criticism that has developed around the question of adaptation usually follows from the assumption that film and the novel have "natural" affinities as narrative forms, and therefore adaptation-analysis (that is, analysis of the novel as source, the film as a "faithful" or "distorted," "adequate" or "inadequate" rendition of it) tends by definition to be a-historical and limited only to the most isolated aesthetic concerns.

This is not to say that the whole question of adaptations should be discarded as hopelessly unhistorical. While literary adaptations have existed since the beginnings of cinema, the classical Hollywood cinema has a special relationship to literary sources. In adapting traditional novels as well as best-sellers, the classical Hollywood cinema promises that the reading experience will be recaptured in the movie theatre. And perhaps more fundamentally, the adaptation of traditional novels to the screen coincides with the attempt to define cinema as middle-class entertainment.

Nearly all criticism of the novel-film connection has been bound by the question of artistic superiority. If, in the early years, theorists of the cinema had to defend this new art form as different from the theatre, in later years the novel would take the place of theatre as rival. Hence in his defense of cinema vis-à-vis the novel, George Bluestone, in his 1957 study *Novels into Film*, insists that it is erroneous and fruitless to examine whether a filmed adaptation is "faithful" to its literary source. Rather, Bluestone defends film as an autonomous production: "In film criticism, it has always been easy to recognize how a poor film 'destroys' a superior novel. What has not been sufficiently recognized is that such destruction is inevitable. In the fullest sense of the word, the filmist becomes not a translator for an established author, but a new author in his own right."[13] Bluestone's approach is informed at all levels by an insistence on autonomy, and thus all relations between film and the novel are collapsed into the single question, can the film "stand on its own"?—"The final standard, the one to which we must always revert, is whether, regardless of thematic, formal, and medial mutations, the film stands up as an autonomous work of art. Not whether the film-maker has respected his model, but whether he has respected his own vision."[14] What begins as a way of defining cinema as an art form in its own right leads to the pursuit of aesthetic auton-omy and individual authorship. Films and novels are thus connected in a way that has nothing to do with history, nothing to do with any consideration other than: Does the novel provide a point of departure for a "good film"? A false coherence is doubly bestowed, to the novel and to the cinema.

The reverse of Bluestone's defense of cinematic authorship is found in Lester Asheim's study of twenty-four film adaptations of novels ranging from *Pride and Prejudice* to *Alice Adams*, from *Anna Karenina* to *The Grapes of Wrath*, in which he meticulously records what changes and additions were made in each case. Asheim's conclusions could be read as a series of indictments of an inferior art form: "The assumed level of audience comprehension is generally lower for the film than for the novel." "The importance of the romantic love story is stressed to a greater extent in the film than in the novel." But most fundamental is Asheim's indictment of the film industry. [15] If filmed adaptations are simplistic in relation to their literary sources, then, according to Asheim, it is primarily because of the industrial control of the cinema. Asheim defines the cinema as a monolithic culture industry, rigidly and unilaterally controlled by the myth of the mass audience.

Traditional analyses of adaptations tend to focus on authorship almost exclusively: from the work of one author, the filmmaker as *auteur* creates either an autonomous (Bluestone) or a simplified (Asheim) work. If, then, adaptation analysis upholds a mythical connection between the novel and film, the notion of author is central to the myth. The evolution of the notion of authorship in the cinema has focused primarily on the role of the film director. But if there is any single individual most responsible for exploiting and refining the connections between novels and films in the 1940s, it is film producer David O. Selznick. In the 1930s, Selznick had established a reputation based on adaptations of classics like *David Copperfield* and *A Tale of Two Cities*. Undoubtedly the key film in his career was *Gone with the Wind* (1939). From the purchase of the rights to Margaret Mitchell's novel to the search for the right actress to play Scarlett, from the changes in directors to the censorship problems over that classic line, "Frankly my dear I don't give a damn," the production of *Gone with the Wind* has become a fixture in Hollywood mythology. It is tempting to dismiss Selznick as merely an entrepreneur, a producer whose spectacular production of the novel would accentuate film as a showcase for comic-book adaptations, at the expense of narrative and aesthetic possibilities. *Gone with the Wind* was not the first novel to be purchased for the screen, but according to Selznick, this was the first novel purchased before it was a commercial success. [16] Hence the production of *Gone with the Wind* marks an important turning point in the film-novel relationship: the tie-in principle, between film studios and various companies whose products would be shown on screen, enlarges its scope to include the novels upon which films were based. Selznick remarked that snoods became a popular headdress as a result of the film.[17] Now this is nothing new in the history of Hollywood, since the purpose of tie-ins is to create demands for certain products. But what is new about the tie-in principle here is that novels themselves became, after *Gone with the Wind*, commodities on a par with snoods. Buy the snood and you adopt a Scarlett- or Melanie-like identity; buy the novel and you recapture the experience of seeing the film.

If the film *Gone with the Wind* would profit from the success of Mitchell's novel, there would be other films, especially those based on classic novels, which would be instrumental in increasing the sales of the literary source. One editor of a French publishing house, somewhat excessive in his enthusiasm, even claimed that *Jane Eyre* was practically unknown until the film version made it a popular novel.[18]

The tie-in principle has had some unfelicitous results from an aesthetic point of view. Yet the increasingly intimate interdependence of novel and film is an essential component of the institutional quality of cinema. For reading and film viewing would be considered, more and more, as analogous experiences. One sign of the analogy is the appearance of novels in advertisements for films based on them, an increasingly common practice in the 1940s. An interesting advertisement for *Random Harvest* (1942), based on James Hilton's novel, appeared in *Variety*.[19] A man and a woman are seated next to each other in a train, and the face of each is obscured by the book he/she is reading: he, *Mrs. Miniver*, she, *Random Harvest*. *Mrs. Miniver*, a 1942 film, had been a huge success, and featured Greer Garson, as does *Random Harvest*. Thus on one level the advertisement is a simple attempt to create an audience-carryover from one film to the other. The advertisement suggests, as well, that seeing the films is a kind of necessary complement to reading the novels. But there is more. It is easy to imagine a sequel to this advertisement, with the man and woman dropping the books to their laps and looking, instead, at a movie screen, for they could as easily be spectators in a movie theatre as passengers on a train. Doubtless they would look at each other, and then, who knows? A bit of romance might ensue. Novel and film, male and female; these are natural combinations, and reading is, the advertisement suggests, a solitary activity perfectly matched by the more social activity of movie-watching.

Selznick's reputation as a producer, at least in terms of adaptations, is divided almost equally between the classics (*David Copperfield*, *A Tale of Two Cities*) and more contemporary novels (*Rebecca*, *Since You Went Away*). It was later in his career that Selznick turned to contemporary novels, as if the adaptation of the classics were an apprenticeship of sorts. With varying degrees of success, Selznick brought to all of his productions the sense of adaptations as remembered acts of reading. An appropriate image of this remembrance is Selznick's description of how, when filming the classics, he always used the copies that his own father had given him: "When we were in England on the *David Copperfield* search for locations, second-unit shots, casting, research, etc., I lugged with me every place we went the old-fashioned red leather copy of *Copperfield*, which my father had given me, with its tiny type on bad paper and its heavy binding. Half sentimentally, half superstitiously, on most of the classics that I have purchased from the books he first suggested I read, I used the very volumes that he gave me."[20] Hence the movie-producer son carries on the tradition of the book-loving father.

David O. Selznick is suggestive of how the definition of cinema as a narrative experience akin to the novel, the increasing institutionalization of film narrative, would occupy a curious hypothetical space between pure entrepreneurialism and nostalgic memories of personal ties. This juxtaposition is revealed, for instance, by Selznick's comments on Sergei Eisenstein's script for an adaptation of Theodore Dreiser's novel *An American Tragedy*: "I have just finished reading the Eisenstein adaptation of *An American Tragedy*. It was for me a memorable experience; the most moving script I have ever read. It was so effective, that it was positively torturing. When I had finished it, I was so depressed that I wanted to reach for the bourbon bottle. As entertainment, I don't think it has one chance in a hundred."[21]

In film history and theory, few novels have such a mythical relationship to the cinema as Flaubert's *Madame Bovary* (1857). Amongst those works which have had a particular influence on the cinema, and which might indeed be called "cinematic novels," *Madame Bovary* holds a place right next to the works of Dickens. Flaubert's novel is full of narrative devices which seem to anticipate the language of cinema. Best known is the scene at the agricultural fair where the distribution of various ribbons and prizes alternates with Rodolphe's attempted seduction of Emma Bovary. The pace of the alternation becomes quicker and quicker, and the length of each scene shorter and shorter, so that an increasingly tight network of juxtaposition and commentary is created. Eisenstein described the scene as "one of the finest examples of cross-montage of dialogues, used with the . . . intention of expressive sharpening of ideas."[22]

The "cinematic" techniques evidenced in *Madame Bovary* might be taken as indicative of the importance of Flaubert's work, and of *Madame Bovary* in particular, in reshaping and redefining the very scope of narrative fiction. *Madame Bovary* was published in the 1850s, predating the first moving pictures by forty years. The novel both engages with and departs from the realist tradition. If there seems to be a "cinematic" quality to the novel, it may have more to do with *Madame Bovary*'s status as both "classical" and "modernist."

One critic describes the status of Flaubert's novel: "After the appearance of *Madame Bovary,* one either tried to write a book that was like it or one tried to write a book that was not like it."[23] Given this awesome stature, one can perhaps imagine nothing but dismal results in the way of cinematic adaptations of *Madame Bovary.* This is not necessarily because cinema inevitably destroys the complexities of novels. A novel like *Madame Bovary* is inscribed, simultaneously, within the traditions of realism and modernism. Given the links between cinematic adaptations and the institutions of realism, a film adaptation of a novel like *Madame Bovary*—as well as of novels like *Ulysses, To the Lighthouse,* or *A Remembrance of Things Past*—can undoubtedly only be seen as a stress on the realism at the expense of the modernism.

Alternatively, one might look at cinematic renderings of such novels as "hidden" deconstructions, searches for cinematic equivalents of narrative devices, texts which may appear realistic but when tested against other criteria are not. While I do not doubt that many American films do, indeed, have more to them than the simplifying mechanisms of "adaptation" would suggest, the danger of such an approach is that the "hidden" text is indeed so well hidden that it ceases to have much to do with the actual experience of film viewing. While there is much more ambivalence in the Hollywood cinema than usually meets the eye, it is an ambivalence rooted in the historical conditions of film viewing, in a narrative experience which mediates the spheres of private and public existence. The complexities with which I am concerned are not simply those of an individual text, but rather the complexities engendered by a juncture of texts, viewers, and history. It is worth keeping the dangers of simple-minded deconstruction in mind, because the film to which we now turn, Vincente Minnelli's *Madame Bovary* (1949) is particularly susceptible to such misreading.

In Minnelli's film, the story of Emma Bovary (portrayed by Jennifer Jones) is framed by Flaubert's trial. The film opens in a courtroom where accusations are made. Flaubert (portrayed by James Mason) has "committed an outrage against public morals and established customs. . . . [He] has created a character, a French woman, who is at once a disgrace to France and an insult to womanhood." Flaubert speaks in his own defense. Thus the story of Emma Bovary unfolds as if told to a courtroom of angry citizens. Flaubert is heard at several points in the film as a voice-over narrator. At the conclusion of the film, we return to the courtroom, and Flaubert sums up his defense: "I maintain that there is truth in her story, and the morality which has within it no room for truth is no morality at all. . . . Truth lives forever. Men do not." The film closes with a righteous-looking Flaubert gazing upwards, while titles inform us that Flaubert's acquittal was a "triumphant moment in the history of the free mind."

My interest in Minnelli's film has to do, not with the adaptation of the events in *Madame Bovary*, but rather with how the trial functions as a framing tale for the novel. In Minnelli's film, the novelistic is articulated through the context of authorship. What Minnelli did or did not do with cinematic style in *Madame Bovary*, or the process of selection and change that informed the adaptation of the novel (in the film, for example, Charles Bovary refuses to perform the club-foot operation on Hippolyte) are thus less significant than how authorship is represented in the film.

Minnelli's *Madame Bovary* gives to the author the role of narrator within the film. Narration in *Madame Bovary* embodies contradictory stances, from the sudden shift, in the first chapter of the novel, from a first person plural to an omniscient (although omniscient in a very problematic sense) point-of-view, to the complex ways in which narration may be said to chime with Flaubert's famous statement, "Madame Bovary, c'est moi." That Minnelli makes the narrator a principal character in the film suggests that this is a potentially instructive example of how the cinema, in posing the problem of narration, works through its own myths of authorship and narrative.

Minnelli's film is frequently referred to as an instance of how Hollywood maligns the true substance of classical literature. George Bluestone referred to the film as an "illustrated lecture." He compared the framing of the novel via Flaubert's trial to the appearance, in Flaubert's novel, of the beadle at the Rouen church who persistently follows Emma and Léon, wanting to show them every important artifact in the church.[24] Geoffrey Wagner has described the film in these terms: "For MGM Vincente Minnelli chose to make a child's color book of adultery, as seen through 'emancipated' American eyes. The over-simplification was such as to attain at times a kind of genius."[25]

If the plot and substance of Flaubert's novel are "oversimplified" in the film *Madame Bovary*, then we might consider for a moment whether the same is true of the trial. Minnelli described the "historically accurate courtroom proceedings" as the device which "progressed the story more than any other device used in the film." The trial foregrounds the very important role of censorship in Hollywood. In his memoirs, Minnelli speaks in virtually the same breath of the courtroom scenes in the film, and the censorship problems that were posed ("The censors found virtually every suggestion of sex inadmissible").[26]

In 1856, Flaubert published sections of *Madame Bovary* in the journal *Revue de Paris*. He was tried, along with the publisher and the editor of the journal, for "outrage to public morals and to religion." The trial consisted largely of the reading aloud of lengthy excerpted passages followed by a brief commentary on their offensiveness. The strategy of the defense was often to reread the passages and put them into context, thus challenging what was often seen as a "partial" and selective reading of Flaubert's work. There is, then, a certain truth to Minnelli's retelling of *Madame Bovary* in a courtroom setting, although Flaubert never spoke in his own defense.[27]

Flaubert never doubted that the trial was a political tactic directed, not against him but against the *Revue de Paris*, known as a liberal journal. The journal had already received two warnings. As Flaubert noted in a letter to Maurice Schlesinger, "in order to suppress the journal with one stroke, for immorality and anti-religion, blasphemous and licentious passages were excerpted at random from my book."[28] In a sense, Flaubert was a pawn in his own trial. He himself would write, however, chiming more with the conclusions drawn from the acquittal in Minnelli's film, "my cause was the cause of all contemporary literature. It is not my novel that is under attack, but all novels and the right to create them."[29]

The courtroom frame of the film is highly selective, and devoted to that ambiguous ideological entity, the "free mind." Within this framing device, where the figure of an author speaks in his own defense, is a certain conception both of authorship and of its relationship to the classical Hollywood cinema. Flaubert appears as a defendant. He is silent as the charges against him are read; then he speaks on his behalf. As he begins to tell the story of Emma, Flaubert's voice becomes that of a narrator, introducing his characters and putting them into context. The story of Emma is firmly established as the center of our attention when, at the Rouault farmhouse where Charles has come to tend Emma's father, the doctor's look is captured by the beautiful young Emma. The romantic intrigue has been launched. From this moment on, Flaubert's voice appears at selective moments, providing narration and commentary simultaneously. Thus the changes in Flaubert's role as narrator take place when certain laws of the classical text—like the articulation of desire—have occurred.

Flaubert's most extensive commentary follows the breakfast at the Rouault farm during which the attraction between Emma and Charles is clearly defined. Still addressing the court, Flaubert says: "Here gentlemen is the monster . . . Here is the disgrace to France, the insult to womanhood. Emma Rouault, the flower beyond the dunghill. How had she grown here? The kitchen drudge who had dreamed of love and beauty." A condensed representation of Emma's youth accompanies Flaubert's commentary. The passage corresponds to the famous section of the novel where Emma's dependence on romantic fiction is revealed. Here is how the cinematic Flaubert describes Emma's adolescence in the convent at Rouen, with particular attention to the novels through which her romantic fantasies developed: "Novels. Novels. She lived in a world of love, lovers, sweethearts, persecuted ladies, fainting in lonely pavillions, horses ridden to death on every page." However much one might object to the "translation," as it were, of Flaubert, the passage is not completely out of keeping with the way in which Emma's relation to fiction is described in the novel. The narration changes focus with Flaubert's adoption of a "we": "Here in these books, in these pictures, we had taught her that the strange was beautiful and the familiar, contemptible. We had taught her to find glamour, excitement, in the far away. And only boredom in the here and now. We had taught her what? To believe in Cinderella." This "we" supposes a unity of fiction—of all fiction. And more important, Flaubert has suddenly adopted, vis-à-vis Emma, the voice of paternalistic authority: we created her, we are responsible for her.

Flaubert's commentary next appears during the "peasant wedding"

("The cruelty. The drunkenness . . ."). His voice provides a bridge as we see Emma and Charles leave in a carriage and arrive in Yonville, where Charles is to set up a medical practice. Flaubert's words give symbolic resonance to the scene: "He took her away from the squealing pigs, from the dunghill beside the door." The commentary ends over images of Emma as she awakens in the morning after her wedding night. "Was Emma the first bride to weep while the bridegroom slept? Or the last? Tristan. Lancelot. Love in a Scotch cottage. Love in a Swiss chalet." Flaubert's commentary is beginning to sound like the very books which have so polluted Emma's imagination. From the wedding to the first morning in Yonville, the primary function of Flaubert's commentary is to recall that flashback to Emma's youth; and to inscribe a tension between the "real" (what we see on screen) and the literary, the romantic (Flaubert's commentary). Flaubert's voice has a similar function in another scene at Yonville. Emma has busied herself with home decoration and the accumulation of consumer objects. A visit from a count from Vaubyssard, who will later invite Emma and Charles to a ball, rekindles Emma's discontent. She sees the count laughing at the country yokels at a party. Emma retreats to the attic, where the pictures from her former bedroom are located. She suddenly decides that she wants a child, and Flaubert's commentary again bridges the past and the present, the "real" and the "fictitious." "New dreams of old," he says. "The dark hours of a woman's life when old dreams perish and new dreams are born."

Flaubert's commentary disappears during a large portion of the film. He is silent, as it were, during the ball at Vaubyssard where Emma is ecstatic, Charles drunk and miserable; while Emma's friendship with Léon Dupuis grows; when she meets Rodolphe and is later courted by him at the agricultural fair; during the preparation for the clubfoot operation; during the developing affair with Rodolphe; and as Emma's debts to the merchant Lheureux increase. The climactic event of the film, the event which will mark the beginning of Emma's downfall, is Rodolphe's rejection of her. She has talked Rodolphe into running away to Italy with her, and as she makes her arrangements to leave, Rodolphe makes his own arrangments to avoid the plan. As a result, Emma falls into a deep depression and is only restrained from killing herself because Charles stops her. Here, during Emma's desolation, Flaubert's voice reappears over a series of images in which time is condensed: "Was it sickness?" he asks. "If sickness, was it of the body or of the soul?"

One might ask why this voice, so central and so present at the beginning, can disappear during such a large portion of the film, aside from the obvious reason that once voice-over narration has established the story, it can continue quite well on its own. There is a shift in the tone of *Madame Bovary*, from narration to spectacle. The central moments of the film during which Flaubert is silent are scenes—the fair, the ball, the operation—in which the reader/viewer's relation to Emma's story is one of spectator more than one of listener or reader. Hence Flaubert's trial is a framing device in yet another way, enclosing what is primarily a tale of spectacle with voice-over narration.

Flaubert's voice fades as his function as narrator is effectively dispersed, displaced onto other characters in the film. Indeed, virtually every male character will adopt, in relation to Emma, a role that resembles the perspective of Flaubert the narrator. Lheureux the merchant watches Emma, seemingly aware of her attraction to Léon before she herself is. If Flaubert creates the story of Emma, within that story Lheureux provides much of the incentive for her downfall. Lheureux deals in money and products like Flaubert deals in words and stories. Male characters often utter phrases that are remarkably similar to Flaubert's narration and commentary, again suggesting that the role of narrator has been displaced onto other characters. When Emma tells Charles that she wants him to perform the clubfoot operation, he tells her that "this is storybook." And when Emma tries to convince Rodolphe to run away with her, he says, "this is where dreams leave off."

Madame Bovary creates a kind of authorship in which easy mobility from the position of writer to the position of fictional characters is assured. In simplest terms, we might say that the film is built upon a referential fallacy. Had Minnelli chosen to begin his film a bit earlier in time, in Charles's story rather than in Emma's, we might well imagine an attempt to "show," in all its intricate detail, the hat which Charles Bovary wears on his first day in the schoolroom.[30] One has the impression, indeed, that the filmed version of *Madame Bovary* was constructed around the literalization of Flaubert's famous remark: "Madame Bovary, c'est moi."

But let us put aside, for the moment, this naïve articulation of authorship, and the relatively silly comments ("the kitchen drudge who had dreamed of love and beauty") attributed to Flaubert, and come back to the context within which authorship is defined: a courtroom, the law. In other words, this is a public sphere in which the author is *made accountable* for his work. In that public sphere, the novel is told in such a way that the novelist merges with the characters he has created. Flaubert is both father and lover. The position he occupies in relation to Emma straddles paternalism and sexual desire. And the figure of Flaubert could also be described as both author and reader, author as father and reader as lover. The author is the genesis of the object of desire; the lover is the consumer of that object. Flaubert gives birth to Emma, describing at length the genesis of her character in storybooks. Then Flaubert keeps silent, moving towards the other pole, in order to consume the tale he has created.

The position of Flaubert in Minnelli's film recalls the way in which Roland Barthes has described the myth of authorship: "The *explanation* of a work is always sought in the man or woman who produced it, as if it were always in the end, through the more or less transparent allegory of the fiction, the voice of a single person, the *author* 'confiding' in us." Barthes identifies the preoccupation with authorship as "the epitome and culmination of capitalist ideology."[31] The author is the central personnage of readerly discourse. Barthes's perspective on authorship is an appropriate grid for *Madame Bovary*, and particularly appropriate is Barthes's utilization of an image of paternity: "The Author is thought to *nourish* the book, which is to say that he exists before it, thinks, suffers, lives for it, is in the same relation of antecedence to his work as a father to his child."[32]

To the notion of the author as unquestioned center of a meaningful text, Barthes opposes a notion of writing which is "the destruction of every voice, of every point of origin." Within the multi-levelled network of writing stands the reader: "a text is made of multiple writings, drawn from many cultures and entering into mutual relations of dialogue, parody, contestation, but there is one place where this multiplicity is focused and that place is the reader, not, as was hitherto said, the author."[33] I would argue that even if *Madame Bovary* seems to passively reflect the vision of the author as unquestioned center, there are signs of a certain decentering. For Flaubert's voice is, simultaneously, that of father and lover, author and reader. I am not suggesting that Minnelli's film is, in the terms of S/Z, a "writerly" rather than a "readerly" text; but rather that Flaubert's role in the film draws our attention to the strain within the myths of authorship, as they are perpetrated in Hollywood cinema.

Relevant to this context is another American film constructed around such myths of authorship. *The Life of Emile Zola* (directed by

William Dieterle, 1937) announces itself, in its opening credits, as fictionalized history: "This production has its basis in history. The historical basis, however, has been fictionalized for the purposes of this picture." Zola's life is thoroughly narrativized in the film. The painter Cézanne becomes a character, a friend of Zola's who conveniently provides artist's illustrations every now and again. The Dreyfus affair becomes the climax of Zola's existence. In fact, the Dreyfus affair is used in a way not unlike the trial as framing device for *Madame Bovary*, for both are historical events reshaped by the demands of narrative. These narrative demands concern the position of authorship defined within the spheres of private and public life. In both films, "real" historical events become arenas where the author intervenes as a mediating presence. Indeed, in *The Life of Emile Zola*, the Dreyfus affair appears as a barometer of the changes in the author's life. Near the conclusion of the film, we see two events which appear parallel to each other. Zola is working on what he calls his most important work, and Dreyfus is restored to his former position in the army. The two spheres—one of official history, the other of one individual life—are brought together in one integrated moment at the conclusion of the film as we see two ceremonies. One is for Dreyfus. Just as he asks where Zola is, we hear a newspaper-seller shout: "Zola is dead!" The other ceremony is a memorial for Zola, during which the last lines of the film are spoken: "He was a moment of the conscience of man."

Most interesting in *The Life of Emile Zola* is the way in which the genesis, the "nourishment" (to use Barthes's term) of a particular novel is described. Early in the film, Zola and his friend Cézanne are sitting in a café where a woman rushes in, clearly running away from someone or something. Cézanne and Zola invite her to sit with them so as to protect her. Each man responds to the woman in the way particular to his art: Cézanne draws her, Zola talks to her. Speaking of her past, the woman cries as she tells Zola: "I wish I could tell you about it!" The chance encounter in a café and the ensuing conversation is stage one in the evolution of a novel. Stage two occurs in the woman's room, where the first object we see is a "diary" in close-up, lying in her drawer. She describes the details of her life to Zola: the men who left her, the child that died. The viewer familiar with Zola's work can anticipate the name he calls her: Nana. Cézanne brings his sketch of Nana to the room, and Zola writes her name on it: "That's what I'll call my book," he says. Such is the way that novels are written, in the cinematic imagination.

We cut from Nana's room to a store window, now replete with *Nanas*. Later Zola takes the book as a gift to Nana's room, where her name, only "Nana," is printed on the door. Outside the building, soldiers are marching, and when Zola asks where they are going, the reply is: "To Berlin." This is a partial view of the conclusion of Zola's novel. Nana dies at the end of the novel, while soldiers in the street prepare to march "To Berlin." The conclusion of the novel is based on the disjuncture between private and public spheres, between the individual life and official history, a disjuncture marked by a rigid separation between the world of men and the world of women.

Nana is evoked in this film to trace an itinerary of authorship. The itinerary begins in the public space of the café where Nana is pursued by the law, and moves to the private space of her room. We move from a chance encounter to intimate conversation. This vision of authorship combines the processes of writing and image-making, as if authorship were filling in the information for a portrait, giving it—as the character of Zola says—a name. Novel-writing is, in short, direct address, intimate friendship. *Nana* may conclude differently in Zola's novel than in this film, but the terms at least are similar. As author, Zola mediates between the individual existence and the social sphere in which it is narrated.

Emma Bovary undergoes a transformation in Minnelli's film which is not unlike the creation of Nana as one moment in the myth of authorship. Authorship is defined, constantly, as simultaneous readership. Hence Zola had access to a privileged "reading" of Nana's diary, and Flaubert disappears, as it were, into his own characters. The myth of authorship thus created is based on the separation of male and female spheres, and their identity with public and private space, respectively. Emma Bovary maintains, we are led to believe, a private life which it is the duty of Flaubert to illuminate by bringing it into the public sphere. Hence the courtroom becomes, within the film, a spatial equivalent of the novel itself.

The profound and intimate connections between authorship, male identity, and the public sphere can be gauged by looking at the excessive lengths to which a classical film text has to go in order to create a film about *female* authorship. Consider *Devotion* (directed by Curtis Bernhardt, 1946), for instance, a film about the Brontë sisters. A love triangle is created between Charlotte, Emily, and Mr. Nicholls. Emily, we are told, was madly in love with Mr. Nicholls. But her love was unrequited, and because she understood the dynamics of tragic love she wrote *Wuthering Heights*. Mr. Nicholls loved only Charlotte, and after Emily's death the two walk across the moors, arm in arm. Mr. Rochester of *Jane Eyre* has found his equivalent in Mr. Nicholls, and Emily becomes the source, it seems, of the mad wife in the attic. Zola's relation to Nana, and Flaubert's to Emma, may have sexual overtones, but they are never *reducible* to sexual desire. For authorship encompasses the roles of father and lover, writer and reader, held in what must indeed be at some points a precarious balance. Only for a woman author, within the logic of the classic text, can writing be the direct result, whether positive or negative, of a romantic attachment.

These film versions of authorship are images in miniature of how the novel has become a part of the institution of cinematic narrative. Authorship is, at once, the imaginary figure of coherence described by Barthes; and it is the reader, diffused throughout the text. The exaggerated form that the myth of authorship takes in *Madame Bovary* is emblematic. Authorship combines the functions of reading and writing, public record and private reality, father and lover.

Readership and Spectatorship

Central to the classical American cinema is a myth of authorship, and the importance of adaptations of nineteenth-century novels has to do largely with the sustenance of that myth. Parallel to the function of authorship in the relationship between the novel and film is that of readership. Consider, for example, the Robert Stevenson–directed adaptation of *Jane Eyre* (1944). There are many omissions and condensations in this film, some of which are examined by Asheim.[34] And following Bluestone, we might consider how successfully the Brontë novel is used as a point of departure to create an "autonomous" work of art. But there is another kind of work in this film, irreducible to either a celebration or a denial of authorship. The film begins with a close-up of a leather-bound volume of *Jane Eyre*, and closes with a symmetrical close-up of a page marked "The End." Such a "framing" of a film with reference to its literary source is common to many Hollywood adaptations of the period. *Jane Eyre* suggests some of the implications of this parallel between book cover and screen, between page and frame.

Throughout this film, pages from the book appear on the screen as structuring devices, with specific passages illuminated. The adult voice of Jane (Joan Fontaine) reads these passages aloud in voice-over. Occasionally these pages correspond to actual passages from *Jane Eyre*, but by and large they do not. "Chapter one," for example, on screen, begins: "My name is Jane Eyre. I was born in 1830, a hard time." This is a far cry from the actual opening of Charlotte Brontë's novel: "There was no possibility of taking a walk that day. We had been wandering, indeed, in the leafless shrubbery an hour in the morning."[35] These imaginary passages in the film form one of the many strategies by which the novel is condensed for the screen version. They recall producer David O. Selznick's description of "bridging scenes":

> I have discovered that the public will forgive you for any
> number of omissions—particularly of subordinate material
> which is not directly connected with the main plot—but it
> won't forgive you for deliberate changes. For that reason I have
> found it best to make the bridging scenes which span the omis-
> sions as suggestive as possible. That is, by picking up dialogue
> and even phrases from other parts of the book and using such to
> construct the bridging scenes, the audience is given the illusion
> of seeing and hearing that with which they are already
> familiar.[36]

The "illusion of seeing and hearing": such a description of those "well-beloved" works brought to the screen suggests an interesting parallel between the itineraries of reading and viewing. The pages are selectively illuminated, light separated from dark, and thus the arrangement of words on a page is not unlike the arrangment of figures in a landscape. The female voice narrates, while we read what she has ostensibly "written." The female character is thus simultaneously a reader and a narrator within the film.

The reading process represented in the film is of a special type. One might certainly criticize the substitutions that occur in the film and dismiss them in the terms used by Asheim: "The assumed level of audience comprehension is generally lower for the film than for the novel."[37] But Charlotte Brontë's novel has a rather unique status, for, like Emily Brontë's *Wuthering Heights*, it is a nineteenth-century classic frequently read by adolescent girls. The distortions of Brontë's novel in the illuminated pages on screen are as much the reflection of an adult's memory of the adolescent experience of reading this novel, as they are the result of a film industry determined to simplify for its mass audience at all costs. Jane Eyre is adapted to the screen in such a way, then, that film viewing becomes, through the book, through the novel, a form of memory of a certain kind of reading.

Memory is essential to the way in which the itineraries of reading and viewing are intertwined in this film. The film is structured so as to constantly refer to associations of the reading process, and to integrate those associations into the act of film viewing and comprehension. And thus the film version of *Jane Eyre* presents itself as a fantasy of how we remember the novel. I am reminded here of how Sergei Eisenstein spoke of Charles Dickens: "All of us read him in childhood, gulped him down greedily, without realizing that much of his irresistibility lay . . . in that spontaneous, childlike skill for storytelling."[38] At the heart of D. W. Griffith's narrative skill was, according to Eisenstein, an understanding of the importance of that "childlike skill." Similarly, many of the cinematic adaptations of classical novels evolve from an understanding of the special function of reading in childhood and adolescent fantasies of the self in relation to the world. An essential component of classical film narrative is the memory recaptured by the experience of film viewing, and recaptured twice over: there is the memory of childhood, and the memory of reading. Cinematic adaptations evoke childhood memories of reading, and the transaction between viewer and screen is shaped by the contours of family identities, with the figure of the author as lover and father, as narrative authority.

Orson Welles' *Citizen Kane* (1941) brings together in a particularly striking way the implications, for classical film narrative, of the myths of authorship and readership inherited from the middle-class novel. *Citizen Kane* is less about one man's life than it is about the very possibility of telling that story in the first place. The film begins with the death of Charles Kane, and moves to a newsreel obituary. We then witness a series of interviews with Kane's acquaintances, conducted by the journalist Thompson whose assignment is to discover the significance of Kane's last word, "rosebud." That enigma has become one of the most classic in film history. Rosebud may represent lost innocence and mother-love, but it represents equally forcefully the impossibility of a facile understanding of one individual's life.

Yet it is not just any individual life which is impenetrable, but the life of an individual who has become a public figure. In the scene where the sled called Rosebud appears, when Mr. Thatcher comes to fetch the child Kane and take him away to the city and to wealth, it is as if Kane crosses an absolute threshold separating private and public spheres. Indeed, there is virtually no other private sphere in Kane's world after he leaves his home. First wife Emily seems to be as important as the President's niece as she is as Kane's wife, and second wife Susan Alexander is quickly transformed by Kane into a failed public figure herself.[39] The very structure of the film is informed by the potential negotiation of private and public spheres—from the newsreel, a collection of documents about the public man that is narrated by an authoritative voice-over, to the quest, a collection of different perspectives which make up a mosaic of glimpses into the private life concealed beneath the public façade. *Citizen Kane* does not correspond uniquely to what I have called the fantasy of reconciliation, nor to the nightmare of reification. Private and public selves never are totally integrated, but neither can it be said that *Citizen Kane* puts forth a private sphere invaded by the forces of the public sphere. For the private sphere in *Citizen Kane* remains, quite simply, separate and unknowable. And even if one accepts a dime-store Freudian explanation of Rosebud, the knowledge that Kane suffered all his life from separation anxiety is, to say the least, somewhat anti-climactic.[40]

More important than the figure of Kane himself is the attention given, in *Citizen Kane*, to the particular position of the film spectator vis-à-vis the complicated journey from public to private existence. As a reflection on spectatorship, *Citizen Kane* is a turning point of sorts in the history of the relation between classical film narrative and the novelistic tradition. Of central importance in *Citizen Kane* is the particular way in which the film spectator is implicated in the process of discovery of the enigma. To be sure, we are given privileged access to the meaning of Rosebud, but it would be a mistake to ignore the irony with which such privileged access is given. For the spectator within the film, that character who mirrors our own relation to the screen, is Thompson, and not his boss Rawlston, who is convinced that Rosebud will unlock a hidden meaning in Kane's life.[41] Thompson concludes his failed search with the remark that there is no single word or sign which could explain a man's life. And the "No Trespassing" sign appears at the end of the film as it did at the beginning, reminding us that Rosebud solves everything, and nothing at all.[42]

Yet Rosebud may not really be the object of Thompson's search. Robert Carringer argues persuasively that the little glass globe with its snow scene is endowed with much more narrative significance, and it is towards this object that Rosebud always leads us. Carringer writes: "The little glass globe (not Rosebud) is the film's central symbol. A mediating symbol of inner and outer, of subjective and objective, it stands at once for what we have seen and seek to recover, the psychic wholeness of Kane, and for the totality of Kane as a force, the man whose life and works are empires and private worlds. The shattering of the globe (not the appearance of Rosebud) is the film's main symbolic 'event.' "[43] That globe is, we recall, the object we see at the moment of Kane's death at the beginning of the film. It seems to occasion the utterance of "Rosebud," and once smashed on the floor, it is a lens through which we see Kane's room and an arriving nurse. We see another such globe on a bureau in Susan Alexander's apartment at the moment that Kane speaks of his mother and his childhood. The snow scene in the globe recalls, of course, the scene in the film of Kane's youth when Thatcher comes to take him away. And it recalls as well the estate of Xanadu, constructed by Kane as if to possess the glass globe on a large scale.

The glass globe links present and past, private and public selves. Xanadu has a similar function, but now in nearly hysterical proportions. Carringer says that the glass globe "condenses the whole experience of Xanadu, his last and most ambitious monument to himself."[44] For Xanadu is a private sphere erected as a public monument, within which there is nothing but space, never private but not quite public either. The narrative function of the glass globe in *Citizen Kane* is reminiscent, on several levels, of what writer Christa Wolf calls "miniatures," bits and pieces of the past, the results of a "furtive process hard to avoid, a hardening, petrifying, habituating, that attacks the memory in particular." Wolf writes: "We all carry with us a collection of miniatures with captions, some quaint, some gruesome. These we occasionally bring out and show round, because we need confirmation of our own reassuringly clear feelings: beautiful or ugly, good or evil. These miniatures are for the memory what the calcified cavities are for people with tuberculosis, what prejudices are for morals: patches of once active life now shut off. At one time one was afraid to touch them, afraid of burning one's fingers on them; now they are cool and smooth."[45] For Kane the globe is a miniature of lost innocence, and for the viewer, an equally forceful miniature of the very possibility of recapturing that past. How appropriate that Wolf should describe these miniatures as the province of cinema, and should then go on to insist that "prose should try to be unfilmable."[46] Indeed, *Citizen Kane* is informed by a resistance to that very process which, following Wolf's metaphor, is particularly characteristic of the cinema.

Citizen Kane puts forth a vision of private and public existence riddled with ambiguities. The ambiguity of the *quest* for the private man, and not the private man himself, is foregrounded in the film. Thus in *Citizen Kane* the transaction between viewer and screen in the public sphere of the movie theatre has become problematized. And perhaps the most striking ambiguity of all in *Citizen Kane* is that the film tells a story which, it insists, somewhat in the spirit of Christa Wolf, is "unfilmable."

That the evolution of spectatorship is tied to the function of readership is suggested in a different way by the presence of characters who function primarily as "spectators within the film," like the journalist Thompson in *Citizen Kane*. Whether major characters or not, the primary function of these figures is to establish narrative perspective. As is the case with many of the devices of film narrative, equivalences could be established between the use of the spectator within the film, and the forms of narration and point-of-view that occur in the novel. The intertextual links between novel and cinema are more strongly suggested, however, by the fact that frequently spectators within the film are identified as *readers*. Readership thus becomes a form of narrative participation incorporated into cinematic narrative.

In George Cukor's *Gaslight* (1944), there is a rather comic, elderly woman character who is constantly in the vicinity of the central action of the film, but never directly involved in it. She lives in the same neighborhood where the murder of opera singer Alicia took place, and is thus a bystander to the crime which determines the narrative development of the film. Throughout the film this woman functions as an observer, sometimes as a busybody who tries to glean information from servants, sometimes as a gossip who thoroughly enjoys discussing the past and present affairs of her neighbors. This character is first introduced to us in a train compartment she happens to share with Paula (Ingrid Bergman), the central female character of the film. The elderly woman is reading a suspense novel, which she describes for Paula: a man, who has murdered six wives and buried them in his basement, has just taken a new wife. This novel parodies the film we are watching. The elderly woman has, she tells Paula, only reached page one hundred, and so she is certain that there is still more to come. Indeed there is, for the woman becomes a kind of reader of the equally suspenseful plot that thickens in her own neighborhood.

Gaslight's incorporation of a reader into its narrative reminds us of how, in the development of the middle-class novel, the conditions of readership were gradually and persistently incorporated and embedded into the narrative. We recall the significant resonances of Elizabeth's development as a reader in *Pride and Prejudice*, for instance. We have already seen this process at work in the early years of motion picture history: films would cease to bear titles like *Grandpa's Reading Glass*, but those figures of vision would still be apparent, here and there and across the narrative structures of later films. So too within the classical Hollywood cinema there is the development of the novelistic in such an "embedded" way. The example of *Gaslight* is particularly striking, for the conditions of (cinematic) observation are precisely those of readership.

Spectatorship in the cinema evokes parallels between watching a film and reading a novel, and in this sense incorporates readership into the classical cinema. In a more general way, spectatorship in the cinema is structured by the relationship between private and public existence. The separation of private and public spheres to which the middle-class novel responds has, in the era of cinema, changed dimensions. Narratives of private and public life have been appropriated from one set of historical circumstances to another. The development of consumerism in the early twentieth century is an essential aspect of the changing relation between private and public spheres. With consumerism, the reification of the private sphere appears to be complete. In his study of the evolution of consumerism, for instance, Stuart Ewen describes how the home became increasingly perceived as a kind of factory in its own right: "As the housewife assumed more of a factory-operative status, the home became a place where the values of factory production, and the conditions if not the pay of the wage worker, were replicated and reinforced on a day-to-day basis."[47] The class dimensions of consumerism were essential to the reification of the private sphere. An imaginary ideal of homogeneity was put forth, whereby working-class and middle-class aspirations could be united around the pursuit of leisure and goods.[48]

We have seen how the early motion pictures offered glimpses of consumerist ideals; and how the audience for moving pictures developed, like the very phenomenon of consumerism, in cross-class terms. An important aspect of the classical cinema is the way in which the movie theatre seems to provide a space in which class differences temporarily dissolve. I do not mean that working-class and middle-class audiences would respond to films in identical ways; rather, film narrative would work on multiple levels, so that different class-defined responses would be condensed within a single film.

The relationship between private and public spheres, as a narrative theme and structure, would become an essential means to cut symbolically across class lines. Consider the film *My Sister Eileen* (1942), for example, in which two sisters, Ruth and Eileen, leave their Columbus, Ohio, home to look for work (Ruth as a writer, Eileen as an actress) in New York City. The Greenwich Village apartment they share—their private space—is constantly invaded by external forces, usually male figures, representing professional, sexual, or proprietal authority. The two sisters make uneasy accommodations by adopting a variety of family roles in relationship to each other: Eileen acts as housewife when her older sister goes out to look for work; Ruth comforts and gently disciplines her younger sister as a mother would a child; and when the sisters are frightened by the street activity that keeps them from sleep, they share a not-quite conjugal bed. The women's world is more gently invaded by another male figure, Ruth's professional mentor, who accepts her first story for publication and conveniently falls in love with her at the same time. The romantic resolution of the film marks a restoration of order, as the union of male and female coincides with the readjustment of private and public space to complementary rather than conflicting spheres.

Central to that resolution is the question of class. Ruth and Eileen leave a middle-class existence in a town which symbolizes a middle-class way of life, to live in an ethnic, working-class neighborhood. The middle-class life they leave represents security and boredom; the working class environment they enter may represent danger, but it is also full of color and excitement. The editor whose entrance into Ruth's life allows a balance of personal and public selves is also a mediator of class differences. He promises *both* middle-class security and the vivacity of an urban environment. Viewers of this film encounter the potential mediation of class differences, but in order to arrive at that conclusion they can follow quite different paths. To a middle-class audience, the Greenwich village characters correspond to comic ethnic stereotypes, while to a working-class urban audience, the trials and tribulations of two middle-class provincials must have been laughable and amusing.

Given the historical parallels between cinema and the emergence of a consumerist culture, it is perhaps tempting to define American cinema as an agent of consumerist culture. Such a definition has been put forth persuasively by Charles Eckert who, in describing how cinema actively contributed to the cause of consumerist culture, says that in the first decades of the twentieth century, "the conditions were right for Hollywood to assume a role in the phase of the capitalism's life-history that the emerging philosophy of consumerism was about to give birth to."[49]

Eckert's explorations into the "almost incestuous hegemony" which characterized Hollywood's connections with big business provide some of the most illuminating evidence for the very special role of cinema within consumerist culture. Inscribed within film from the very beginning, says Eckert, are "innumerable opportunities for product and brand-name tie-ins. But more than this, [motion pictures] functioned as living display windows for all that they contained; windows that were occupied by marvelous mannequins and swathed in a fetish-inducing ambiance of music and emotion."[50] Throughout the decade of the 1930s, films would function as "living display windows." Extensive tie-ins with a variety of manufacturers assured the visibility of specific products and brand-names on the screen. In addition, entire industries would be built around the kinds of clothing and furnishings shown on screen. The female viewer was central throughout. If, in the novels of two centuries before, she occupied a strategic central position in the private sphere, in Hollywood narrative woman was central as consumer, as the strategic center of yet another stage in the relationship between private and public existence.[51]

Central, then, to Eckert's view of Hollywood is the decisive contribution of American cinema to the shaping of consumerist culture. "Hollywood . . . did as much or more than any other force in capitalist culture to smooth the operation of the production-consumption cycle by fetishizing products and putting the libido in libidinally invested advertising."[52] Yet at the same time that consumerism was developing as a major phenomenon of twentieth-century capitalist societies, there persisted the nineteenth-century ideal of family life as a separate, isolated realm. Zaretsky writes that in the twentieth century, the "proletariat itself came to share the bourgeois ideal of the family as

·a 'utopian retreat.' "[53] If consumerism is built upon the reification of the private sphere, that ideal of a haven, of a "utopian retreat" persisted. And with a contradictory twist, that ideal was often actively foregrounded as a central image in advertising.

While it is true that moving pictures became, in Eckert's words, "living display windows" for the products of consumer society, the movies had an equally important function in the maintenance of the ideal of the private sphere as a privileged, separate realm. Cinema is a form of spectacle, governed by consumerist principles. Cinema is also a narrative form, governed by principles not so quickly nor so easily assimilable to the phenomenon of consumer society. Thus as spectacle and narrative, cinema emerges both from the new consumerist culture and from the eighteenth- and nineteenth-century novelistic tradition. The classical American cinema is spectacle and narrative; a vehicle for consumerism and a link to a narrative tradition. Put another way, the classical American cinema is an arena where the contradictions of the changing dimensions of private and public life are enacted.

Within the public space of the movie theatre, private fantasies are indulged: this has been a relative constant in the history of narrative cinema. But the contours of that public space, and of the transaction between viewer and screen, are always determined by specific historical conditions. In the 1940s those conditions led directly or indirectly to World War II. If the space of the movie theatre allowed a temporary dissolution of class differences, and if films were constructed to allow different forms of class identification, then moving pictures would serve an important function in the war effort. And if cinema of the 1940s explored in depth the relation of private and public spheres, it was in part because private and public existence had become problematized in American social life. The symbolic mediation of private and public life thus spoke to a kind of historical urgency.

The demands of war economy meant a heightened awareness of private and public life, the most striking symptom of which was the participation of women in the war industries. Indeed, the ways in which women were encouraged to take on work outside the home during the war is a fascinating case study of how consumerist culture would be grounded in a curious contradiction whereby the private sphere was at once a refuge from, *and* an extension of, the public sphere. One thinks of the various wartime images of women created by advertising, and Rosie the Riveter in particular stands out, dressed in overalls and carrying a lunchpail to the factory. However emancipated Rosie the Riveter might have appeared, the image of the working woman still focused on woman's traditional place in the private sphere. The popular image of woman which evolved during the war years suggested that American women had never worked outside the home before (even though women had in fact been entering the job market steadily for decades), and that women had never performed factory work before (even though they had been working in factories for years).[54] In particular, it was assumed that if women worked to support the war effort, they were *really* working for their men. One newspaperwoman spoke, typically, of the "deep satisfaction which a woman of today knows who has made a rubber boat which may save the life of her aviator husband, or helped to fashion a bullet which may avenge her son."[55] In short, then, the image of Rosie the Riveter and her compatriots corresponded to a pre-war ideal. Thus historian Leila Rupp writes that "the appeals used to recruit women for war work strengthened the impression that the public Rosie was, inside her overalls, the same prewar woman who cooked, cleaned, and cared for her family."[56]

One could of course criticize these images of women as blatant distortions of the real situations of women workers, but the goal of advertising, after all, is to create myths, not to reproduce reality. Yet the myth thus created is anything but simple. Rupp points out that Rosie the Riveter is an "exotic creature" who seems somehow out of place in the public sphere of men's work, and so the potentially jarring quality of the image is softened by the appeal to women's traditional roles as wives and mothers.[57] Perhaps during any war, the relation between private and public spheres is bound to be problematic. But particular to 1940s America is that the institutions of consumerism, advertising in particular, were firmly in place. Never before had there been such fastidious orchestrations of the possible harmonious interchanges between the two spheres—the battlefront and the homefront, the world of men and the world of women. The home would be regarded, simultaneously, as a recuperative refuge *and* as a battlefront. If American films of the 1940s, whether specifically devoted to war themes or not, revealed a profound ambivalence towards private and public life, it is because the culture was straining under the tension of different ideals of private and public existence. Emblematic of that strain was the wartime woman worker. Her participation in war industries suggests an integration of the private and the public, but she was constantly addressed (through advertising in particular) as if she were a pure creature of domesticity.

We know that film attendance peaked during the war, and given the number of men overseas, women viewers were more visible than usual. Some theatre managers commented on the increasing number of unescorted females who were attending moving pictures.[58] Given the strategic importance of women's roles vis-à-vis the private and the public, we might look at how, in the 1940s, women were addressed as film viewers.[59] Newsreels were shown with virtually all feature films, and a strategy first developed in Detroit to attract women to the newsreels is an interesting example of how cinema's narrative capacities were adapted to wartime conditions. Noting that women were less inclined than men to be interested in newsreels, exhibitors put together a one-hour program, focusing when possible on footage of areas where Michigan soldiers had been sent. Advertisements were put in the newspapers offering free admission to mothers and wives of soldiers, who were asked to send in the names of their relatives in service. The program proved to be a smashing success, leading to an extended run and similar programs in other cities. The drawing card, of course, was the possibility of identifying loved ones. On opening day in Detroit, one woman saw a newsreel of a plane landing in Egypt, and recognized the plane as her son's from its number and nickname. And when she returned home that day, there was a letter from him confirming what she had just seen at the movie theatre.[60] One can hardly imagine a more striking mediation of the personal and the social: newsreel journalism becomes a narrative of family life. And it comes, perhaps, as no surprise that, as *Variety* reported, "it is believed numerous identifications are erroneous and it does not detract from the mounting interest. Houses have reported that different families have asked for film snips of the same soldier, both insisting he is their son."[61]

Not all film viewing in the 1940s would be so explicitly conditioned by the war, or by the possible connections between private and public life evidenced in this particular marketing strategy. But all commercial films of the period would connect to the war in one way or another. For the problematic relationship between private and public existence was not a simple result of the war, but rather was a fundamental aspect of that society which had undergone the transformation of consumerism.

David O. Selznick and the glass globe in *Citizen Kane*, cinematic versions of authors in *Madame Bovary* and *The Life of Emile Zola*, are suggestive of the changing dimensions of classical film narrative in the 1940s. The influence of the novel is in evidence from the earliest years of cinema. But in the 1940s, something changes. The confluence of increased production costs, a growing consciousness of the institutional quality of the medium, and an increasingly close relationship— with varying shades of mercantilism—between film and the novel, created a cinematic narrative institution of new depth and maturity. Kane, Selznick, and James Mason as Gustave Flaubert: these are the figurative sons of D. W. Griffith, and Kane's glass globe and Selznick's well-worn copy of *David Copperfield* are 1940s analogues to the sword that inspired *His Trust/His Faithful Trust*, the object which in Griffith's memory of childhood and then on the screen, represented the scope of narrative.

And casting an eye toward the film audience, the woman wartime worker is heir to another tradition. She may not be appropriately designated as Griffith's daughter, but the woman spectator in the 1940s, whether seeking imaginary narrative reconciliations of the two spheres or looking for loved ones in newsreels, is the descendant of two other traditions: that of the woman reader, and that of the immigrant spectator. Like them, American women viewers of the 1940s exemplify the changes in private and public existence which would be enacted in a variety of ways in the movie theatre.

Five

NARRATIVES OF AMBIVALENCE

A *Female Point of View*

Narrative in American films of the 1940s is built on a simultaneous encounter with, and a repression of, the contradictions of middle-class ideals. In many films the contradictions of private and public existence are made visible. To be sure, there are some films which are built explicitly upon a "consumerist" principle and which seem far removed from the nineteenth-century novel. Musicals like *Babes in Arms* (1939) and *For Me and My Gal* (1942) immediately come to mind, and Charles Eckert describes the preference evidenced in many films for settings with product-display potential, like beauty parlors and living rooms.[1] On the other hand, some films seem to have little to do with the practices of tie-ins and consumerist ideals, films which have appropriated in a naïve way the mythology of the novel, and in particular its concern with the family. *Life with Father* (1947), or *I Remember Mama* (1948), for instance, evoke a nostalgia-ridden memory of the family as resting on firm ideological ground. But the nature of private and public existence in mid-twentieth-century America, and the function of the classical American cinema as narrative form, are most clearly demonstrated in those films where resonances of consumerism and of the middle-class novel are equally present, the one sometimes reinforcing, sometimes contradicting the other. In *Rebecca* (1940), a Selznick production, and Hitchcock's first American film, the female hero of the film attempts to deal with her fears of her husband's first wife by defining herself through a consumerist ideal of beauty (black satin and pearls) copied from a fashion magazine. But her situation is complicated by the echoes of another kind of identity, more properly and immediately novelistic, represented by a mansion which seems to offer the nostalgic ideal of another time and another place. In Michael Curtiz's *Mildred Pierce* (1945), the female body strains between two different sets of functions. On the one hand there is the mannequin, exemplified by Joan Crawford's trademark clothing. On the other hand there is the mother who cannot really function as a mother as long as consumerist values reign supreme.

Both *Rebecca* and *Mildred Pierce* have a direct relationship to the novel-form, since they are adaptations of the novels by Daphne Du Maurier and James Cain, respectively. While Du Maurier's novel is somewhat reminiscent of a nineteenth-century novel like *Jane Eyre*, it is according to the conventions of the twentieth-century gothic novel, and James Cain is far removed from the nineteenth-century novel. Yet the adaptation of these novels to the screen raises central questions concerning the cinematic connection to the middle-class novel. In *Rebecca*, the connection focuses on the exploration of space, and in particular the space of a house; and in *Mildred Pierce*, the connection focuses on a plot device, the conventions of the mystery with the proverbial question: "Who did it?"

Cinematic uses of the gothic and the mystery evoke narrative definitions of the private and the public in the traditional novel. One of the stock features of the gothic is the mansion, attributed with a wide range of supernatural and psychological effects. Such personifications of the house may reveal preoccupations with the mystical and the occult that go far beyond the development of capitalist production. But frequently the house of gothic literature reflects, in exaggerated form, those ambivalences about the private sphere that have emerged in a variety of other ways in Western narrative fiction. The character traumatized by the gothic mansion is often a woman (as is the case in *Rebecca*). Thus the gothic plot becomes a working-through of female fears about the private sphere and its connections with the world beyond. Conversely, mysteries often recount the disentangling of the private sphere from the public, via the efforts of a male protagonist. In *Mildred Pierce*, the role of the police inspector is to separate Mildred's devotion to her daughter from the laws of the social order. The mystery of Monte Beragon's murder is solved at precisely the same moment that private and public spheres seem to be restored to balance.

Rebecca and *Mildred Pierce* also identify spectatorship in ways parallel to readership. In *Rebecca*, images have a problematic status, particularly since the most pervasive image of the film is the invisible presence of the first wife who dominates the mansion. This image is made visible by the fictions that surround Rebecca. The heroine of *Rebecca* must learn, quite simply, how to read. The question is one of intelligibility, of articulating the past in a balanced relation to the present. In *Mildred Pierce*, the issue is posed in different but related terms: Mildred becomes a storyteller of her own past, and she must constantly be brought back to the present by the efforts of her listener, the police inspector.

The examples of classical film narrative cited in the preceding chapter suggest that cinema has acquired, from the middle-class novel, a set of preoccupations concerning authorship and readership which have determined the evolution of film narrative in relation to the spheres of private and public life. But in at least one area, that of sexual difference, the cinema seems to be taken up with and structured by an excessively rigid dualism when compared to the novel.

The films cited in the previous chapter suggest that narration, in film narrative of the 1940s, assumes a male subject: the myth of authorship so persuasively demonstrated in Minnelli's *Madame Bovary* is defined by a male vantage point of the author as father and lover, and the ways in which spectatorship is problematized in *Citizen Kane* focus on the journey of a male reporter in search of the identity of a male public figure. One of the ways in which film narrative may be said to depart from the nineteenth-century novel is in its excessive sexual polarization. As many feminist critics in particular have argued, one of the distinctive features of the classical cinema is its obsessive orchestration of sexual difference.[2] Although it is much too simplistic to ascribe this obsession to film as a "visual" form as opposed to the novel as a "verbal" one, there is something to be said for the affinity between a preoccupation with sexual difference and a preoccupation with image. What is more specifically characteristic of the cinema is not just the preoccupation with sexual difference per se, but also the way in which other forms of difference, and that of social class in particular, are subsumed by sexual polarity. In the traditional cinema, in other words, the discourse of class is submerged by the discourse of sexual difference.

The examples referred to in the previous chapter suggest an analogy between male and female difference, and the poles of authorship and spectatorship. By and large, however, discussions of the classical Hollywood cinema have assumed the spectator to be male. In speculating on the female wartime viewer recruited to the newsreels, I think we see something of the same phenomenon as with women readers of the eighteenth century: their responses evoke, in bold form, the contours of spectatorship in general. But in terms of the films themselves, enunciation in the classical cinema does function primarily in terms of the male subject. In the two films to which we now turn, the female point of view foregrounds the function of cinema in the 1940s in relation to the spheres of private and public life. Female narration is posed as both a problem and as a possibility. As narratives of the private and the public, Hitchcock's *Rebecca* and Curtiz's *Mildred Pierce* suggest that in the classical cinema, the social function of film is intimately tied to the very possibility of a female point of view. In both cases, the preoccupation with sexual difference displaces a preoccupation with social class, and so the two films are particularly instructive examples of the convergence of sexual and class dynamics in cinematic narratives of the private and the public.

Rebecca, *or Possession*

Rebecca is a tale of obsession and paranoia. In both Daphne Du Maurier's novel and Alfred Hitchcock's rendition of it, the standard formula of gothic literature (a young woman in a frightening house involved in an ambiguous relationship with a man) becomes an exploration of a woman's perceptions of the complexities of sexual and class identity.[3] *Rebecca* is above all a tale of possession. The story unfolds in a hypothetical space where different kinds of possession intersect: the sexual possession of a woman by a man and of a man by a woman; the economic possession of property; and the possession—whether supernatural or psychological—of one mind by another.

Rebecca tells the story of a young woman (Joan Fontaine in the film) working as a paid companion for a boisterous rich woman, Mrs. Van Hopper. They vacation at Monte Carlo and meet the wealthy and mysterious Maxim de Winter. Little is known of Maxim except that his wife, the beautiful Rebecca, has been dead for a year, and that he is the owner of the fabulous estate of Manderley. De Winter takes a liking to the shy young woman and much to her surprise (not to mention Mrs. Van Hopper's), he proposes marriage. The couple moves to Manderley, where the heroine quickly becomes obsessed with thoughts of Rebecca. She imagines Rebecca, through the various stories and recollections she pieces together, as everything she is not: beautiful, vivacious, sexually attractive. More important, she is convinced that her husband is as obsessed by Rebecca as she is, and that he is still madly in love with his former wife. The obsession is fueled by Mrs. Danvers, the housekeeper, who is totally devoted to the memory of Rebecca and maliciously set upon destroying the new Mrs. de Winter. When truth is revealed in *Rebecca*, however, it is diametrically opposed to the heroine's suspicions. Rebecca had died in a boating accident. The boat and her body are found, and an inquest is ordered to discover the true cause of her death (Maxim had identified another body as Rebecca's). The discovery frees Maxim to confess to his new wife. Maxim despised Rebecca, who was a wife in name only. She agreed to be mistress of Manderley in exchange for the freedom to live—primarily in the beach cottage adjacent to the house—a life of sexual freedom. Maxim was responsible for Rebecca's death—deliberately in the novel, accidentally in the film (due to the pressures of censorship: a hero cannot be a murderer). Rebecca had taunted her husband with her pregnancy by another man. Yet another truth is then revealed: Rebecca was dying of cancer, and she deliberately provoked her husband to murder her as a final sadistic revenge. Maxim is absolved of any guilt as another fiction is accepted as truth: that Rebecca killed herself. Mrs. Danvers, in her own moment of revenge, sets fire to Manderley and is consumed by the flames. And so the heroine and Maxim live, as the saying goes, happily ever after.

The overall narrative structure of *Rebecca* consists of three parts. Manderley is a claustrophobic estate saturated with real or imagined memories of Rebecca. It is framed, in the first and third parts of the film, by two different public spheres. The first section of the film takes place in Monte Carlo. Through the comically boisterous and obnoxious character of Mrs. Van Hopper we perceive Monte Carlo as a place where the bored rich come to be seen. This is a public sphere of hotel lobbies and luxurious restaurants, defined by upper-class values and leisure. Only for "I" is this a place where work actually occurs. (The heroine is never given a name; I will refer to her as "I," as she is named in the film script).[4] Maxim rescues "I" from the superficialities of Monte Carlo and Mrs. Van Hopper. He is, indeed, a Prince Charming who carries the heroine off to his magic castle.[5]

The third section of the film takes place within another public sphere, that of the law. After Rebecca's body is found by fisherman, and evidence of possible foul play is discovered, an inquest is held. Maxim's guilt is suspected by Jack Favell, Rebecca's cousin and lover, and the ostensible father of the (imaginary) child. Once it is discovered that Rebecca suffered from cancer, her death is ruled a suicide and Maxim is cleared of any wrongdoing. The inquest is a narrative rite of passage, for it dispels the threat of Rebecca and validates the marriage of Maxim and "I."

From one public sphere, Maxim and "I" retreat to Manderley, and then enter another public sphere, that of the law. Like its novelistic predecessors, the negotiation of private and public in *Rebecca* is marked by the intersection of class and sexual identities, even though the discourse of class is submerged by the discourse of sexuality. Social class functions in *Rebecca* in a complex way. Hitchcock remarked that his first American film could easily have been British, given the actors, script, and setting.[6] To an American audience in the 1940s, this aristocratic context speaks at once to cultural clichés of European "tradition," and to the threat of destruction of a way of life. It is tempting, and perhaps too easy, to invoke the authority of the nostalgia or escape factor, whereby the aristocratic context would function as utopian in both senses of the word, as no-place and as idealized place. But *Rebecca* separates the aristocrat from the space he inhabits: indeed, as a monument to aristocratic privilege, Manderley must be destroyed.

In class terms, *Rebecca* does indeed present a fantasy, but one which is complicated by its own contradictions. Manderley is threatened by two outsiders: "I," and the middle-class values represented by the law. Middle-class values triumph only when "I"'s desires can be successfully harnessed to those of middle-class institutions. The marriage of Maxim and "I," then, is only genuinely consummated once Manderley is destroyed. The fantasy here is a vision of class that has virtually nothing to do with labor, industry, or capitalism. This is not to say that work is absent from the film; but of the main characters, only "I" and Mrs. Danvers work, and their work is overlaid with other implications. For both women, "work" is a sign of the confusion of private and public realms. And if "I" is rescued from the tiresome job of paid companion, the job description nonetheless describes perfectly the ideal of marriage presented in the film.

In sexual terms, *Rebecca* explores female fears of heterosexuality, and Tania Modleski has made a convincing case for *Rebecca* as a *female* oedipal narrative.[7] In Du Maurier's novel, the heroine is the first-person narrator. That she is not named in Hitchcock's film is even more striking, for with the exception of the opening scene (an imaginary dream-like return to Manderley), there is no parallel first-person narration to thus naturalize the absence of a name. This nameless heroine is also without parents. Indeed, she strikes one as a foundling. Her father died, she tells Maxim, the summer before—that is, at about the same time that Rebecca died. If "I" and Maxim have both lost a loved one, it is suggested that Maxim is in fact a substitute father to the woman. When "I" tells Maxim that her father, an artist who painted the same tree over and over again, had a theory that "if you should find one perfect place or thing or person you should stick to it," Maxim tells her, "I'm a firm believer in that myself." From the outset, "I" has an ambiguous relation to Maxim, for it is just as tempting to describe her as his daughter as it is to see her as his wife.

Manderley occupies the center of *Rebecca*. The mansion has an ambivalent status in the film, stemming precisely from the confusion as to who really "owns" it. There is something of Pemberley (Darcy's estate in *Pride and Prejudice*) in Manderley: Like Pemberley, the mansion seems to combine the values of nature and civilization. But Manderley lies next to the sea, rather than to an adjacent woods (as is the case with Pemberley). The associations of Rebecca with the sea (her cottage was on the beach; she died in a boating accident) suggest an ominous mansion, a house haunted with memories not of balance and harmony and integration, but of turpitude, violence, and secrecy. There is something of Darcy in Maxim de Winter. But the essential question raised concerning Maxim is never asked apropos of Darcy: Does he own the mansion? Or is he possessed by the woman who so dominates it?

If Manderley is somewhat reminiscent of Pemberley, it is more often, in the eyes of "I," like a Grandet household, ruled not by gold but by the obsessive memories of Rebecca. Indeed, the function of the mansion in gothic fiction in general might be seen as an extreme form of the function of the house in *Eugénie Grandet*. Central to nearly all gothic fiction is the house—or castle, or chateau—as a site of fear and yet possible comfort (once the source of fear is removed). In their discussion of gothic literature, Norman Holland and Leona Sherman describe the function of the castle as follows: "The castle admits a variety of relationships between itself and the novelent [i.e., the reader, or the consumer of literature] and between itself and the characters of the novel. It becomes all the possibilities of a parent or a body. It can threaten, resist, love, or confine, but in all these actions, it stands as a total environment in one-to-one relation with the victim, like the all-powerful mother of earliest childhood. The castle becomes the entire world of possible relationships for its prisoner."[8] This is precisely the role of Manderley vis-à-vis "I." The mother-connection is particularly interesting. Even though "I," in a brief mention of her parents, quickly dismisses her mother (she died years before) in order to describe her father's notion of art, mother figures are ominously present in the film. First there is Mrs. Van Hopper, and then the malevolent housekeeper, Mrs. Danvers. "I"'s behavior as paid companion to Mrs. Van Hopper affects her behavior at Manderley, but it is never quite clear whether she functions as a "paid companion" to her husband—or to Mrs. Danvers. In other words, the position of surrogate mother occupied by Mrs. Van Hopper early in the film is taken up, simultaneously, by Maxim and by Mrs. Danvers. And again the question is raised about Maxim: Does he, or Mrs. Danvers, "own" his wife?

Holland and Sherman also attempt to come to terms with why, in the genre of gothic fiction, we find conventions particularly appropriate to the female experience of the male-female couple and of sexuality. During the central portion of *Rebecca* at Manderley, there is a tension between past and present tense. It appears to "I" that there is, in fact, *no* present tense except for that defined by the projected presence of a dead woman. Through that tension all others—especially that between male and female—are experienced. What Holland and Sherman describe as the essential tension between inside and outside represented by the gothic castle could also describe, in Hitchcock's film, the tension of past and present—a tension which is, in *Rebecca*, a form of the tension of inside and outside: "Just as a child of either sex might interpret its psychosocial surroundings by means of the inner and outer space of its own body, so the gothic novel provides a polarizing of inside and outside with which an adult woman, particularly in a sexist society, might symbolize a common psychosocial experience: an invaded life within her mind, her body, her home, bounded by a social structure that marks off economic and political life as 'outside.'"[9] Indeed, Manderley represents for "I" an "invaded life"—invaded primarily by the signs of possession of Manderley that are so ubiquitous in the house. Nowhere is a portrait of Rebecca to be found, but her signature and her initials, like stamps of ownership, are everywhere. And of course Rebecca's possession of the house is also perceived by "I" as possession of Maxim, who becomes a fearsome and separate "other" for the film's heroine.

Manderley is not quite a public space, not quite a private space, nor is it an integrated moment between the two spheres. Rather, it is an ambivalent projection of both private and public space. The couple's arrival at Manderley signals the ambiguity. At Mrs. Danvers' order, the entire household staff is lined up like a veritable army, and the new Mrs. de Winter behaves clumsily, as if on stage with a severe case of the jitters. Indeed, the space of Manderley is transformed into a kind of theatre, and "I" becomes obsessed with what she imagines to be the disapproving gazes of all members of the house. Of course the glacial gaze of Mrs. Danvers *is* disapproving. But for "I," the look of Mrs. Danvers condenses the look of the "other," any other, including her husband. Thus "I" cannot really regard Manderley as a home, and the watchful eye of Mrs. Danvers is a reminder of what a fantastic home this once was. Manderley is also a museum of sorts: we are told, when the couple arrives, that the public is allowed to visit once a week. In Du Maurier's novel, these public visits are mentioned when the heroine notices, from a distance, Mrs. Danvers with someone else at a window (the guest is later revealed to be Jack Favell).[10] The heroine describes herself, in the novel, as one of the "public" when the servant Frith shows her the house: "feeling . . . that he considered me as he would one of the public visitors, and I behaved like a visitor too, glancing politely to right and left."[11] In the film, the public is never visible and these visits are not mentioned after the initial reference to them. Rather, the inhabitants of Manderley, and Mrs. Danvers first and foremost, function quite adequately as representatives of the public eye.

Within Manderley, there is little sense of the connecting areas of the house. We have no idea where "I" and Maxim sleep. This spatial disorientation corresponds to "I"'s sense of fragmentation. There is no real sexual architecture in *Rebecca* to correspond to novels like *Pride and Prejudice* or *Eugénie Grandet*, where there is a clear separation along the axis of male-female difference. There is a female space in *Rebecca*, that of Rebecca. But this female space is all-encompassing, like obsession itself, or like the distinctive perfume that "I" associates with Rebecca in the novel. Thus Rebecca's room, in the west wing of the house, is not opposed to another space, like that of Maxim; rather, the room exists as the interior counterpart to another space, the beach cottage, equally defined by Rebecca. The west wing of Manderley is the center of the house. "I" senses from the start that this is forbidden territory, and when she finally timidly ventures forth, she finds Mrs. Danvers adoring the room as if it were a shrine. In some ways, Rebecca's room is reminiscent of the secret room in Monsieur Grandet's house where he keeps his gold for contemplation: the remembrances of Rebecca are, for Mrs. Danvers, like so many pieces of gold. She has preserved all of Rebecca's things, from her hairbrushes to her nightgown. She has preserved, in other words, all of the accoutrements of femininity, all of the signs of a vivacious woman who is—as the portrait of Maxim on the bureau indicates—simultaneously a devoted wife. And the beach cottage, in conjunction with the room, offers to "I" the spectacle of a woman who is at once a part of nature and civilization, who is adventuresome and domesticated, who is devoted to her husband and independent. Rebecca seems to have lived, in other words, a perfectly integrated existence. She has become, for Mrs. Danvers (and for Maxim as well, "I" assumes) a mediator through whom all experience is gauged.

Rebecca's room in the west wing is a kind of magnetic field within Manderley to which "I" gravitates, and in terms of mise-en-scène, the most important spatial elements of Manderley are the west wing and the beach cottage. As narrative space, then, Manderley is the embodiment of a contradiction, activated by "I"'s presence. Manderley signifies neither the integration and promise of reconciliation of Pemberley, nor the contamination of the private sphere by capitalist value, as in *Eugénie Grandet*. Manderley is contaminated by Rebecca, but it is contamination presented in the illusory form of integration. If the house is a body, then so too is narrative perspective defined at every level by the body of Rebecca. If film narrative combines image-making and storytelling, then Rebecca is a figure of their imaginary coherence. This imaginary coherence is central, for the narrative intelligence of the film is largely identified with "I."

The issue of narration in film has been problematic, since the fluidity and diversity of the various techniques that comprise point of view and perspective in film make the designation of a narrator extremely difficult. One of the most interesting features of *Rebecca* is how a problem of narration is handled. The film opens with the voice-over narration of "I" over a subjective camera shot of the entry to Manderley. While the purpose of this scene seems to be an evocation of the novel (Selznick wanted the film to remain as close to the novel as possible[12]), a similar use of first person, now marking the beginning of the departure from Manderley, occurs when Maxim confesses to his wife. As he describes the night of Rebecca's death, the camera moves as if it were Rebecca, while Maxim—speaking in the first person—re-creates the scene.

In a film so taken up with memory, with the past as a mysterious entity which controls the present, it is interesting that there are no flashbacks—unless, of course, one takes the entire film, given the opening dream scene, as a flashback. However, there is one pivotal scene in *Rebecca*, a fold upon which the entire film turns, and which could be (loosely) described as a flashback. This is the home-movie sequence, the one obvious addition to the Du Maurier novel.[13]

Halfway through the scenes of the film that take place at Manderley, Maxim and "I" look at home movies from their honeymoon. "I" enters the drawing room wearing a new dress and a new hairstyle (the latter suggested by Maxim's sister Beatrice), attempting at least to look more the part of mistress of Manderley. Maxim is unimpressed and in any case he is more preoccupied with threading the projector. They begin to watch the home movies. The film breaks, and as Maxim is repairing the projector, Frith enters the room to tell Maxim about some household difficulties. In an earlier scene, "I" accidentally broke a china cupid in the morning room formerly used by Rebecca, and in her embarrassment, she hid the pieces in a drawer. Mrs. Danvers discovered the loss and accused a servant of the theft. In the scene that follows, a humiliated "I" must tell Mrs. Danvers what really happened. The home movies then resume, but Maxim and "I" have an argument "off-screen" as it were. "I" expresses her paranoia and self-deprecation more strongly than at practically any point in the film, and she again interprets Maxim's reaction as a sign that he is still attached to Rebecca.

The presence of Rebecca finally causes an eruption between the couple, a return of the repressed, that is, of Rebecca. All other scenes may lead back to the image of Rebecca, but not with the same implications for narration in the film as this one. The scene is a fold in the film in the sense that all of the scenes which follow it have a symmetrical relationship to those which came before it. After the home-movie scene, "I" encounters Jack Favell, who has come to visit Mrs. Danvers, and we eventually discover that he and Crawley—with whom "I" had previously discussed Rebecca—were the objects of Rebecca's flirtations. "I" finally penetrates the west wing of the house, thus entering a space, the contours of which had been suggested initially by the beach cottage. The costume ball, where "I" is fooled by Mrs. Danvers into wearing a costume identical to one worn by Rebecca the year before, is the culmination of the process of humiliation begun when "I" broke the china cupid and hid the pieces for fear of encountering Mrs. Danvers. The concluding episode at Manderley occurs at the beach house, where Maxim finally explains the events which led up to Rebecca's death, and this scene rhymes with the home-movie scene, providing closure.

In the home-movie scene, Maxim and "I"'s memories of their own past are intruded upon by Mrs. Danvers, and by "I"'s own obsession with the ubiquitous Rebecca. When Maxim finally tells his own story, describing a more distant yet nonetheless present past, he and "I" merge into a kind of union which prevents the intrusion of either Rebecca or her representative, Mrs. Danvers. If "I" must learn how to read, then Maxim must learn how to narrate, and confession is the necessary prerequisite to the public ritual of the trial which will permit validation of a particular kind of contract.

The home-movie sequence focuses on two forces which are present throughout *Rebecca*: storytelling and image-making. The two realms are fused, via the home movies and the characters' responses to them. If *Rebecca* is a film about the way in which a woman must discard certain fictions, certain images, and accept certain others, then these elements are foregrounded in the home-movie sequence in a particularly striking way.

Home movies bring images of the couple from social surroundings into the home for individual contemplation. It is the very nature of home movies to be simple narratives connecting public image and private space. For once Maxim and "I" seem to enjoy a self-sufficient relation of harmony without the intrusion of Rebecca or Mrs. Danvers. And via the home movies, Manderley seems to belong to this couple.

Harmony is quickly disturbed by the appearance of Mrs. Danvers, and "I" must confess her childish behavior both to her and to Maxim. The film breaks just before the incident takes place, as if announcing the intrusion. But already, from the beginning of the sequence, there is a disturbance in the harmonious relation between the couple in the drawing room and the couple on the screen. Just before "I" enters the drawing room, we see an image from a magazine: a model dressed in a black satin gown, wearing pearls. If the home movies remind us of the earlier section of the film at Monte Carlo, so does this image: during one of their outings, "I" told Maxim that she would like to be "a woman of thirty-six, dressed in black satin with a string of pearls." Maxim replies cryptically that "you've blotted out the past for me more than all the bright lights of Monte Carlo . . . please promise me never to wear black satin or pearls or to be thirty-six years old." "I" adopts this identity, for this is how she imagines Rebecca to be. Indeed, Rebecca's mark is present. "I"'s dress bears a garland of artificial flowers, and when she enters the room she stands near a vase of flowers—real flowers—which dwarf her own imitation. We recall that flower arranging, as Beatrice said earlier, was a talent that Mrs. Danvers learned from Rebecca. Predictably, Maxim asks "I" what she has done with herself. And in any case, "I"'s new disguise does not change her perception of herself as a naughty child. Thus, in the course of the scene, there are two conflicting images of "I": a happy young woman enjoying her honeymoon, and a child caught doing something wrong.

The home movies quickly become a focal point of discord, and the briefly represented promise of harmony is dispelled. The discord revolves, as always, around the continual presence of Rebecca—present in the clothes worn by "I," in the discussion of the china cupid, and in "I"'s interpretation of Maxim's reactions as regret for Rebecca. The home movies focus that presence in a variety of ways. The screen on which the movies are projected seems, at first, an extension of the happy life of the couple. But soon a disjunction is operative between "on" and "off" screen space, as the words exchanged between Maxim and "I" are in conflict with the happy images on the screen. As a result, the home movies become more and more visible as a fiction, an imaginary unity of male and female sharply distinct from the couple that exists "off" screen.

Watching themselves on the screen, Maxim and "I" are simultaneously spectators and objects of spectacle. But there is a difference between Maxim's and "I"'s identities in this respect. As they sit down to watch the movies, "I" watches as one who has just entered the room as an object of spectacle, whereas Maxim has been setting up the projector. Maxim is more defined as a spectator, and is more in control of the spectacle, than his wife. This sexual polarity corresponds, of course, to the way in which women and men have had opposing roles in cinema as in virtually all visual arts, as object of spectacle and spectator, respectively. Similarly, there is a difference between the images of Maxim and "I" that appear on the screen. Virtually all of the images of "I" show looks that are *contained*: she looks either at other objects in the frame, like a waiter or geese, or she looks at the camera that is being held by Maxim. Maxim also gestures at the camera, but more characteristic is the direction of his look off-screen. Twice we see images of Maxim alone, and both are the same image, though reversed. Maxim is seen looking through a pair of binoculars, and the object of his vision is never specified. Like a movie camera, binoculars are instruments of vision: within the home movies, as in the drawing room where they are screened, Maxim is identified with the production of images (the binoculars, the projector).

Maxim is also identified with sources of illumination: he runs the projector, turns the lights on and off. Maxim stands in front of the screen during an argument with "I": cast across his face are the light and shadows of the film, his body thus blocking the projection of an image. When he steps away we see the image: Maxim again looking through his binoculars. The reappearance of this image—it first appeared before the film broke—signals a look which is not only undirected, but vacant. Maxim's attention, within the "fiction" of the home movies, is directed elsewhere, like a vacant eye. There are two kinds of separation that occur at this moment in the film. First, the separation between Maxim and "I" is signalled by the different relations of each character to the image and to the camera. And second, there is a separation between two views of the couple: the one, defined in the film we are watching, and the other, in the home movies watched by us, spectators of the film, and by them, spectators within the film. The most immediate consequence of this separation is the even more radical separation of past from present, of a utopian past from problematic present. And for "I," her relation to Maxim thus becomes just as much of a spectacle as her life at Manderley.

The final image of the home movies shows Maxim and his wife together, hugging: they are finally, within the "fiction" of the home movies, brought together in a kind of happy ending. But there is an enormous gap between the couple in the room and the couple on the screen, a difference marked by the camera on the tripod. In the previous home-movie scenes, one character was filmed by the other. But now the camera has become not an extension of the couple, but an eye as vacant as Maxim's gaze through the binoculars. In the home-movie sequence, metaphors of vision, of image, of fiction, create an absolute separation of male and female space, of image and reality. This separation will not be healed until Maxim tells another story, the ostensible "real" story of what occurred between him and Rebecca.

One might also describe the home movie scene as the moment when Maxim becomes, for "I," completely fused with the others in the mansion—i.e., with Mrs. Danvers, and with the memory of Rebecca. Later in the film Mrs. Danvers tells "I" that she wonders whether

Rebecca watches Maxim and "I" when they are alone together. The camera on the tripod is a fitting figure for Rebecca's omniscient eye. For "I," the watchful eye of Rebecca has been present throughout her stay at Manderley. The camera on the tripod in the home movies marks the fusion of Rebecca's eye with the eyes of Maxim. From the outset, "I" is unable to distinguish between the perceptions of Mrs. Danvers and the perceptions of other characters, especially Maxim. That inability to distinguish reaches a climax in the home movie scene. Every statement "I" hears about Maxim's first wife becomes one more piece of proof of a superior person, held in esteem by all, adored by Maxim. "I"'s reaction to Crawley's image of Rebecca is particularly interesting. When she asks the manager of Maxim's estate what Rebecca was "really like," he reacts somewhat awkwardly and uncomfortably, and finally admits that she was the "most beautiful creature" he had ever seen. "I" assumes, here as always, that Crawley utters an objective fact, one more instance of public opinion voting in favor of Rebecca's superiority. It is only when Maxim tells "I" the true story of his relation to Rebecca that Crawley's attitude and remarks are revealed to be the results of Rebecca's power over him. "I" is incapable, however, of distinguishing between personal histories and public opinion.

In coming to Manderley, "I" feels as though she is treading on someone else's territory, intruding on another's private space. All the while, of course, she assumes that she has violated Maxim's private space. Rather, what "I" penetrates is the web of fictions and tales that have been constructed around the figure of Rebecca. For what Rebecca incarnates is the power of storytelling: through the image of Rebecca, characters' capacities for myth-making and storytelling are intensified. We eventually discover that Rebecca was an instigator of fictions, not because of her unquestioned superiority and brilliance, but because of the contradiction between appearance and reality that so dominated her existence. On the surface a devoted wife, underneath a seductress; in the public eye a perfect woman, in private engaged in a loveless marriage; seemingly a great admirer of men but at heart contemptuous of them. What initially appears to "I" as a single unified story, universally agreed upon, turns out instead to be a story full of cracks and contradictions. Perhaps the most fundamental of these contradictions is that in the public eye, Rebecca died an untimely death; she was a beautiful young woman tragically killed. To the two men who knew her best, Rebecca died bearing a child. But the story revealed by the doctor is that Rebecca was going to die anyhow. The disease that was killing her was hidden from public view, and what would eventually kill her is understood by Maxim and Favell as the source of life rather than death. Once this contradiction is revealed, then the coherence of all other fictions about Rebecca falls apart.

"I" goes through a narrative process whereby the mechanics of fiction are dismantled, and narration in *Rebecca* thus assumes a problematic quality. The heroine begins as the terrified listener of stories, until she herself becomes the center of another fiction. This fiction is the life of the couple. At the center of all of the stories that are told in *Rebecca* stands a certain conception of the couple. Maxim and "I" emerge as an authentic couple only when they themselves accede to *another* fiction, one as equally rooted in falsehood as all the endless stories of Rebecca's perfection. This is, of course, the fiction of Rebecca's suicide. The disjunction between public image and personal life is the very basis for the resolution of the narrative in terms of the couple.

In Daphne Du Maurier's novel, there is no question as to whether Maxim actually murdered Rebecca. He did. In Hitchcock's film, however (and again, because of the demands of censorship—a hero cannot be a killer), Maxim may have wanted to kill Rebecca, but her death was technically an accident. In the novel, Maxim's firm commitment to his new wife purifies him of the crime he has perpetrated. But in Hitchcock's film, "guilt" and "innocence" are not so easily defined. *Rebecca* is one film in which the demands of censorship make for a far more ambiguous meditation on the life of the couple than one might suspect. Ultimately, the film *Rebecca* never really reveals "truth"—the intrigue is somewhat deceptively developed in this way. Rather the narrative process of the film reveals the substitution of one fiction for another. If truth is revealed, it is only to quickly establish another fiction. For "I," one set of fictions are dismantled and another set takes its place. This is the narrative price paid, let us say, for the emergence of the couple in a requisite "happy end."

Mildred Pierce *and Family Business*

The protagonist of *Rebecca* is obsessed by the image of an other, the presence of Rebecca diffused throughout the mansion. The gothic conventions of *Rebecca* make for a public sphere somewhat archetypically drawn. We now turn to a film in which the relation between the self and the image of an other is complicated by the dynamics of a public sphere defined by work and business. Mildred Pierce builds a successful business enterprise and engages in a loveless marriage, all for the sake of her greedy, malevolent daughter Veda. The striking physical resemblance between the two women (portrayed by Joan Crawford and Ann Blyth) suggests that the typology of opposition— good versus evil, self-sacrificing versus ruthlessly selfish—is undercut by profound identity.

The relation of mother and daughter in *Mildred Pierce* is the configuration through which all other relations—male and female, father and daughter, female and female—are represented. *Rebecca* explores female fantasies of the male-female couple, with Rebecca and Mrs. Danvers functioning as malevolent mother figures whose destruction is necessary in order for "I" to assume her place in the middle-class institution of marriage. In *Mildred Pierce*, it is a malevolent daughter whose power must be dispelled. The relationship of parent and child in *Mildred Pierce* evokes the relationship of male and female, suggesting the common dynamic of the sexual and the parental. Michael Curtiz's film is in no way as explicit as James Cain's novel in representing mother-love as profoundly erotic. As with Maxim's murder of Rebecca in the Du Maurier novel, the specifically erotic language of Mildred's love for Veda in Cain's novel is repressed in the film version of *Mildred Pierce*. Mildred and Veda's mother/daughter relationship is a nightmarish fantasy of mother-love carried to its most exaggerated, and perhaps most logical, extreme. Veda, as "other" to Mildred, may not be as ephemeral a gothic figure as Rebecca. Veda is horrifying in a different way, for she is the embodiment of those contradictory elements which in *Rebecca* are constantly evoked but never actually represented in concrete form.

The major change in the film version of James Cain's novel is the addition of a murder. The plot of *Mildred Pierce* is told primarily in flashback, the events of Mildred's life recounted to a police officer so as to discover "who killed Monte Beragon." The film begins with the murder of Monte, but we do not see the killer. Monte gasps "Mildred!" as he dies, clearly making Mildred the prime suspect. She is taken to the police station and begins to tell the story of her life. Four years before, husband Bert was out of a job and Mildred was a housewife. An argument leads to their separation, and Mildred becomes a waitress. She quickly learns the restaurant business through a combination of ambition and skill and she opens her own chain of restaurants. To be sure, Mildred works out of economic necessity. But her ambition is motivated by her obsessive love for, and her desire to please, her obnoxious daughter Veda. Mildred is the mother of two daughters, but the younger, Kay, quickly disappears in the film. Kay is a sweet, good-natured tomboy. She is, one might say, a "normal" daughter. For that reason, she has virtually no function in the film, and she dies (of pneumonia) as a sacrifice of sorts to Mildred and Veda. Mildred gets involved with a wealthy playboy, Monte Beragon, whom she meets when she leases his property for her first restaurant.

Several times during the course of the film, we return to the "present tense" of the police station. The officer in charge, Inspector Peterson, finally reveals that Veda killed Monte. Mildred only married Monte because it was a way of acquiring his elegant mansion and luring Veda back to her. But Mildred's scheme turns against her, on two counts. Monte, with the help of Wally Fay—Bert's former business partner who helped Mildred get started in her restaurant business—cheats her out of control of her business. Soon afterwards, Mildred discovers Monte and Veda in a passionate embrace. But it is Veda who kills Monte when he tells her he has no intentions of marrying her. Mildred agrees to help her daughter avoid the police, responding to Veda's pleas that Mildred is responsible for her daughter's behavior. Indeed, Mildred protects Veda up until the end. We discover that the detective has known the truth all along. He brings Veda into the same room as Mildred, pretending that Mildred has told them everything. Veda takes the bait, and her reaction is, of course, confirmation of her guilt. Hence Veda is punished, while Mildred leaves the police station with Bert. Reunited, they walk together into the dawn.

Mildred Pierce rearranges the material of Cain's novel and in so doing asks the classic question: Who did it? From Cain's novel, Curtiz's film retains the image of California as a mythical site of industrial society, where tract housing and sunny climates create a bizarre image of paradise. In order to create a mystery from Cain's novel, *Mildred Pierce* uses many of the conventions of film noir. Film noir is concerned with characters, most of whom are undesirable or fast on their way to becoming so, caught in webs of crime, vice and deception. Film noir also refers to a visual style, where emphasis is on extreme shadows and light and dark contrast. Sylvia Harvey offers this definition: "Film noir offers us again and again examples of abnormal or monstrous behavior, which defy the patterns established for human social interaction, and which hint at a series of radical and irresolvable contradictions buried deep within the total system of economic and social interactions that constitute the known world."[14] Marginality is a given in the world of film noir, and disequilibrium is the rule. Central to such disequilibrium is a vision of a world in which social orders are eminently corrupt, personal relations deceptive, and families nonexistent or at best far-removed.[15] In short, the conventions of film noir do not allow for an easy fit between the personal and the social, and if the private and public spheres of film noir are held in any balance, it is in function of their equal corruption.

Mildred Pierce is not a film noir *per se*. Rather, one of the most distinctive characteristics of the film is its mixture of film noir and melodrama. Joyce Nelson has described how the film alternates between a present tense (the police station) in the style of film noir, and flashback sequences which are essentially melodramatic in tone, more evenly illuminated and less inclined to adopt the sharp angles characteristic of film noir.[16] Hence, as Nelson says, two discourses are juxtaposed in *Mildred Pierce*: the discourse of the law (articulated in film-noir style, the voice of which is the police inspector Peterson), and the discourse of Mildred. Whereas the detective obsessively repeats the same demand for truth, which will result in a clear-cut distinction between victim and murderer, Mildred's discourse "stresses the gradual changes within her life over a long period of time, the gradients within the various relationships, the importance of context for action and behavior, the triadic nature of interrelationships rather than binary oppositions."[17]

Mildred's account of her life reveals an existence where private and public realms are hopelessly confused. Men, for the most part, do not work (Bert is unemployed during most of the film, and Monte Beragon has made a "science" out of loafing). Women do. In this respect, *Mildred Pierce* directly reflects certain aspects of the culture of post–World War II America. For *Mildred Pierce* reflects the consequences of women's entry, during World War II, into the job market. Mildred Pierce is hardly Rosie the Riveter, and it is not war that gets her into the restaurant business. There are, however, connections between Mildred's transition from housewife to successful businesswoman, and the situations of many American women in the 1940s. Having entered the job market, women were expected to make a quick retreat so as to accommodate returning soldiers. We know that many women who held wartime jobs would have preferred to keep on working.[18] *Mildred Pierce* reminds us of the propaganda campaigns which, in encouraging women to work in the first place, emphasized the temporary nature of the jobs. June Sochen argues, in this context, that *Mildred Pierce* "acted as a piece of social control for women. . . . Mildred Pierce had to be destroyed to eliminate any troublesome thoughts held by working mothers. Rosie the Riveter and Mildred Pierce had to go home again."[19]

But to see *Mildred Pierce* in this narrow prescriptive function is to miss the point, for the film engages with the contradictions of women's work, and elaborates a fantasy of the conflicting identities of sexuality, work, and family. At the center of the confusion between private and public stands Mildred's equally confused relation with her daughter Veda. Narration unfolds in the films as an interweaving of two discourses. The voice of the law constantly brings Mildred's account of her life back to the question: Who killed Monte Beragon? Eventually the disorder recounted by Mildred will be regulated by the intervention of the law. The interweaving of two discourses corresponds to an alternation between the perspectives of private and public existence. Mildred *confesses* her life as if "telling" a soap opera; the police officer distills it all into a matter of public record. And so a public sphere emerges through the narrative structure of *Mildred Pierce*: the public sphere of the law. The law is represented as a relationship between a man and a woman in a room, the man unquestionably the more powerful of the two. The law is at once the "truth" that will be committed to public record, and a configuration of a male-female relation. This male-female relation is a relation between storyteller and listener. Throughout most of the scenes in the police station, Inspector Peterson appears to be listening attentively to what Mildred narrates. But we discover that he is, in fact, much more of a storyteller in his own right.

The truth that is revealed in *Mildred Pierce* is Veda's guilt. But there is another discovery as well, that Inspector Peterson knew all along that Veda was guilty. In some ways Peterson is like the various legal forces in *Rebecca* which authenticate the marriage of "I" and Maxim. But Inspector Peterson does not really substitute one fiction for another (as is the case in *Rebecca*); rather, his narrative authority relies on his capacity to reveal the truth. *Mildred Pierce* makes Peterson both spectator and narrator within the film. Peterson is never seen outside the room where he questions Mildred, and when he reveals that he had known the truth all along, his relationship with Mildred resembles that of analyst and patient, for Inspector Peterson is adept at reading Mildred's story between the lines.

Peterson's role as narrator-detective evokes a common narrative device of many classical films: the investigator, whether a police official or a private detective, whose activities of observation and deduction mirror the quintessential cinematic gestures of looking and telling. The origins of detective fiction are instructive in this regard.

The detective story is a nineteenth-century invention, and Edgar Allan Poe is most often credited with the invention of the genre. "Murders in the Rue Morgue" (1841) has been called the world's first detective story.[20] Poe's detective, C. Auguste Dupin, so gifted in the art of "disentanglement," lives an extremely isolated private existence. His only companion is a male friend, the narrator, who writes: "Our seclusion was perfect. We admitted no visitors. . . . We existed within ourselves alone."[21] Dupin has separated himself absolutely from the realm of the everyday, and this separation allows him the position of privileged spectator with an acutely developed "faculty of resolution."[22] Dupin's private sphere is so isolated that no light is ever admitted into the apartment. The narrator says, "We busied our souls in dreams—reading, writing, or conversing"; and when night falls, the two men seek, "amid the wild lights and shadows of the populous city, that infinity of mental excitement which quiet observation can afford."[23] That Dupin's skill is defined through such an entrenchment in privacy suggests a narrative form in which a fantasy of control of the public sphere is operative. For the public sphere, in "Murders in the Rue Morgue," is shaped by newspaper stories and the incapacities of the police to decipher them.

Dupin's analytic skills are demonstrated twice. First he makes a comment to his companion-narrator that is a precise response to what the narrator has been thinking about—in silence. Dupin then explains his deduction step by step, proving his own contention that "most men, in respect to himself, wore windows in their bosoms."[24] From penetration of the innermost thoughts of his companion, Dupin moves to analysis of the story proper, the murders in the rue Morgue. The analysis begins with study of the newspaper stories and concludes at the scene of the crime. The itinerary of detection involves a movement from private to public, from the penetration of one man's thoughts, to analysis of the public records of newspaper accounts. If the reader of Poe's story is fascinated by Dupin's powers of detection, it is not just his scientific skill that elicits admiration, but also his skill in bringing together the spheres of private and public existence, of encompassing the personal and the social in his analysis.

In Mildred's account of her own life, another public sphere emerges, that of work and business. From the very beginning of Mildred's story, the public sphere of work is separated from its traditional male associations. Men are rarely portrayed in relation to work. When they are the portrayal is ambiguous. Such is the case with Wally Fay, with whom it is never clear where the financial ends and the sexual begins. Thus the two public spheres of *Mildred Pierce* have different sexual compositions. The public sphere of the law is represented through a clear distinction between male and female roles, between truth and falsehood. In the public sphere of work, the roles are not traditional and the distinctions are unclear. The function of the law will be to impose that distinction, and to contain Mildred's story within the structures of the law. But whether the law succeeds in doing so is another question.

As the plot of *Mildred Pierce* thickens, private and public realms become increasingly confused. Mildred may be a successful businesswoman, but there are constant echoes of the home in this public sphere of work. In her first "flashback," to life on Corvalis Street, Mildred says: "I was always in the kitchen. I felt as though I'd been born in a kitchen and lived there all my life, except for the few hours it took to get married."[25] There is a striking similarity between this description of domestic life, and the words that Mildred uses to describe her first job in the restaurant: "In three weeks I was a good waitress. In six weeks I felt as though I'd worked in a restaurant all my life" (p. 125). In some sense, of course, Mildred *has* worked in a restaurant all of her life—only it was called a home.

Hence when Mildred enters the public sphere of work, her identity is still shaped by traditional female associations with the home. The private sphere of the family and the public sphere of business are both run by women's work. And what of the private sphere of intimate relationships? In *Mildred Pierce*, family ties and sexual ties do not always overlap. Mildred leases her first property from Monte. The business transaction clearly has more to do with Monte's attraction to her than with good business sense. Indeed, Wally Fay's attempts to talk Beragon into letting Mildred have the property without a down payment are unsuccessful. Beragon flatly refuses until Mildred makes the request. Monte then agrees. Throughout the film, it is never quite clear when "property" and "investment" refer to business, and when they refer to sex. Monte stops at the restaurant to check up on his "investment," and his eyes and the camera's linger on Mildred's legs. Later Mildred will move into Monte's mansion, in a combined marriage and business deal. The deal marks the complete invasion of personal relations by business interests. When Monte leans over to kiss his bride-to-be, Mildred places her glass next to his and refuses the kiss with the words: "Sold. One Beragon" (p. 217).

Thus there are virtually no boundaries between private and public space. Yet boundaries do remain between the realm of the family and the realm of sexuality. Veda's function in the film is to transgress those boundaries by her desire to sleep with her mother's husband. In her own way, Mildred operates according to the same logic as her daughter. Early in the film, Mildred is horrified at Veda's suggestion that she marry Wally Fay, whether she loves him or not, so that they can live in a nice house with a maid. But Mildred eventually comes around, eager to marry Monte in order to regain Veda's affections. When Mildred and Monte meet, their attraction to each other seems to have little to do with Mildred's attachment to Veda. In the course of the film, however, Veda grows up and in becoming a sexual being she defines the terms of Mildred and Monte's relation.

But from the outset, there is a narrative connection between Mildred's attraction to Monte and her attachment to Veda. When Monte takes Mildred to his beach house, they swim and later passionately embrace. The scene occurs just before the death of Kay. Mildred is thus punished for her brief moment of illicit passion. If one triangle links Mildred, Monte, and Kay, another links Mildred, Monte, and Veda. Mildred's passionate moment with Monte is framed by the departure of Veda and Kay with their father to Arrow Beach for the weekend, on the one hand; and Kay's death on the other (she caught pneumonia at the beach and was rushed home). When Kay and Veda are preparing to leave home for the beach, Kay comes downstairs to ask Mildred where Veda's bathing suit is. Returning to the bedroom, Kay coughs—the only sign that she might be ill—and Veda briefly wonders whether there will be any boys at Arrow Beach. "If there are," says Kay, "they'll find you. Don't worry" (p. 142). After the children have left, Mildred goes to work to prepare for the opening of the restaurant. Monte comes by and convinces her to take off the afternoon. At the beach house, Monte tells Mildred to pick a bathing suit from a large closet just full of bathing suits. "They belong to my sisters," Monte says. Mildred replies: "There's nothing like having a big family" (p. 148). Later, before making a toast to "brotherly love," Mildred comments that "they all seem to be my size." Monte replies: "I like them in your size" (p. 151).

The scene at the beach house is the first re-appearance of the site of the murder since the opening shots of the film. The image of Mildred with Monte suggests that she is indeed the missing link, the murderer. Perhaps more important, there is a subliminal connection established between sex and death—a connection which will be displaced, in the following scenes, onto the death of Kay. If Mildred is "punished" by Kay's death, then it makes sense that she might eventually pay for her sexual transgression by killing Monte. If Mildred's "guilt" is suggested, in this scene, as both lover (to Monte) and mother (to Kay), the fit between those two terms moves, indirectly, through Veda. Veda, we recall, couldn't find her bathing suit, and when she does, she wonders about "boys." Monte's cliché'd comments about brothers and sisters and bathing suits in the closet foreshadow the eventual, semi-incestuous relationship that will transpire between him and Veda. Adolescent Veda, wondering about the boys at the beach, is already designated as the figure in whom the sexual and the familial are conflated.

And then there is a simple object of clothing, the bathing suit. In the relations between characters that develop in *Mildred Pierce*, and Mildred and Veda's relation, in particular, pieces of clothing acquire symbolic dimensions. That there is something unhealthy about Mildred and Veda's relationship is suggested during the first scene of the flashback, in the Pierce home. Mildred has bought a dress for Veda, and it is delivered during an argument between Bert and Mildred. The arrival of the dress coincides with Bert's departure—an indication, perhaps, that their rocky marriage has more to do with Mildred's devotion to Veda than with Bert's attachment to his apparent lover, Mrs. Biederhof. Mildred overhears Veda in her bedroom as she complains to Kay that the dress is cheap and unattractive. Veda says that she will never wear it. Veda scorns what Mildred offers as not good enough.

The dress defines both Mildred's connection to Veda, and the relation of both mother and daughter to the world. What connects Mildred and Veda is always what separates them—no matter what Mildred offers Veda, it is never quite good enough. I am reminded of the way in which, in *Eugénie Grandet*, Eugénie sees in the gold chest a souvenir of her love for Charles, while her father can only see a certain amount of gold. Like Eugénie, Mildred imagines objects as signs of the affection of the people who give them. And like Monsieur Grandet, Veda can see objects only as extensions of herself. Mildred offers gifts to Veda, wanting Veda to have what she never had, and showering her with affection. Mildred expects the objects she offers to fulfill virtually every need, financial and emotional. Her fantasy is that the object can be both valued in itself and seen as an expression of affection. For Veda, however, objects are reified, belonging to no one but herself.

Human beings and objects become increasingly interchangeable in *Mildred Pierce*, and this interchangeability is one mark of the confusion of private and public spheres. At the beginning of Mildred's flashback, the home that we see corresponds to stereotypical images of domestic bliss. Discord is introduced when we discover that Bert is unemployed. But it is not that discord which begins the real reification of the private sphere of the Pierce home. Reification is marked, instead, by the entrance of an object, the dress, into the house. In the universe of *Mildred Pierce*, relations between mother and daughter and clothing initiate disorder.

When Mildred gets a waitressing job, she conceals it from Veda. Mildred comes home from work one day to discover that Lottie, her black maid (portrayed by Butterfly McQueen) is wearing her (Mildred's) waitress uniform. Mildred confronts Veda with the knowledge that "you've been snooping around ever since I got this job" (p. 130). Veda knew about her mother's job and created a humiliating scene so as to dramatize her discovery. By giving her mother's waitress uniform to the maid, Veda symbolically takes control of the house. Veda taunts her mother: "My mother, a common waitress" (p. 130). Mildred slaps her. Immediately regretful, Mildred attempts to placate Veda by saying, it appears, whatever comes into her mind. Mildred says she is only working as a waitress so that she can open her own restaurant. Even though Veda will eventually see owning a restaurant as just as degrading as waitressing (she later tells Mildred that she is sick of her "chickens and her pies" [p. 200]), the thought of being rich is enough to make her embrace her mother wildly. This object of clothing, the waitress uniform, initiates another stage of Mildred's position in the world of work. In the process, the relationship between Mildred and Veda begins to look like a relationship between worker and boss. Marxists have often commented on how, within the family, the structures of class society are reproduced: the husband is like the boss, and the wife like a worker. The same could be said of the Pierce family, except that it is Veda who is like a boss, and Mildred like the exploited worker. And the black woman becomes an object onto which the conflict of mother and daughter is displaced.

In the conflation of private and public spheres, of family and business, characters are distinguished on the basis of how actively they contribute to this conflation. Mildred is not just driven, in a simplistic way, by excessive mother-love; she is also unable to distinguish between the personal and the social. But for Veda, as to a lesser extent for Wally Fay (who helps Veda arrange a "marriage" and false pregnancy that will get her $10,000), sex and money are virtually the same thing: there is no private sphere separable from the public sphere. In this way Veda's function as mirror image of her mother is most crucial, for Veda articulates what is repressed in virtually every other character in the film, and especially her mother. One exception, perhaps, is Mildred's friend and business associate, Ida (portrayed by Eve Arden). She expresses, humorously and innocuously (because Ida does not have the power of sexual attraction, in the film, that Veda has), the same philosophy as Veda. But whereas Ida has retreated from the world of relations with men, Veda is an active participant in that world. Indeed, Veda enthusiastically pursues the conflation of private and public spheres, as her scheme for marriage and annulment so amply demonstrates. In the confrontation between Mildred and Veda that follows the exposure of Veda's scheme, the physical resemblance between the two women is more marked than at any previous point in the film. Veda has adopted motherhood as a fiction. And that fiction of motherhood is dangerously close to Mildred's own.

With Mildred's help, Veda creates another fiction: the fiction of her own innocence. The first time we see Veda and Mildred together in the film is before the flashback, when Mildred returns home to find Veda and two police officers. Veda expresses (feigned) concern. Once they have left the house, the two men tell Mildred that they didn't want to say anything in front of Veda. They then inform Mildred that Monte is dead. In this scene, the representatives of the law are ignorant of Veda's role in the crime, but by the conclusion of the film she is discovered, captured, and punished.

Mildred Pierce traces, then, the disorder that reigns when the worlds of work and home overlap too extensively: men become weak, women become powerful, children become spiteful. At the conclusion of the film, Mildred is reunited with Bert, and they leave the police station together. It appears that after a long delay, the couple functions, once again, as a means of restoring private and public spheres to a relation of harmony. Mildred has retreated from the public sphere (her business is in shambles) that Bert has re-entered (he has gotten a job). As we see the couple leave the police station, however, there is a disturbance in this vision of order. In the foreground of the image, two cleaning women are on their knees, scrubbing the floor. Contained within the same image are two visions of private and public space: the couple, representing the idealized balance of male and female, work and home; and the two women, representing a less idealized balance where women's work is a constant, whether in the home or in the official realm of work. If the conclusion of *Mildred Pierce* provides a fantasy of reconciliation, it also suggests that the boundaries between home and work are very tenuous. The final images of the film represent the contradictions of private and public, female and male spheres, as much as the desirability of their reconciliation. The final image of the film functions as the underside of the discourse articulated by Veda throughout the film. There is a grain of truth in that discourse. For women, private and public spheres are, indeed, one and the same.[26] Inspector Peterson may impose the distinction between guilt and innocence as the narrative resolution of the film, but the resolution is a limited one. The two public spheres of *Mildred Pierce*—business and the law—remain separate. The only sign of their connection is the ironic image of the two cleaning women on their knees.

In both *Rebecca* and *Mildred Pierce* there is a problem of narration. In both films the problem of narration is solved, so to speak, by invalidating a female point-of-view. Rebecca's status in Hitchcock's film is like an omniscient narrator, and for the heroine of the film, the power of that narrative can only be dispelled once "I" is identified with middle-class institutions. The "truth" that Maxim tells of his relationship to Rebecca can have narrative consequences only once that identification has taken place. In *Mildred Pierce*, Mildred's story is incorporated into Inspector Peterson's, and her attempt to assume guilt for the murder of Monte is dismantled by his revelation of the truth. Given that the figure of narrative authority in both cases is male, it is thus tempting to read these films as imposing the hierarchy of sexual difference. But in both films, there is a separation between the men with whom the women find their so-called rightful places, and the men who function simultaneously as figures of the public sphere and of narrative authority. In *Rebecca* the participants in the inquest remain distinctly separate from

Maxim, and as we have seen in *Mildred Pierce*, the detective and the husband are of two different worlds. Male identity does not assume a coherent form, but is rather split across the dividing line separating private and public existence.

Rebecca and *Mildred Pierce* use different conventions (the gothic, film noir and melodrama), different settings (the English countryside, Southern California) and different narrative devices, but the stories they tell are strikingly similar. For central to both films are the narratives of private and public life inherited from the tradition of the middle-class novel. Both films are inhabited by the visions of integration and of reification. If the films adopt an ambiguous stance vis-à-vis those visions, it is a function of how narrative itself is problematized.

While both films designate narrators within the film, these are not narrators which can be compared easily to the narrators of novels, given that the narrating intelligence of a film is virtually irreducible to a single figure. The ambivalent position of narration in *Rebecca* and *Mildred Pierce* is a function of conflicting discourses. These discourses expose, rather than repress, the contradictions of class and gender identity.

Rebecca and *Mildred Pierce* evoke other examples from the history of narrative, but these are not films which simply "remind" us of other narratives. Both films take as their point of departure the problematic fit between private and public existence and the attendant implications for sex and class difference. But they also take as their premise the dissolution of the public sphere. The law permits narrative resolution, but in *Rebecca* it is pure fiction, and in *Mildred Pierce* it is immediately visualized in contradictory terms. The law, whether in the form of a courtroom or a police station, allows absolute answers, rigid hierarchies of right versus wrong. That such legal resolutions must be sought at all might be read as symptomatic of the impossibility of such resolutions in any other context. The public sphere that legitimates "I"'s marriage to Maxim, or Mildred's innocence and (presumed) return to her first husband, is first and foremost one of image, of language, of representation. In other words, the public sphere has a purely discursive function. The public sphere of the law allows facile resolutions, but *Rebecca* and *Mildred Pierce* put such resolutions into question.

IN THE MARGINS
OF CLASSICAL
FILM NARRATIVE

In describing the connections between the novel and the cinema, I have suggested that from its very beginnings, middle-class narrative has spoken to a persistent historical need, if not always to integrate private and public spheres, then at least to comprehend the connections between them. As we have seen, the historical dimensions of private and public life, and their corresponding narrative forms, have changed shape. Yet what I have described is still a continuous history, that of middle-class culture. It is one thing to examine an impressive apparatus like the classical Hollywood cinema and conclude that this apparently monolithic system is in fact full of more contradictions than meets the eye. Beneath the ideologically complicit surface of American cinema there are profound ambivalences. It is something else again to generalize from there, and to assume that contradiction is the basis of *all* narrative systems. Throughout this study I have looked at narrative in an ideological context. In this conclusion to my study, I would like to shift that ideological perspective a bit, to turn away for a moment from the contradictions within classical film narrative, and to look instead at how the narrative tradition illuminates films of the post-1940s era, films which do not have the same relationship to middle-class ideals as the classical American cinema. My purpose here is not to engage in a series of analyses of texts, comparable to those analyses that have preceded, but rather to open up a series of questions about the social status of cinema in relation to private and public existence.

One of the most intriguing coincidences in film history is that at about the same time that cinema was increasingly defined as emblematic art form of twentieth-century capitalist society, the first socialist society in history was also encouraging the development of a cinema every bit as emblematic of socialist ideals. This was Soviet cinema of the 1920s, when film was utilized in the creation of a socialist public sphere. Throughout the 1920s artistic experimentation flourished in the Soviet Union, and innovative cinematic works were produced by filmmakers like Pudovkin, Eisenstein, and Vertov. By the end of the decade, tight bureaucratic controls were imposed. Even though the peak of Soviet revolutionary cinema in the 1920s predates the high point of American classical cinema by two decades, Soviet revolutionary cinema of the 1920s also worked within and against a narrative tradition. One thinks immediately, of course, of how Sergei Eisenstein designated Charles Dickens as the forefather of the montage principle. [1]

Perhaps the most obvious contemporary political response to the classical narrative cinema is the contemporary Cuban cinema, which in some ways is continuous with the principles that informed Soviet film of the 1920s. Consider *The Other Francisco* (directed by Sergio Giral, 1974), for instance, a film which demonstrates in a particularly striking way the relevance of the narrative tradition to socialist culture. The film is based on the first Cuban novel about slavery, and alternates between two different readings, or possible adaptations, of it. One might be called the more "faithful" adaptation, reproducing scenes from this novel about a romance between two slaves and the eventual suicide of the man. The second reading asks, rather, where such a romanticized view of slavery comes from. From this perspective, scenes from the novel are enacted and read against the grain simultaneously. There are two voice-overs in the film, corresponding to these two readings: one representing the author of the novel, who is seen at the beginning of the film reading aloud to an appreciative audience of wealthy folks; the other, clearly the voice of contemporary Cuba, which attempts to construct a portrait of the "other" Francisco, that is, the slave who does not fit the conventions of literary genre.

The narrative project of *The Other Francisco* is built upon the historicization of narrative, and the one voice represents what is repressed by the other. The novel of Francisco's life represents an attempt to impose a certain convention of a novelistic private sphere on a life that resists it; Francisco hangs himself in desperation when the slave he loves is sent away. While the revolutionary voice in the film acknowledges the strategy involved in creating a romance out of Francisco's life (the novel was nonetheless censored when it first appeared), it insists on the essential lies of such novelistic portraits. The point is not so much that *The Other Francisco* puts forth the "truth" of slavery as opposed to the "lies" of bourgeois art, but rather that the way in which this film creates a (cinematic) public sphere is by questioning how the two spheres intersected in the original novel in the first place.

However much one might question the place of traditional narrative in socialist filmmaking, there is no question that Cuban cinema is formulated in opposition to the ideals upon which the classical American cinema is based. There are, of course, other ways in which and other perspectives from which the assumptions of classical film narrative are challenged.

For instance, in many French films of the 1960s, and in the work of Jean-Luc Godard in particular, narrative structures became increasingly informed by self-reflexivity, an encounter with the particular qualities of cinema as a narrative and novelistic institution. Yet in the early 1960s, at least, these encounters had little to do with an ideological parti pris. The term which James Monaco uses, "existential semiology," to describe Godard's early work, is not one of which I am particularly fond, but it does suggest how difficult it is to name an artistic practice that is hardly ideologically complicit, but which cannot really be considered contestatory either.[2]

Godard's 1962 film *Vivre sa vie*, for distance, is a film told in twelve "episodes," a summary of each given in chapter-like titles, about Nana who becomes a prostitute and is eventually killed. Like most of Godard's films, this intrigue is of less interest in and of itself than for the inquiries it initiates into the nature of the image and of representation. One of the most striking things about *Vivre sa vie* is that practically the entire film takes place in public spaces: cafés, parks, restaurants, streets. Only in the final episode of the film is there any representation of private space, and then it is quickly interrupted.

Nana, of course, is also the name of the novel by Emile Zola, and Godard does much more than quote the source in *Vivre sa vie*. I have described how the novel and novel-reading often become, in the classical cinema, figures of narrative perspective: the elderly woman reader and gossip in *Gaslight*, for example. *Vivre sa vie* is constructed, precisely, on a query into such equivalences. One of the most famous scenes in *Vivre sa vie* shows Nana at the movie theatre, where she watches Carl Dreyer's film, *La Passion de Jeanne d'Arc*. The identification of Nana with the screen is "framed," as it were, by two images that denote sexual commodification: a stranger puts his arm around Nana's shoulder in the theatre, and after the film he is irritated when Nana wants to say good night, after he paid for her ticket. How reminiscent this structure is of the first chapter of Zola's *Nana*, when preparations for Nana's appearance on stage are made. Whenever anyone speaks to manager Bordenave about his theatre, he sharply interrupts with : "You mean my brothel!"[3]

There are many narrative quotations in *Vivre sa vie*, ranging from Poe's "The Oval Portrait" to Dreyer's film, and if Zola's *Nana* is of particular interest, it is because this novel raises so many issues relevant to film narrative. There seems to be no moment of real connection in *Vivre sa vie* between the private and the public. In the final episode of the film, the private space represented with the voiceless young man is so distanced, and Nana is portrayed here as she has been in other scenes in the film, looking out the window towards another space, as if that privileged realm is always "off-screen."

In Zola's *Nana*, there is a constant movement back and forth from private to public space. The novel seems to follow in the tradition of the nightmare of reification we see in Balzac, for Nana's personal life is a miniature of the public sphere surrounding it. The novel traces a disintegration, a disorder resulting from the breakdown of boundaries between the private and the public, between male aggression and female passivity.

At the conclusion of the novel, the women characters are in Nana's hotel room at her deathbed, while the men wait outside, for fear of contamination. A crowd has gathered in the streets, and men are being recruited to go to war by a man who walks up and down the street shouting "To Berlin! To Berlin!" The conclusion of Zola's novel is an appropriate text through which to read the conclusion of Godard's film. Nana also dies in the film, if not tucked away in a hotel room attended to by other prostitutes. And what of the crowds? There is no major historical event, but there are a crowd of people at the conclusion of *Vivre sa vie*: they are lined up to see Truffaut's film *Jules et Jim*. Hence the only public sphere that can be represented with any certainty, in this film, is that of the cinema itself.

One of the most striking aspects of *Vivre sa vie*, indeed of Godard's work in general, is the sexual dimension: an image of woman examined as the most complex and telling instance of the relations between desire and representation, and the metaphor of prostitution a central figure for the narrative motifs of exchange and transaction. Yet another response to the classical American cinema is to be found in the work of women filmmakers who confront issues similar to Godard's, but from a female perspective. One of the most significant connections between different films by women directors is the relationship between private and public spheres. The narrative strategies of many women's films have focused on disjunctures of private and public space.

Dorothy Arzner was one of the few female directors to have been successful during the 1930s and 1940s in Hollywood, and several of her films are suggestive of a critical foregrounding of the relationship between the private and the public.[4] *Craig's Wife* (1936), based on a stage play by George Kelley, shows us a woman so obsessively concerned with her house that nothing else is of interest to her. Harriet Craig married as "a way towards emancipation . . . I married to be independent." If marriage is a business contract, then Harriet Craig's capital is her house. Indeed, Harriet's sense of economy is pursued with a vengeance, and the men in the film are the victims, explicit or not, of her obsession. It is Harriet's husband who married for love, not money; and in the subplot of the film, a friend of Walter Craig is so obsessed by his wife's unfaithfulness that he kills her and then himself.

As an adaptation, Arzner's film is quite faithful to the Kelley play, but with an important difference. At the conclusion of the film, virtually everyone has cleared out of Harriet's house: her niece has left with her fiancé, her servants have either quit or been fired, and Walter has finally packed up and left in disgust. Harriet, who has actively pursued the separation of private and public realms, now seems pathetically neurotic and alone. The widow next door brings Harriet some roses. In Kelley's play, Harriet has become a mirror image of her neighbor. Both are women alone, to be pitied. But virtually the same scene is acted out quite differently in Arzner's film. The neighbor represents Harriet's one last chance for connection with another human being. Thus the figure who, in the play, is a pale echo of Harriet, becomes in the film the suggestion of another identity. Yet the otherness of the neighbor is deceptive at the same time, for she is a stereotype of effusive femininity.

Harriet Craig's neurosis is an extension of consumerist ideals, and her living room is like a department store display. But the products on display, from furniture to clothing to Harriet herself, are designated as the symptoms of a neurosis, and not presented in a naturalized way as innocent objects in a happy, healthy consumer society. Hence, women's relationship to domestic space is problematized in Arzner's film.

The representation of domestic space has been a central element in the works of some contemporary independent women filmmakers who explore the relations between cinematic narrative and female subjectivity. Some filmmakers, such as Chantal Akerman, have insisted upon the representation of real time on the screen. Akerman's 1974 film, *Jeanne Dielman, 23 Quai de Commerce, 1080 Bruxelles*, is constructed around real time, and gives detailed attention to the everyday gestures of a woman. Akerman has said: "I give space to things which were never, almost never, shown in that way, like the daily gestures of a woman. They are the lowest in the hierarchy of film images . . . But more than the context, it's because of the style. If you choose to show a woman's features so precisely, it's because you love them. In some way you recognize those gestures that have always been denied and ignored."[5]

Virtually all of the films of Marguerite Duras are informed by a principle of duration. In *Nathalie Granger* (1973), the space of a house inhabited by two women is explored and recorded. There is little condensation of time. Gestures, looks, aimless wanderings, household tasks—these are also "marginal gestures" which form the body of this film. But then there is a climax, of sorts. A traveling salesman enters the house and tries to convince the two women to buy a washing machine. He finally discovers that they already have the washing machine that he is trying to sell. The traveling salesman is one of the few male presences in the film. At the beginning of the film, we hear a radio announcer's broadcast about two killers loose in the area, and a husband (one assumes he is a husband) leaves. In the traditional cinema, the broadcast and the husband's departure would be the first clues that the women in the house are soon to be murdered. But that plot never thickens. Rather, the film creates a sense of anticipation never fulfilled, and opens up a hypothetical space between the private and the public.[6]

There are many other directions one could pursue leading from the classical America cinema to other kinds of film practice, aside from those I've sketched here. If these examples, from Cuban cinema to Godard to women's cinema, raise other questions about classical film narrative, we return to what is perhaps the most basic question concerning film and ideology. To what extent does the ambivalence I have described serve to uphold and affirm ideology, and to what extent, rather, does it serve to contest and challenge it? There is no simple answer to this question. And in any case, it is impossible to ascribe firm ideological characteristics to a medium that will always be determined by the historical conditions in which it is screened.

I have described the function of cinema vis-à-vis private and public existence in two basic contexts: the experience of film viewing, on the one hand; and the internal structure of narrative texts, on the other. It should be obvious that the themes of private and public space are "no accident," as it were, and that if I privilege these themes it is because they connect so directly with the situation of film viewing. While it seems obvious that any discussion of film and ideology should be grounded firmly not only in texts but in how they are received, this has not always been the case. And in any case, it is not so obvious just how one can speak of audience responses. For even once one affirms the importance of audiences, there are other problems, like the tendency to describe spectators as passive sponges, or the equally problematic tendency to overly romanticize the interaction between spectator and screen, and to thus consider film viewing as a kind of political consciousness-raising.

Any look to the past of classical film narrative by necessity is, at least in part, determined by the present status of film narrative. In many contemporary American films, forms of ambivalence not exactly identical to, but still akin to what I've described in 1940s films, are prevalent. The ambivalence usually turns on what have become key political and cultural issues of the 1970s and 1980s, like feminism and gay rights. Julia Lesage describes this phenomenon as "structured ambivalence": "Any of us may like a film because it has a 'good portrait' of x or y but that sympathetic element (i.e., sympathetic to us) has been structured into the film to allow for a certain amount of criticism."[7] *Ordinary People,* for example, has been praised and condemned by viewers with common ideological beliefs: praised for its attempt to show men trying to deal with emotions and for its reversal of standard family roles; and condemned for what amounts to a portrayal of the mother as the evil bitch, and for a narrative momentum designed to get rid of her. An understanding of this film, as any film, in relation to ideology, is better focused on how and why that ambiguity is produced, and how viewers respond to it, rather than which reading is the more "correct" one.

Ultimately the ambivalence of classical film narrative is a necessary component of any evaluation of film and/as ideology. For the cinema is *both* spectacle and narrative, a "living display window" and a continuation of the narrative tradition. And so too can narrative in all its forms be understood as a mode of critical understanding *and* as a form of ideological complicity. The same applies to visions of integration of private and public spheres. To be sure, the very conception of the private and public as separate realms serves an ideological end by the assignation of sex and class identities. But at the very same time, the search for connections between the two realms, whether in the solitude of reading Honoré de Balzac or Jane Austen, or in the public space of a movie theatre, is a fantasy of integration, and in this sense the ideology of film narrative needs to be evaluated not only for what it represses, but for what it gives expression to.

NOTES

Introduction

1. Analogies with poetry have by and large been limited to the avant-garde cinema. Kristin Thompson suggests that the short story is one of the most significant, yet least explored influences on classical film narrative. See *The Classical Hollywood Cinema: Film Style and Mode of Production to 1960* (New York: Columbia University Press, 1985), pp. 165–73.

2. Hugo Munsterberg, *The Film: A Psychological Study* (1916; reprint, New York: Dover, 1970), p. 18.

3. Vachel Lindsay, *The Art of the Moving Picture* (1915; reprint, New York: Liveright, 1970), pp. 108, 193, 197–98.

4. John Fell, *Film and the Narrative Tradition* (Norman: University of Oklahoma Press, 1974).

5. Nicholas Vardac, *Stage to Screen: Theatrical Method from Garrick to Griffith* (Cambridge: Harvard University Press, 1949).

6. Robert C. Allen, *Vaudeville and Film, 1895–1915: A Study in Media Interaction* (New York: Arno Press, 1980).

7. Ibid.

8. Fell, *Film and the Narrative Tradition.*

9. See, for example, Yon Barna, *Eisenstein: The Growth of a Cinematic Genius* (Bloomington: Indiana University Press, 1973), p. 74.

10. Sergei Eisenstein, "Dickens, Griffith and the Film Today," in *Film Form*, ed. and trans. Jay Leyda (1949; reprint, Cleveland: World Publishing Company, 1957), p. 206. See also Robert Richardson's discussion of this essay in *Literature and Film* (Bloomington: Indiana University Press, 1969), chap. 3.

11. Eisenstein, "Dickens, Griffith and the Film Today," p. 206.

12. Alexandre Astruc, "Naissance d'une nouvelle avant-garde: la caméra-stylo," *L'Ecran français*, no. 144 (March 30, 1948); George Bluestone, *Novels into Film* (1957; reprint, Berkeley: University of California Press, 1973).

13. Marie-Claire Ropars, *De la littérature au cinéma* (Paris: Armand Colin, 1970), chap. 3.

14. Susan Sontag, "A Note on Novels and Films," in *Against Interpretation* (New York: Dell Publishing Company, 1969), p. 245.

15. Ropars, *De la littérature au cinéma*, chaps. 3 and 4.

16. See, for example, the essays in Eric Rentschler, ed., *German Film and Literature: Adaptations and Transformations* (New York: Methuen, 1986).

17. See, for example, Alan Spiegel, *Fiction and the Camera Eye: Visual Consciousness in Film and the Modern Novel* (Charlottesville: University Press of Virginia, 1976).

18. See, for example, Seymour Chatman, *Story and Discourse: Narrative Structure in Fiction and Film* (Ithaca: Cornell University Press, 1978).

19. David Bordwell, Janet Staiger, and Kristin Thompson, *The Classical Hollywood Cinema* (New York: Columbia University Press, 1985), p. 81.

20. Janet Bergstrom, "Alternation, Segmentation, Hypnosis: Interview with Raymond Bellour," *Camera Obscura*, no. 3–4 (1979): 89–90.

21. Marthe Robert, *Origins of the Novel*, trans. Sacha Rabinovitch (Bloomington: Indiana University Press, 1981); Sandy Flitterman, "That Once Upon a Time of Childish Dreams . . . " *Ciné-tracts*, no. 13 (1981): 14–26; and Stephen Heath, "Film Performance," *Ciné-tracts*, no. 2 (1977): 14.

22. Colin MacCabe, "Realism and the Cinema: Notes on Some Brechtian Theses," *Screen* 15, no. 2 (1974): 7–27.

23. Roland Barthes, *S/Z*, trans. Richard Miller (New York: Hill and Wang, 1974), p. 4.

24. Ibid.

25. Tony Tanner, writing of the novel in relationship to family life, says that the novel is a ". . . paradoxical object in society, by no means an inert adjunct to the family decor, but a text that may work to subvert what it seems to celebrate." See *Adultery in the Novel: Contact and Transgression* (Baltimore: Johns Hopkins University Press, 1979), p. 4.

26. For an analysis of the concepts of the private and the public in Western social and political thought, see Jean Bethke Elshtain, *Public Man, Private Woman* (Princeton: Princeton University Press, 1981).

27. For discussions of mediation as a concept in Marxist literary theory, see Fredric Jameson *The Political Unconscious* (Ithaca: Cornell University Press, 1981), pp. 39–44; and the collective text, "Literature/Society: Mapping the Field," *Working Papers in Cultural Studies*, no. 4 (Spring 1973).

28. Raymond Williams writes: "The most damaging consequence of any theory of art as reflection is that, through its persuasive physical metaphor (in which a reflection simply occurs, within the physical properties of light, when an object or movement is brought into relation with a reflective surface—the mirror and then the mind), it succeeds in suppressing the actual work on material—in a final sense, the material social process—which is the making of any art work. By projecting and alienating this material process to 'reflection,' the social and material character of artistic activity—of that art-work which is at once 'material' and 'imaginative'—was suppressed. It was at this point that the idea of

reflection was challenged by the idea of 'mediation.'" See *Marxism and Literature* (New York: Oxford University Press, 1977), p. 97.

29. See Williams, *Marxism and Literature*, p. 99; and Kenneth Neill Cameron, "The Fallacy of 'The Superstructure,'" *Monthly Review* 31, no. 8 (January 1980).

Chapter One

1. Ian Watt, *The Rise of the Novel* (Berkeley: University of California Press, 1957).
2. See ibid., chap. 1 ("Realism and the Novel Form").
3. Ibid., p. 63.
4. A. O. J. Cockshut remarks on the "double character" of love in the Western novel, as both private and public institution. See *Man and Woman: A Study of Love and the Novel, 1740–1940* (London: Collins, 1977).
5. Hannah Arendt gives a historical overview of the definitions of private and public life in *The Human Condition* (Chicago: University of Chicago Press, 1958), chap. 2 ("The Public and the Private Realm").
6. Richard Sennett, *The Fall of Public Man* (1974; reprint, New York: Vintage, 1978), p. 16.
7. Several critics have analyzed the social differences between tragedy and the novel in terms of the increasing separation of private and public spheres in Western societies. Everett Knight writes, for instance, that the "real difference . . . between renaissance tragedy and the novel lies in the disappearance, after Racine, of a type of humanity (the noble) in which the public and private realms could not be separated." See *A Theory of the Classical Novel* (New York: Barnes and Noble, 1970), pp. 48–49. Georg Lukacs speaks in similar terms in *The Historical Novel*, trans. Hannah and Stanley Mitchell (London: Merlin Press, 1962), pp. 128–38.
8. Such intentions are signalled even in the preface of Defoe's novel: "If ever the story of any private man's adventures in the world were worth making public, and were acceptable when published, the editor of this account thinks this will be so" (*Robinson Crusoe* [New York: Penguin, 1965], p. 25.) About the preface, John J. Richetti has written: "This preface claims that Crusoe has connected the public and the private, implying that in being himself he has lived the kind of private existence that is of 'public' interest." See *Defoe's Narratives: Situations and Structures* (Oxford: Clarendon Press, 1975), p. 24.
9. Some critics define the genre of the novel exclusively in terms of the

private sphere. See, for example, Knight, *Theory of the Classical Novel*, p. 53.

10. Or, as Terry Eagleton suggests, the *novel* must accept those terms: "The tragic irony of the text is that it can ensure the victory of Clarissa only by fetishizing her." See *The Rape of Clarissa* (Minneapolis: University of Minnesota Press, 1982), p. 85.

11. Arnold Kettle has described *Clarissa* in terms of the opposition between love and money: "The conflict of *Clarissa*—the individual heart versus the conventional standards of the property-owning class—is one of the essential, recurring conflicts of the modern novel, as of all literature of class society. It is the conflict of love (i.e., human dignity, sympathy, independence) versus money (i.e., property, position, 'respectability,' prejudice), which lies at the heart of almost all the novels of Fielding, Jane Austen, the Brontës, Thackeray, unalike as they are in almost every other respect." See *An Introduction to the English Novel*, vol. 1 (London: Hutchinson House, 1951), pp. 66–67.

12. Daniel Defoe, *Robinson Crusoe* (New York: Penguin, 1965), p. 28.

13. Eagleton, *The Rape of Clarissa*, p. 56.

14. Marthe Robert describes Friday as Crusoe's "adopted son, Robinson Crusoe's spiritual heir." See *Origins of the Novel*, trans. Sacha Rabinovitch (Bloomington: Indiana University Press, 1981), p. 95.

15. For a discussion of the relationship between the private and the public in *Clarissa*, particularly concerning epistolary form and the representation of space, see Christina Marsden Gillis, *The Paradox of Privacy: Epistolary Form in* Clarissa (Gainesville: University Presses of Florida, 1984).

16. Eli Zaretsky, *Capitalism, the Family, and Personal Life* (New York: Harper and Row, 1976), p. 29.

17. Ibid., p. 30.

18. Philippe Ariès, *Centuries of Childhood*, trans. Robert Baldick (New York: Vintage, 1962), p. 398.

19. Ibid., pp. 406–7.

20. Watt, *The Rise of the Novel*, pp. 188–89.

21. Sennett, *The Fall of Public Man*, p. 98.

22. Henry Fielding, *Tom Jones* (Baltimore: Penguin, 1966), p. 51.

23. Karl Marx, *A Contribution to the Critique of Political Economy* (New York: International Publishers, 1970), p. 49.

24. Georg Lukacs, *History and Class Consciousness*, trans. Rodney Livingstone (Cambridge, Mass.: MIT Press, 1971), p. 83.

25. Ibid., p. 91.

26. Ibid., pp. 91–92.

27. Ibid., p. 93.

28. Lukacs, *The Theory of the Novel*, trans. Anna Bostock (Cambridge, Mass.: MIT Press, 1971), p. 56.

29. Lucien Goldmann, "La Réification," in *Recherches dialectiques* (Paris: Gallimard, 1959), p. 71.

30. Goldmann, *Towards a Sociology of the Novel*, trans. Alan Sheridan (London: Tavistock, 1975), p. 6. Goldmann's analysis of homology is not without problems. See, for example, Fredric Jameson, *The Political Unconscious* (Ithaca: Cornell University Press, 1981), p. 44.

31. In his study of the changing nature of the public sphere from the eighteenth century to the present, for instance, Richard Sennett's major area of analysis is the city—particularly the cities of London and Paris. He speaks of the "claims of civility," which originated in the city, as opposed to the "claims of nature" within the family (*The Fall of Public Man*, p. 18). Those claims of civility entailed a highly coded set of social rituals, which permitted interactions between relative strangers. The rituals of London and Paris in the eighteenth century were remarkable for their anonymity. Sennett writes that "in the population formation of both cities, a special sort of stranger played a critical role. He or she was alone, cut off from past associations, come to the city from a significant distance. Indeed, in describing the population of their cities, Londoners and Parisians in a decade like the 1720s resort to images of these outsiders as 'motley,' 'amorphous,' 'questionable,' 'unformed' " (p. 18). The forms of social behavior which emerged as specifically urban have characteristics similar to the "fragmentation of the human subject" described by Lukacs: "As labour is progressively rationalised and mechanised his lack of will is reinforced by the way in which his activity becomes less and less active and more and more *contemplative*" (*History and Class Consciousness*, p. 89). In a similar vein, Goldmann describes the increasing passivity of human beings: "market economy masks the historical, human qualities of social life, transforming man into a passive element, into a *spectator*" ("La Réification," p. 79). Goldmann's use of a theatrical metaphor returns us to the city as public space, which functioned, according to Sennett, like a stage where citizens adopted the roles of actors and spectators.

32. Goldmann, "La Réification," pp. 76, 77.

33. Ann Foreman, *Femininity as Alienation: Women and the Family in Marxism and Psychoanalysis* (London: Pluto Press, 1977), p. 73.

34. Ibid., p. 74. See also Jean Bethke Elshtain, *Public Man, Private Woman* (Princeton: Princeton University Press, 1981).

35. See Sheila Rowbotham, *Women's Consciousness, Man's World* (1973; reprint, Baltimore: Penguin Books, 1974), p. 53.

36. Joan Kelly, "The Doubled Vision of Feminist Theory: A Postscript to the 'Women and Power' Conference," *Feminist Studies* 5 (1979): 217.

37. Foreman, *Femininity as Alienation*, p. 39.

38. See Rayna Rapp, Ellen Ross, and Renate Bridenthal, "Examining Family History," *Feminist Studies* 5 (1979): 174–200.

39. See Renate Bridenthal, "The Dialectics of Production and Reproduction in History," *Radical America* 10, no. 2 (1976): 3–11.

40. Rayna Rapp, in "Examining Family History," develops a particularly lucid argument concerning the danger of replicating the "splits between public and private, workplace and household, economy and family" (p. 175).

41. Carroll Smith-Rosenberg, "The Female World of Love and Ritual," *Signs* 1, no. 1 (1975): 1–29.

42. Ibid., pp. 1–2.

43. Ibid., p. 9.

44. Ibid., p. 11.

45. Ibid., p. 9.

46. Ibid., pp. 20–21.

47. Ibid., p. 14.

48. Peter Bailey, *Leisure and Class in Victorian England* (London: Routledge and Kegan Paul, 1978), p. 17.

49. Gareth Stedman-Jones, "Working-class Culture and Working-class Politics in London, 1870–1900," *Journal of Social History* 7, no. 4 (1974): 485–86.

50. Zaretsky, *Capitalism, the Family, and Personal Life*, p. 61.

51. Stedman-Jones, "Working-class Culture," p. 487.

52. Ibid.

53. Bailey, *Leisure and Class*, p. 106.

54. Ibid., p. 121 (my emphasis).

55. I have described the letters primarily in terms of their function vis-à-vis the private sphere. At the same time, however, it is the function of the epistolary form to combine the private and the public, suggesting once again the impossibility of a fixed separation of the private and the public. As Terry Eagleton writes in *The Rape of Clarissa*, "The letter is the sign doubled, overhearing itself in the ears of its addressee; and in this sense 'public' and 'private' are inseparably interwoven within it" (p. 52).

56. Sylvia Bovenschen, "Is There a Feminine Aesthetic?" *New German Critique*, no. 10 (Winter 1977): 133.

57. Harry Levin, *The Gates of Horn: A Study of Five French Realists* (New York: Oxford University Press, 1963), p. 21.

58. Edward Said, *Beginnings* (New York: Basic Books, 1975), p. 82.

59. Alan Dugald McKillop, *Samuel Richardson: Printer and Novelist* (1936; reprint, New York: Shoe String Press, 1960), chap. 1.

60. The classic study of this phenomenon is, of course, Thorstein Veblen's *The Theory of the Leisure Class* (1899; reprint, New York: Viking Press, 1965). See in particular chap. 3 ("Conspicuous Leisure").

61. Vineta Colby, in *Yesterday's Woman: Domestic Realism in the English Novel* (Princeton: Princeton University Press, 1974), notes the affinity between "cozy interiors" and the act of novel-reading (p. 20).

62. Cited in Watt, *The Rise of the Novel*, p. 44.

63. Robert Halsband, ed., *The Complete Letters of Lady Mary Wortley Montagu*, vol. 3 (1752–1762), (Oxford: Clarendon Press, 1966), p. 134.

64. Halsband, ed., *The Complete Letters of Lady Mary Wortley Montagu*, vol. 2 (1721–1751), pp. 449–50.

65. Ibid., 2: 403.

66. Ibid., 2: 407.

67. Fredric Jameson speaks of the "mapping fantasy or narrative by which the individual subject invents a 'lived' relationship with collective systems." See "Imaginary and Symbolic in Lacan," *Yale French Studies*, nos. 55–56 (1978): 394.

68. Halsband, ed., *The Complete Letters of Lady Mary Wortley Montagu*, 2: 408.

69. Ibid., 3: 32.

70. Ibid., 3: 25.

71. Ibid., 3: 70.

72. Ibid., 2: 443.

73. I have argued, for example, that mediation in *Robinson Crusoe* is in fact the domination of the public sphere over all other concerns. From a different point of view, it is possible to imagine another argument: that it is rather the family, in the form of the father, which dominates all other areas in the novel. This is the basis of Marthe Robert's discussion of *Robinson Crusoe*. See *Origins of the Novel*, chap. 3.

Chapter Two

1. Jane Austen, *Pride and Prejudice*, p. 1. I use the Riverside Edition (Boston: Houghton Mifflin, 1956). Subsequent citations will be indicated in parentheses in the text.

2. See for example, E. F. Halliday, "Narrative Perspective in *Pride and Prejudice*," *Nineteenth Century Fiction* 15 (1960): 65–71.

3. This is suggested by Julia Prewitt Brown, who writes: "Just as the experience of marriage mediates between the individual and society on the level of content, irony mediates between the ideal and the real on the level of form." See *Jane Austen's Novels: Social Change and Literary Form* (Cambridge: Harvard University Press, 1979), p. 25.

4. David Daiches, "Jane Austen, Karl Marx, and the Aristocratic Dance," *American Scholar* 17 (1947–48): 289.

5. Hence Julia Prewitt Brown says that Jane Austen gave meaning to do-

mesticity for the first time in English fiction. See *Jane Austen's Novels*, p. 1.

6. Cited in Mary Lascelles, "Jane Austen and the Novel," in John Halperin, ed., *Jane Austen: Bicentennary Essays* (Cambridge: Cambridge University Press, 1975), p. 236.

7. Judith Newton, *"Pride and Prejudice:* Power, Fantasy, and Subversion in Jane Austen," *Feminist Studies* 4 (1978): 29–30.

8. Mark Schorer, "Pride Unprejudiced," *Kenyon Review* 18 (1956): 80.

9. Ibid., p. 83.

10. The theme of class alliance is also discussed by Alistair M. Duckworth, *The Improvement of the Estate: A Study of Jane Austen's Novels* (Baltimore: Johns Hopkins University Press, 1971).

11. Nina Auerbach points out that as a result, we never get a sense of the collective life of the Bennet family. See *Communities of Women: An Idea in Fiction* (Cambridge: Harvard University Press, 1978), p. 42.

12. Nina Auerbach says: "Mrs. Bennet is perpetually begging any and all eligible males to come to a dinner we have never seen the family at Longbourn eat, as if only in their presence can nourishment present itself" (ibid.).

13. See Auerbach, *Communities of Women*, p. 39; and Newton, "Power, Fantasy, and Subversion," p. 30.

14. Joseph M. Duffy, "The Politics of Love: Marriage and the Good Society in *Pride and Prejudice*," *University of Windsor Review* 2 (n.d.): 17–18.

15. Joseph Duffy says: "Everything about the scene at Pemberley—the house and grounds, the affectionate gossip of the housekeeper, and the appearance and manner of Darcy—is expressive of an equilibrium achieved between the refining power of civilization and the spontaneous regenerative power of nature" (ibid., pp. 22–23).

16. In this sense, Pemberley is somewhat reminiscent of Gaston Bachelard's analysis of the house as a site of integration. See *La Poétique de l'espace* (Paris: Presses Universitaires de France, 1958), p. 26.

17. Duckworth, *The Improvement of the Estate*, p. 125.

18. Ibid., pp. 129–30.

19. Linda Rudich, "Balzac and Marx: Theory of Value," in Norman Rudich, ed., *Weapons of Criticism* (Palo Alto, Calif.: Ramparts Press, 1976), p. 253.

20. Honoré de Balzac, *Eugénie Grandet*, trans. Marion Ayton Crawford (New York: Penguin Books, 1976), p. 248. French text is from the 1964 Garnier-Flammarion edition, p. 189. Subsequent citations will be indicated in parentheses in the text.

21. Lee Baxandall and Stefan Morawski, eds., *Marx and Engels on Literature and Art* (St. Louis/Milwaukee: Telos Press, 1973), p. 115.

22. Rudich, "Theory of Value," p. 246.
23. Eric Auerbach, *Mimesis*, trans. Willard R. Trask, (Princeton: Princeton University Press, 1953), p. 473.
24. For a discussion of the function of objects in *Eugénie Grandet*, see Roland Le Huenen and Paul Perron, "Le Système des objets dans *Eugénie Grandet*," *Littérature*, no. 26 (1975): 94–119.
25. P. M. Wetherill discusses Charles's appearance in the novel in terms of a series of "shocks" that structure the narrative. See "A Reading of *Eugénie Grandet*," *Modern Languages* 52 (1971): pp. 169–70.
26. Rudich, "Theory of Value," p. 254.
27. Roland Barthes, *S/Z*, trans. Richard Miller (New York: Hill and Wang, 1974), p. 39.

Chapter Three

1. Eli Zaretsky, *Capitalism, the Family, and Personal Life* (New York: Harper and Row, 1976), p. 65.
2. Paul Baran and Paul Sweezy, *Monopoly Capital* (1966; reprint, London: Penguin Books, 1973), p. 122.
3. Ibid., pp. 122–23.
4. See Stuart Ewen, *Captains of Consciousness* (1976; reprint, New York: McGraw Hill, 1977).
5. Charles Eckert examines the fundamental connections between American cinema and advertising in "The Carole Lombard in Macy's Window," *Quarterly Review of Film Studies* 3, no. 1 (1978): 1–21.
6. Zaretsky, *Capitalism, the Family and Personal Life*, p. 67.
7. See Robert C. Allen, *Vaudeville and Film, 1895–1915: A Study in Media Interaction* (New York: Arno Press, 1980); and Russell Merritt, "Nickelodeon Theaters, 1905–1914: Building an Audience for the Movies," in Tino Balio, ed., *The American Film Industry* (Madison: University of Wisconsin Press, 1976), pp. 59–79.
8. Robert Allen, "Motion Picture Exhibition in Manhattan, 1906–1912," *Cinema Journal* 18, no. 2 (1979): 9; and Elizabeth Ewen, *Immigrant Women in the Land of Dollars: Life and Culture on the Lower East Side, 1890–1925* (New York: Monthly Review Press, 1985).
9. Allen, *Vaudeville and Film*.
10. William Everson, *American Silent Film* (New York: Oxford University Press, 1978), p. 19.
11. Russel Nye, *The Unembarrassed Muse: The Popular Arts in America* (New York: Dial Press, 1970), p. 364. See also Benjamin Hampton, *History of the American Film Industry* (1931; reprint, New York: Dover Publications, 1970), pp. 13–15.

12. Lewis Jacobs, *The Rise of the American Film* (New York: Teacher's College Press, 1939), p. 12.
13. Garth Jowett, *Film: The Democratic Art* (Boston: Little, Brown and Company, 1976), p. 38.
14. Nye, *The Unembarrassed Muse*, p. 364.
15. G. W. Bitzer, *Billy Bitzer: His Story* (New York: Farrar, Straus, and Giroux, 1973), p. 68.
16. Jowett, *Film: The Democratic Art*, p. 39.
17. Merritt, "Nickelodeon Theaters," p. 64.
18. Ibid., p. 65.
19. Stuart Ewen and Elizabeth Ewen, "Americanization and Consumption," *Telos*, no. 37 (Fall 1978): p. 47.
20. E. Ewen, *Immigrant Women in the Land of Dollars*, chaps. 6–10.
21. Ibid., p. 266.
22. Ibid., p. 163.
23. Ibid., pp. 52–53.
24. Louise Odencrantz, *Italian Women in Industry* (New York: Russell Sage Foundation, 1919), p. 218.
25. Hutchins Hapgood, *The Spirit of the Ghetto: Studies on the Jewish Quarter of New York* (1902; reprint, New York: 1972), p. 91. Cited in Thomas Kessner, *The Golden Door: Italian and Jewish Immigrant Mobility in New York City, 1880–1915* (New York: Oxford University Press, 1977), p. 100.
26. E. Ewen, *Immigrant Women in the Land of Dollars*, p. 127.
27. Analyzing motion picture exhibition in Manhattan, Robert Allen says: "It does appear that the family-oriented, American-minded Jewish community was a more lucrative location for a nickelodeon than the transient, predominantly male Italian neighborhoods." See "Motion Picture Exhibition in Manhattan," p. 9.
28. Ewen and Ewen, "Americanization and Consumption," p. 48.
29. Allen, *Vaudeville and Film*, p. 50.
30. Ibid., p. 51.
31. Peter Bailey, *Leisure and Class in Victorian England* (London: Routledge and Kegan Paul, 1978), p. 182.
32. Gordon Hendricks, "The History of the Kinetoscope," in Balio, ed., *The American Film Industry*, p. 42.
33. Hampton, *History of the American Film Industry*, p. 12.
34. E. Ewen, *Immigrant Women in the Land of Dollars*, p. 224.
35. Ibid., p. 251.
36. Ibid.
37. Merritt, "Nickelodeon Theaters," p. 73.
38. Ibid., p. 74.

39. See, for example, Hampton, *History of the American Film Industry*, p. 31.
40. Noël Burch, *Correction Please: Or How We Got into Pictures*, Pamphlet accompanying his film of the same title. (London: Arts Council of Great Britain, 1979), p. 14.
41. Of the reverse angle, Burch says: "This cut is in fact the true centre of a diegesis which is wholly consubstantial with the complete paradigm of filmic production; and this 'spelling-out' of what was still an 'unimaginable' change of filmic viewpoint, was no doubt a sine que non condition of audience acceptance at that date, of the camera's ubiquity" (ibid., p. 6).
42. Griffith's importance as the "first" true director has been challenged by recent research into the early cinema. See in particular John Fell, ed., *Film Before Griffith* (Berkeley: University of California Press, 1984).
43. D. W. Griffith, "My Early Life," excerpted from Henry Stephen Gordon, "The Story of David Wark Griffith," *Photoplay* 10 (June 1916): 35, 37, 162–65; (July 1916): 124–29, 131–32. Reprinted in Harry Geduld, ed., *Focus on D. W. Griffith* (Englewood Cliffs, N.J.: Prentice-Hall, 1971), pp. 13–14.

Chapter Four

1. Janet Bergstrom, "Alternation, Segmentation, Hypnosis: Interview with Raymond Bellour," *Camera Obscura*, nos. 3–4 (1979): 89.
2. See Christian Metz, "The Cinema: Language or Language System?" in *Film Language*, trans. Michael Taylor (New York: Oxford University Press, 1974), pp. 31–91.
3. Maxim Gorky, quoted in Jay Leyda, *Kino: A History of the Russian and Soviet Film* (New York: Collier Books, 1973), p. 407.
4. Dana Polan, "'Above all else to make you see': Cinema and the Ideology of Spectacle," *Boundary* 2, vol. 11, no. 1–2 (Fall–Winter 1982–83): 131.
5. Roland Barthes, "Writers, Intellectuals, Teachers," in *Image, Music, Text*, ed. and trans., Stephen Heath (London: Fontana, 1977), p. 212.
6. Stephen Heath, *Questions of Cinema* (Bloomington: Indiana University Press, 1981), p. 4.
7. Stephen Heath, "The Cinematic Apparatus: Technology as Historical and Cultural Form," in Stephen Heath and Teresa De Lauretis, eds., *The Cinematic Apparatus* (London: Macmillan, 1980), p. 1.
8. Christian Metz, *The Imaginary Signifier* (Bloomington: Indiana University Press, 1982), p. 7.

9. Ibid., p. 39.

10. Ibid., pp. 110, 64.

11. See Seymour Chatman, *Story and Discourse* (Ithaca: Cornell University Press, 1978).

12. Metz, *The Imaginary Signifier*, p. 94.

13. George Bluestone, *Novels into Film* (1957; reprint, Berkeley: University of California Press, 1973), p. 62.

14. Ibid., pp. 110–11.

15. Asheim's study appeared as a four-part series: "From Book to Film: Simplification," *Hollywood Quarterly* 5 (1951): 289–304; "From Book to Film: Mass Appeals," *Hollywood Quarterly* 5 (1951): 334–49; "From Book to Film: The Note of Affirmation," *The Quarterly of Film, Radio and Television* 6 (1952): 54–68; and "From Book to Film: Summary," *The Quarterly of Film, Radio and Television* 6 (1952), 258–73. The passages cited here are from the final installment, "Summary," pp. 267, 268, and 271.

16. Rudy Behlmer, ed., *Memo from David O. Selznick* (New York: Viking Press, 1972), p. 141.

17. Ibid., p. 237.

18. Cited in Jean Queval, "Le film fait-il vendre le livre?" *Ecran Français*, no. 145 (April 6, 1948).

19. *Variety*, Nov. 25, 1942, p. 19.

20. Behlmer, ed., *Memo from David O. Selznick*, p. 60.

21. Ibid., p. 27.

22. Sergei Eisenstein, "Through Theater to Cinema," in *Film Form*, ed. and trans. Jay Leyda (1949; reprint, Cleveland: World Publishing Company, 1957), p. 12.

23. Alan Spiegel, *Fiction and the Camera Eye* (Charlottesville: University of Virginia Press, 1976), p. 6.

24. Bluestone, *Novels into Film*, p. 198.

25. Geoffrey Wagner, *The Novel and the Cinema* (Cranbury, N.J.: Associated University Presses, 1975), p. 252.

26. Vincente Minnelli with Hector Arce, *I Remember It Well* (New York: Doubleday, 1974), p. 203.

27. For a discussion of the trial in relationship to the novel *Madame Bovary*, see Dominick LaCapra, *Madame Bovary on Trial* (Ithaca: Cornell University Press, 1982).

28. Gustave Flaubert, letter to Maurice Schlesinger, 14 January 1857, in *Correspondence* (Lausanne: Editions Rencontre, 1965), p. 33. My translation.

29. Flaubert, letter to Champfleury, 4 February 1857, in *Correspondence*, p. 47.

30. About Charles's hat, Tony Tanner has written: "It is as if, from the start,

Flaubert is demonstrating that there can be written verbal constructs that the other senses cannot translate: language can create impossible objects that can be read and deciphered, but not seen and experienced." See *Adultery in the Novel: Contact and Transgression* (Baltimore: Johns Hopkins University Press, 1979), p. 238.

31. Roland Barthes, "The Death of the Author," in Stephen Heath, ed. and trans., *Image-Music-Text* (London: Fontana, 1977), p. 143.

32. Ibid., p. 145.

33. Ibid., pp. 142, 148.

34. Asheim, "Summary," p. 268.

35. Charlotte Brontë, *Jane Eyre* (1847; reprint, New York: Penguin, 1966), p. 39.

36. Cited in Margaret Farrand Thorp, *America at the Movies* (New Haven: Yale University Press, 1939), pp. 242–43.

37. Asheim, "Summary," p. 263.

38. Sergei Eisenstein, "Dickens, Griffith and the Film Today," *Film Form*, ed. and trans. Jay Leyda (1949; reprint, Cleveland: World Publishing Co., 1957), p. 201.

39. David Bordwell, "*Citizen Kane*," in Ronald Gottsman, ed., *Focus on Citizen Kane* (Englewood Cliffs, N.J.: Prentice Hall, 1976), says that Kane sees "love solely in terms of power," p. 118.

40. Welles said of Rosebud: "It's a gimmick, really, and rather dollar-book Freud." See Joseph McBride, *Orson Welles* (New York: Viking Press, 1972), p. 44.

41. Joseph McBride says of Thompson: "The reporter, who stands for the audience, also stands for the artist approaching the contradictions of his subject-matter" (Ibid., p. 38).

42. Joseph McBride says: "We see the 'solution' for which we and Thompson have been searching, and we realize that it does in fact solve nothing" (Ibid., p. 42).

43. Robert Carringer, "Rosebud, Dead or Alive: Narrative and Symbolic Structure in *Citizen Kane*," *PMLA* 91, no. 2 (1976): 187.

44. Ibid., p. 191.

45. Christa Wolf, "The Reader and the Writer," in *The Reader and the Writer*, trans. Joan Becker (New York: International Publishers, 1977), p. 190.

46. Ibid., p. 193.

47. Stewart Ewen, *Captains of Consciousness* (1976; reprint, New York: McGraw Hill, 1977), p. 164.

48. See Eli Zaretsky, *Capitalism, the Family, and Personal Life* (New York: Harper and Row, 1976), p. 67.

49. Charles Eckert, "The Carole Lombard in Macy's Window," *Quarterly Review of Film Studies* 3, no. 1 (1978): 2.

50. Ibid., p. 4.
51. Ibid., pp. 6, 19–20.
52. Ibid., p. 21.
53. Zaretsky, *Capitalism, the Family, and Personal Life*, p. 61.
54. See Leila J. Rupp, *Mobilizing Women for War: German and American Propaganda, 1939–1945* (Princeton: Princeton University Press, 1978), p. 177.
55. Ibid., p. 157.
56. Ibid., p. 153.
57. Ibid., p. 151.
58. *Variety* reported on a Pittsburgh theatre manager who said, "Gals have to get their romantic kicks vicariously since Uncle Sam's been pulling so many eligibles out of circulation" (March 11, 1942, p. 1).
59. Yet it should be kept in mind that women have virtually always been regarded as key audiences for Hollywood films. *Variety* (August 4, 1942, p. 3) published the results of a new Gallup poll which claimed that as many men as women went to the movies. The following week a film critic responded: "It is not the percentage of men as against women that counts. It's *how* did *most* of them get there?" (August 12, 1942, p. 12). Whether men go to the movies or not, the critic claims, it is women who do the choosing.
60. The event is described in *Variety*, March 31, 1943, p. 23.
61. Ibid.

Chapter Five

1. Charles Eckert, "The Carole Lombard in Macy's Window," *Quarterly Review of Film Studies* 3, no. 1 (1978): 20.
2. Kaja Silverman writes, for instance: "Classic cinema entertains more than a metaphoric relation to the operations which construct sexual difference; . . . dominant film practice orchestrates the burdensome transfer of male lack to the female subject by projecting the projections upon which our current notions of gender depend." See "Lost Objects and Mistaken Subjects: Film Theory's Structuring Lack," *Wide Angle* 7, nos. 1–2 (1985): 25.
3. For a discussion of the intertwining determinations of sex and class in *Rebecca*, see Alison Light, " 'Returning to Manderley'—Romance Fiction, Female Sexuality and Class," *Feminist Review*, no. 16 (1984): 7–25. Light's discussion focuses on the Du Maurier novel, but is quite pertinent to the film as well.
4. Shooting script for *Rebecca*, Motion Picture Division, Library of Congress.

5. Don Ranvaud discusses the structure of *Rebecca* in terms of three related sections: first, a fairy tale; then, a mystery story; and finally, a detective story. See *"Rebecca," Framework*, no. 13 (1980): 19–24.

6. François Truffaut, *Hitchcock* (New York: Simon and Schuster, 1967), p. 92.

7. Tania Modleski, "'Never to be Thirty-six Years Old': *Rebecca* as Female Oedipal Drama," *Wide Angle* 5, no. 1 (1982): 34–41.

8. Norman Holland and Leona Sherman, "Gothic Possibilities," *New Literary History* 8, no. 2 (1977): 283.

9. Ibid., p. 288.

10. Daphne Du Maurier, *Rebecca* (1938; reprint, New York: Avon, 1971), p. 156.

11. Ibid., p. 70.

12. Truffaut, *Hitchcock*, p. 92.

13. Mary Ann Doane discusses the home-movie scene in relationship to female spectatorship in *"Caught* and *Rebecca:* The Inscription of Femininity as Absence," *Enclitic* 5, no. 2, and 6, no. 1 (1981–1982): 75–89.

14. Sylvia Harvey, "Women and the Family in Film Noir," in E. Ann Kaplan, ed., *Women in Film Noir* (London: British Film Institute, 1978), p. 22.

15. Ibid.

16. Joyce Nelson, *"Mildred Pierce* Reconsidered," *Film Reader*, no. 2 (1977): 67.

17. Ibid., p. 68.

18. See Leila J. Rupp, *Mobilizing Women for War: German and American Propaganda, 1939–1945* (Princeton: Princeton University Press, 1978), chaps. 3, 4, and 6.

19. June Sochen, *"Mildred Pierce* and Women in Film," *American Quarterly* 30, no. 1 (Spring 1978): 9, 13.

20. Howard Haycraft, *Murder for Pleasure: The Life and Times of the Detective Story* (New York: D. Appleton-Century Co., 1941), p. 4.

21. In Edgar Allan Poe, *Selected Writings* (New York: Penguin, 1967), p. 193.

22. Ibid., p. 189.

23. Ibid., p. 193.

24. Ibid., p. 193.

25. *Mildred Pierce*, ed. Albert J. LaValley (Madison: University of Wisconsin Press, 1980), p. 97. Subsequent citations from the screenplay will be indicated in parentheses in the text.

26. Joyce Nelson describes the conclusion of the film as follows: "We are asked to read the final image in *Mildred Pierce* as a positive resolution. . . . Everything and everyone have been put back into their proper places: the murder solved, the murderer found, the couple re-enshrined

in their correct roles, and women back on their knees, keeping the façade clean" (*"Mildred Pierce* Reconsidered," p. 70). See also Pam Cook, "Duplicity in *Mildred Pierce*," in E. Ann Kaplan, ed., *Women in Film Noir* (London: British Film Institute, 1978), pp. 68–82. Here is how Cook describes the conclusion of the film: "As Mildred and Bert walk off into the lift of the new dawn from which all shadow and duplicity has been erased, they turn their backs on another couple, two women in the classic position of oppression, on their knees: an image of sacrifice which closes the film with a reminder of what women must give up for the sake of the patriarchal order" (p. 81).

Chapter Six

1. Sergei Eisenstein, "Dickens, Griffith and the Film Today," in *Film Form*, ed. and trans. Jay Leyda (1949; reprint, Cleveland: World Publishing Company, 1957), 195–255.
2. James Monaco, *The New Wave* (New York: Oxford University Press, 1979), p. 109.
3. Emile Zola, *Nana*, trans. George Holden (New York: Penguin, 1972), p. 48. ("Dites mon bordel!" Zola, *Nana* [Paris: Garnier-Flammarion, 1968], p. 28).
4. See Claire Johnston, "Dorothy Arzner: Critical Strategies," in Claire Johnston, ed., *The Work of Dorothy Arzner* (London: British Film Institute, 1975), pp. 1–8.
5. Chantal Akerman, quoted in Stephen Heath, "Difference," *Screen* 19, no. 3 (1978): 101.
6. I discuss these issues at more length in "The Woman at the Keyhole: Women's Cinema and Feminist Criticism," *New German Critique*, no. 23 (1981), 27–43.
7. Julia Lesage, "Women and Film: A Discussion of Feminine Aesthetics," *New German Critique*, no. 13 (1978): 94.

INDEX

Hitchcock, Alfred, 127, 130, 134, 142, 153. See also *Rebecca* (film)
Holland, Norman, 133, 134
Home, 148; and workplace, 19, 20, 38, 68, 75, 76. *See also* Private and public spheres

Ideology, 8, 9; film and, 160–62
I Remember Mama, 127
Immigrants: and early motion pictures, 71–81, 126; women, 75
Industrialization, 74, 75
Institution, novel as, 32; narrative as, 81; cinema as, 95, 98
Intertextuality, 65–66, 97, 119

Jacobs, Lewis, 72, 73
Jameson, Fredric, 169 (n. 67)
Jane Eyre (film), 114–16
Jane Eyre (novel), 103, 128
Jeanne Dielman, 23 Quai de Commerce, 1080 Bruxelles, 160
Jones, Jennifer, 106
Joseph Andrews, 37
Jowett, Garth, 73
Jules et Jim, 158

Kelley, George, 159
Kelly, Joan, 26
Kettle, Arnold, 166 (n. 11)
Kinetoscope, 77, 81
Knight, Everett, 165 (n. 7)

Law, 110–11, 131, 132, 145, 146, 148, 152, 153, 154
Leisure, 19, 29, 31, 33, 35, 37, 76, 77, 80
Lesage, Julia, 161
Levin, Harry, 32
Life of an American Fireman, 81
The Life of Emile Zola, 111–13, 126
Life with Father, 127

Lindsay, Vachel, 3
Lukacs, Georg, 23, 24, 25, 167 (n. 31)

MacCabe, Colin, 7
McQueen, Butterfly, 151
Madame Bovary (film), 106–13, 126, 129
Madame Bovary (novel), 104, 105, 106–7
Male look, 85–86
Marx, Karl, 17, 22, 41, 52, 97
Marxism, 9, 22, 96, 151; and feminism, 26; and psychoanalysis, 98
Mason, James, 106
Mass culture, 76, 77
Mediation, 9–10
Melodrama, 145
Merritt, Russell, 73, 74, 79
Metz, Christian, 98, 99
Mildred Pierce, 11, 128–30, 142–54
Mimesis, 99
Minnelli, Vincente, 106, 107, 113, 129
Mitchell, Margaret, 102, 103
Modernism, 105
Modleski, Tania, 132
Moll Flanders, 13
Monaco, James, 157
Montage, 4, 88
Montagu, Lady Mary Wortley, 34–38, 66
Mrs. Miniver, 103
Munsterberg, Hugo, 2
Music halls, 30, 77
My Sister Eileen, 121–22
Mystery fiction, 128, 147–48

Nana, 113, 157–58
Narration: in novel and film, 4, 7, 106, 108, 129, 136, 142; first-